IMAGES
of America

BELOIT'S CLUB POP HOUSE

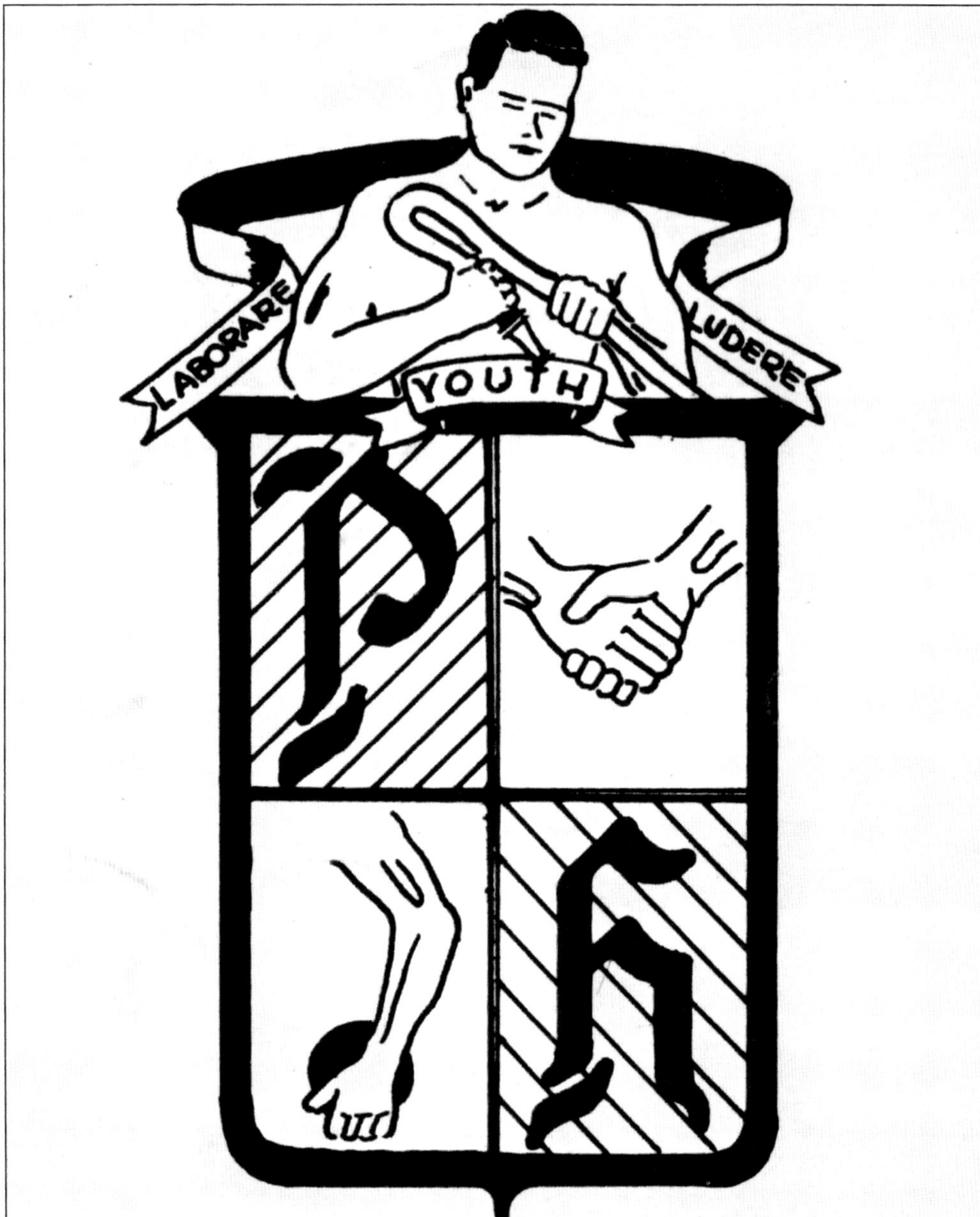

The Pop House logo was designed by Beloit College student Mike Fusello in 1954. It features a shield with the Latin words *laborare* ("to work") and *ludere* ("to play"), flanking the word *youth*. The logo initially was painted on a piece of scrap plywood and was fastened onto the front door of the original Pop House. It was reproduced on membership cards, menus, apparel, and promotional items. (Courtesy of the Pop House collection.)

On the cover: A swing band performs in the main dining room of the original Club Pop House for a chili queen festival during the mid-1950s. Comprised of students from Beloit College, the band would entertain from 8:00 p.m. to 11:00 p.m. for about $3 worth of hamburgers. Over the years, music at the Pop House would feature nationally known acts. (Courtesy of the Pop House collection.)

IMAGES
of America

BELOIT'S CLUB POP HOUSE

Joseph J. Accardi

ARCADIA
PUBLISHING

ISBN 978-0-7385-5209-5

Published by Arcadia Publishing
Charleston, South Carolina

Printed in the United States of America

Library of Congress Catalog Card Number: 2007940597

For all general information contact Arcadia Publishing at:
Telephone 843-853-2070
Fax 843-853-0044
E-mail sales@arcadiapublishing.com
For customer service and orders:
Toll-Free 1-888-313-2665

Visit us on the Internet at www.arcadiapublishing.com

To the memory of George, founder and proprietor of Club Pop House

Contents

ACKNOWLEDGMENTS

My deepest thanks go to Vince Stankewitz, Bernice (Stankewitz) Fairbert, and the Stankewitz family for allowing me to use their photographs from the Pop House collection. This project could not have been accomplished without their cooperation and support. Additionally, I want to express my gratitude to Ken Adamany of Last Coast Producing in Madison for providing photographs, correspondence, and personal stories.

Thanks to Beloit College archivist Fred Burwell for allowing me to scan archives images. Also, thanks to Paul Kerr of the Beloit Historical Society for access to the Builders of Beloit collection. Thanks to Marquette University Cujé Music Collection librarian Bruce Cole for sharing information. Thanks to the Beloit Public Library for access to the local history room. And thanks to my friend Dave Hernandez for his contribution of photographs and memorabilia.

Thanks to the following people for their contributions, whether they were photographs, memorabilia, personal stories, news clippings, or correspondence that helped to make this book possible: Ida and Richard Lenz, Dr. William Fitzgerald, editor emeritus William Behling and sports editor Jim Franz of the *Beloit Daily News*, the *Stateline News*, Mike Fusello, Jon St. John, Kevin Schmale, Tom and Jacqueline Roehl of the Mouse, Turkey Bowl historian David Luebke, Nancy Champion, Jim Wilson, Bob Harrer, John and Fran Tangye, Mike Hutchinson, Bill Torrey, Jerome Elliott, Gary Myers, Tom Tourville, Phyllis Kaplan, Michele Pizza, Gerry Watson, Clark Moriarty, Mike Matheson, Patti Collins, Dee Dee Vince, and many more too numerous to mention who shared comments on the Club Pop House blog. Thank you to Arcadia Publishing and to my editor Jeff Ruetsche and John Pearson for their patience and assistance.

Special thanks to the performers whose Pop House appearances are remembered by so many people through the photographs that became part of the Pop House collection: Layton Zbornik (also known as Jerry Martin), the first rock-and-roll recording artist to perform at the Pop House; Conway Twitty United LP; the Kingsmen; Johnny Green; Bruce Channel; Carl Giammarese; Tommy Roe; Johnny Tillotson; Jim "J. C. Hooke" Pilster; Dana Buck and Brad Palmer; Russell DaShiell of Spiritguitar.com; Janalee and Jim Croegaert of RoughStonesMusic.com; Jimmy "Soul" Holvay; John Furland; Jerry Cadwell; and all the artists for the use of their images.

I want to thank my wife, Sylvia, for her eternal patience and support. And I thank my parents for allowing me to frequent the Pop House. Finally, I thank all the people who made the Club Pop House such a special place and whose happy faces appear in this book.

INTRODUCTION

Imagine cruising across the Portland Avenue Bridge in Beloit on a hot summer day with the windows down. Looking out the passenger window, the Rock River is sparkling in the bright sunlight. With a hasty glance in the rearview mirror, you adjust your sunglasses. The radio is tuned to an oldies station, and the DJ plays "Sugar and Spice." You are transported back in time to the Pop House ballroom and imagine those harmonies are coming from a stage only a few feet away. The music reaches into the very depths of your soul to touch long-forgotten memories. You shiver as a cool wave of nostalgia rushes over you. Above the music, the clamor of a hundred teenagers can be heard talking about last summer's softball tournament, next week's football game, Friday night's basketball game, and this year's candidates for chili queen. Who will win the Turkey Bowl? When is the senior girls' breakfast? You head through the main dining room and make a quick stop at the lunch counter to order a Snead and a Coke, greeting a dozen friends along the way. It is Saturday night at the Club Pop House and all is right with the world.

Such are the memories of a place that served two generations of teenagers coming of age during the 1940s, 1950s, and 1960s in Beloit. Club Pop House was a teen gathering spot unlike any other. To many young people in this midwestern town, the Pop House was utopia. Friday and Saturday nights were reserved for record jams, dancing, and live music performed by countless bands and solo acts. Food, sports, and special events rounded out the activities so that members always had a place to go and something to do when they got there.

Proprietor George Russell Stankewitz was born and raised in Beloit, the son of Lithuanian immigrants. He became friend, father figure, and sometimes boss to hundreds of Beloit teenagers. Stankewitz came up with the idea of a local gathering spot for teens while he was a sophomore in high school, and in 1941, he opened the Club Pop House in the back of his family-run grocery store on the corner of Portland Avenue and Fifth Street near the railroad tracks. He started the club as a place for his friends to hang out, talk about sports, eat a hamburger, and have a soda pop (hence the name Pop House). Membership initially consisted of about 60 high school boys, most of whom were involved in sports. They organized teams to play football, basketball, and softball, often competing with students from Beloit College. Girls were invited to participate mainly as cheerleaders and fans and to serve as royalty for special events and tournaments. It was in 1941 that Stankewitz organized the first Turkey Bowl football game that became an annual tradition on Thanksgiving mornings.

In 1943, George Stankewitz and most of his fellow club members joined the military to serve in World War II. As Stankewitz was preparing to leave, his father told him, "I'll rent out the building while you're gone, but when you come back whoever is there will have to go if you still want the Pop House." Upon completing his distinguished service, marked by numerous citations including a Bronze Star Medal, a Combat Infantry Badge, and a Purple Heart with Cluster for injuries received in the line of duty, Stankewitz was discharged on January 16, 1946, and returned home. After two weeks of rest and renewed gatherings of friends, his father tapped him on the shoulder and said, "If you want to start on that Pop House I'll meet you over there at eight o'clock tomorrow morning." Stankewitz and his father worked on remodeling the building to accommodate a used grill, a jukebox, and a few tables and booths. Stankewitz used money saved from his military pay for the materials and furnishings. His father, on strike from Fairbanks-Morse at the time, helped with converting the space. In return, Stankewitz promised to continue stocking loaves of dark rye Lithuanian bread and some milk for the remaining neighborhood customers. The Pop House reopened on June 11, 1946.

Within weeks a few high school and college students began patronizing the place. Word spread about Stankewitz's friendly manner, the welcoming atmosphere, and the hamburgers. As the business grew, so did the need for more space. The original building was remodeled in 1954. In 1958, Stankewitz moved the business next door to a new building, constructed with the help of customers, many of whom worked for nothing more than hamburgers and fries. An outdoor dance floor was added in 1960. Noise complaints and the persistent threat of bad weather prompted construction of a large dance hall in 1964. Stankewitz liked to refer to it as the "ballroom."

Live music attracted new waves of teens each year to the Pop House where, for $1, one could hear a great band and dance to some of the best entertainment around. The Pop House was witness to the evolution of rock and roll. Two dozen national acts, including Jimmy Gilmer and the Fireballs, the Kingsmen, Tommy Roe and the Roemans, and Del Shannon, and a tidal wave of regional bands all performed there.

The Pop House developed traditions that included an annual chili festival complete with a crowning of the chili queen. It was sponsor to championship softball and basketball teams, sports awards, and recognition dinners for top students and sports teams. More than just burgers and fries, the grill became famous for its specialty sandwiches like the Snead and the Smiley. Also on hand were soft drinks, milk, or a cup of Blast.

One blemish on the Pop House reputation resulted from its status as a club that welcomed members only. Charges of racial bias culminated in a 1965 discrimination suit. The case went to trial later that year, and a jury cleared Stankewitz of the charges, finding that the Pop House operated as a private club and could select its own patrons, a practice not uncommon among business establishments at that time.

There were rules for membership, bylaws, and a board of directors. Prospective members had to be in the 10th grade or above and undergo a review process that included an interview with Stankewitz before receiving a card and a key. In its heyday there were more than 600 active high school–age members in addition to numerous alumni and a waiting list of about 100 more. The rules extended to behavior as well. It was an embarrassment to be kicked out of the Pop House, so most everyone behaved themselves.

In 1972, a new law was enacted in Wisconsin making the legal drinking age 18. Stankewitz reluctantly began serving alcohol in November of that year, effectively excluding the under-18 crowd. With business declining, Stankewitz announced his retirement and closed the Club Pop House in April 1973.

So turn up the radio volume and think back to a more innocent time. How great that tune sounded when you heard the Cryan' Shames perform it live on the ballroom stage. The song fades out. As you shut off the engine and climb out of the car, you remember all the fun you had at the Pop House. There was no other place like it, and there never will be again.

One

Early Years

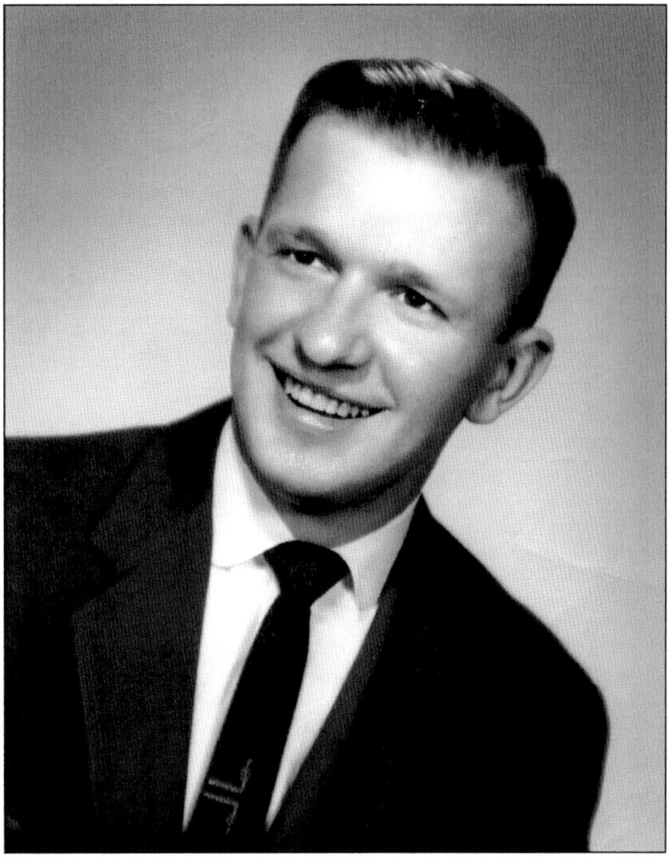

In high school, George "Honest" Stankewitz organized athletic events with friends. Afterward he invited them for sodas and socializing in the back of his family grocery store. The Pop House, a Beloit teen social club that endured for nearly three decades, evolved from this modest beginning. This portrait hung on the Pop House wall, a gift presented to him from grateful students. (Courtesy of the Pop House collection, photograph by Sharpe Studio.)

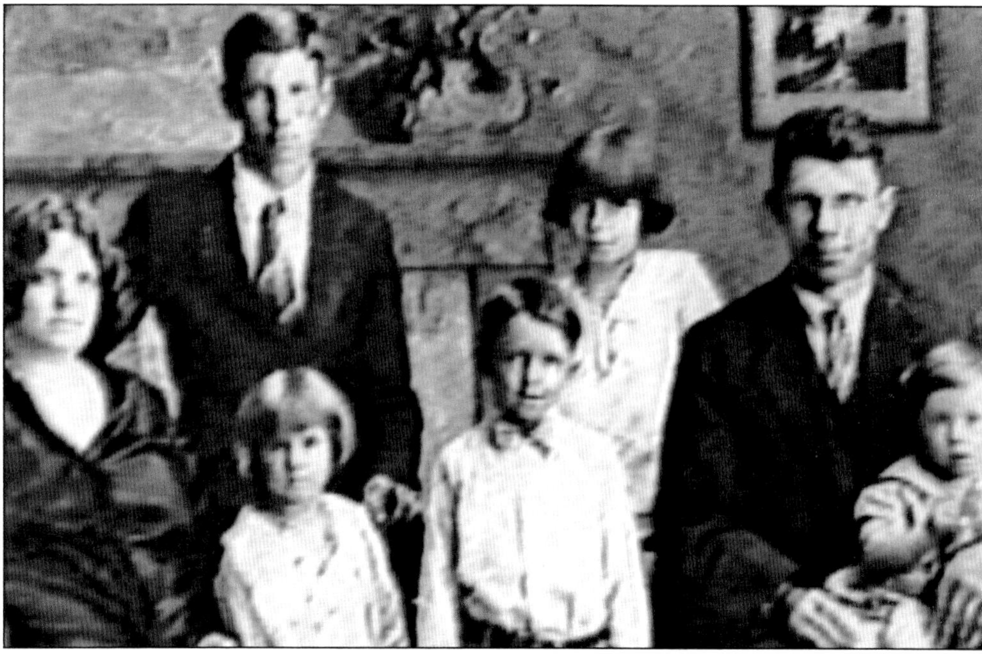

George Russell Stankewitz was born on August 10, 1923, in Beloit, the son of Vincent and Dorothy Stankewitz. Vincent emigrated from Lithuania in 1912 and became a crane operator at Fairbanks-Morse. In this family photograph, George is seven years old. From left to right are Dorothy, Russell, Bernice, George, Ann, Vincent, and Vincent Jr. (Vince). (Courtesy of the Beloit Historical Society)

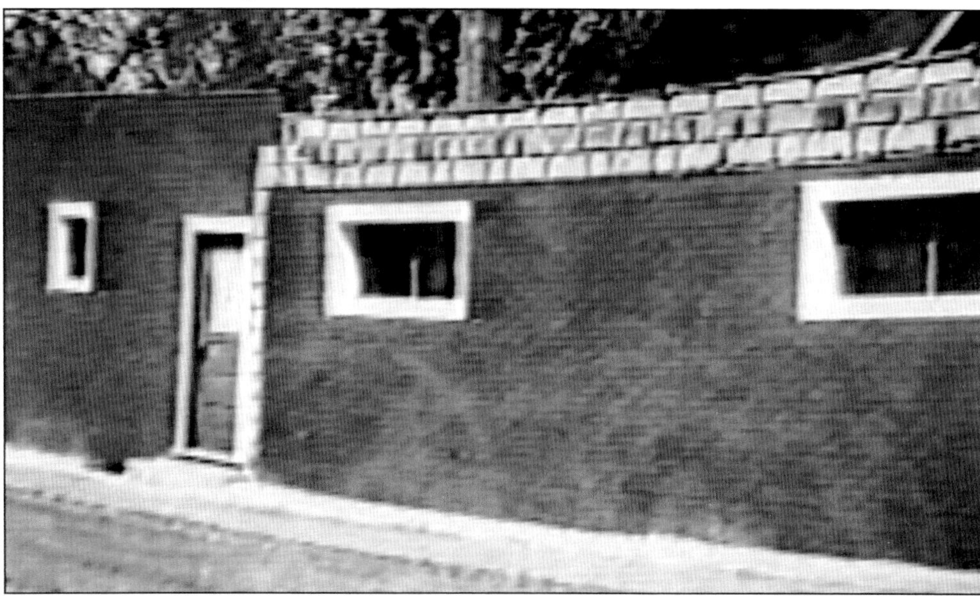

While in 10th grade, George convinced his father to let him run a small grocery business, located at Portland Avenue and Fifth Street. Most of the customers turned out to be fellow students who hung around the store to discuss sports and girls. The original building, pictured here, was built by the elder Stankewitz. The basement was dug out manually with a horse-drawn scoop. (Courtesy of the Beloit Historical Society)

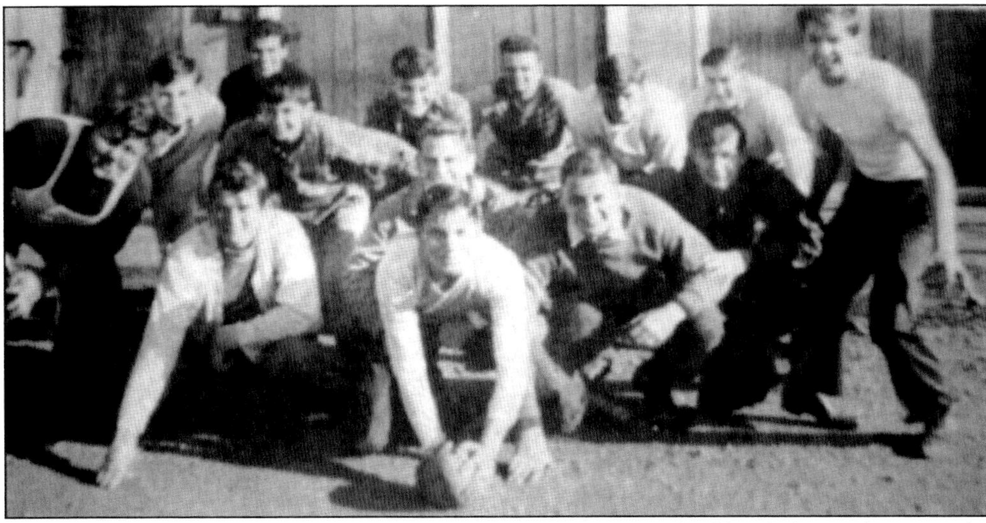

Finding the grocery business boring, George Stankewitz approached his father with a new idea to open an athletic club that would serve refreshments. Soon the Pop House began operating, and the grocery shelves were replaced by booths, a used grill, and a jukebox. The place became a hit with his friends, and in 1941, he organized the first Thanksgiving Day Turkey Bowl football game with them. (Courtesy of David Luebke.)

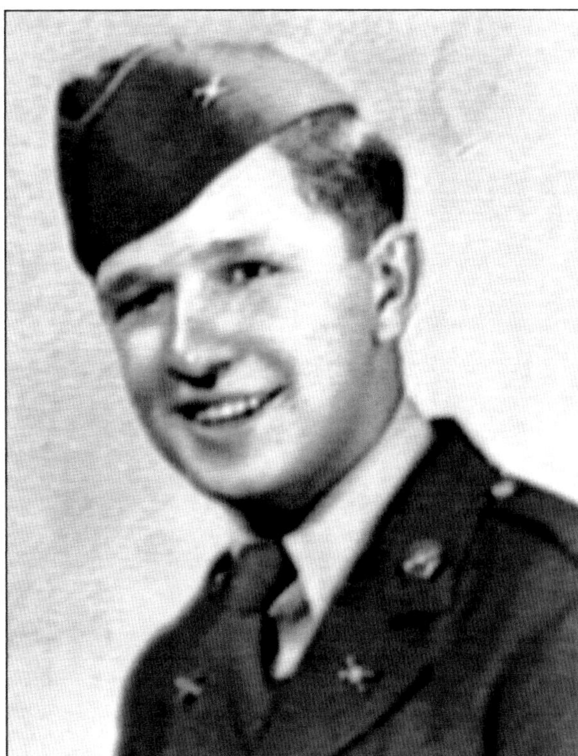

Stankewitz closed the Pop House in 1943 to join the army. Serving as a rifleman in the infantry, he earned the rank of staff sergeant. He entered European combat and was decorated with the Combat Infantry Badge, Bronze Star Medal, and the European Campaign Ribbon with three battle stars. Twice injured, he was awarded the Purple Heart with Cluster. Stankewitz was home on furlough in 1944 in this photograph. (Courtesy of the Beloit Historical Society.)

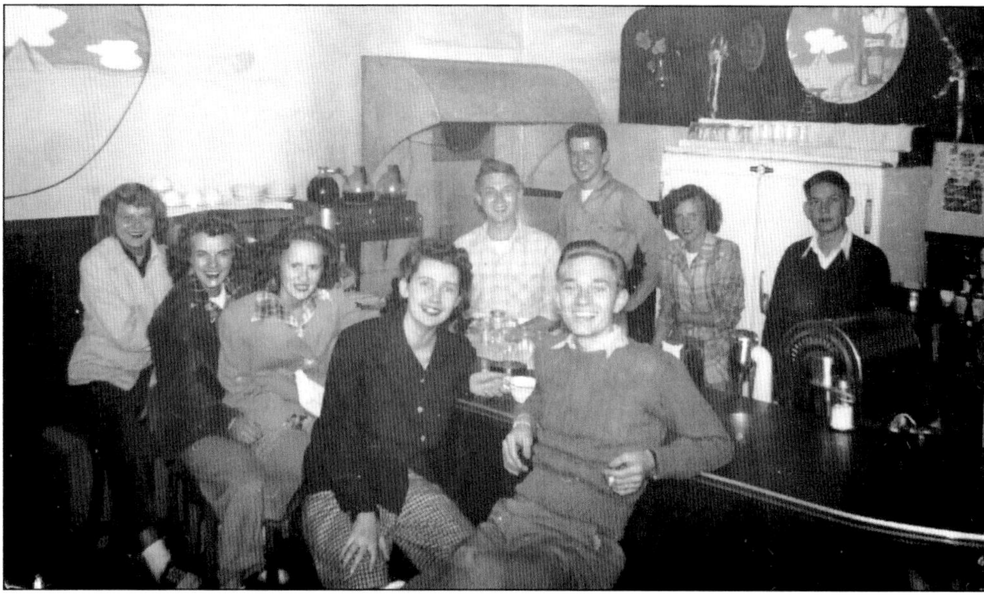

Upon his discharge in 1946, George Stankewitz returned to remodel the Pop House with a lunch counter and dining room. Within weeks he was back in business, serving burgers, organizing events, and providing a hangout for club members. This photograph shows "the gang" in 1947. Seated are, from left to right, Delores (Dee) Podwell, Bev Brack, Ann Dane, Dorothy Pulaski, and Fred "Punk" Warner. Standing are, from left to right, Art Johnson, George Stankewitz, Bev Reimer, and Bill Reinert. (Courtesy of the Pop House collection, photograph by I. R. Andreoni.)

Congratulations
Seniors

It's been one of the most enjoyable years I have spent with your little troubles, big smiles, and glorious victories!

CLUB POPHOUSE
BOARD OF DIRECTORS

By the end of its first year of operation, word spread among students about the genial George Stankewitz, the hamburgers he served up, and the friendly atmosphere of Club Pop House. He showed his appreciation by placing this advertisement in the June 13, 1947, Beloit High School newspaper, the *Increscent*. Three hundred forty seniors graduated that night in a ceremony at Strong Stadium. (Courtesy of Bill Torrey.)

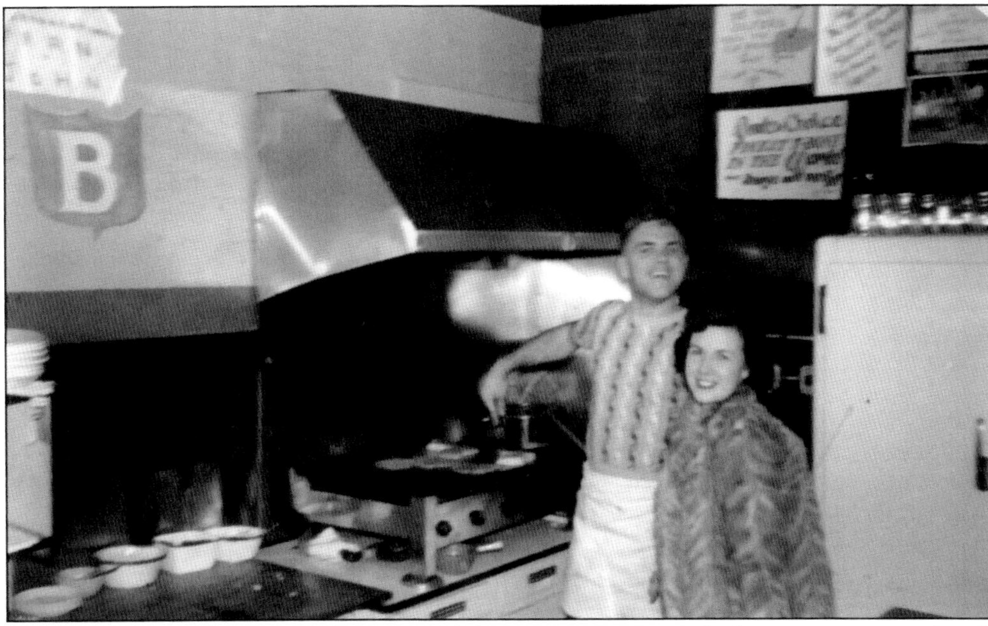

Many hands helped out with the responsibilities of running a refreshment counter and grill. Over the years, Stankewitz hired and trained numerous young "grillmen" to make cheeseburgers, many of whom had never cooked before. Grillman John Tangye poses in the kitchen with his new bride, Fran. Stankewitz held a reception for the newlyweds and posted the sign that reads, "Congratulations Fran and John." (Courtesy of Ida and Richard Lenz.)

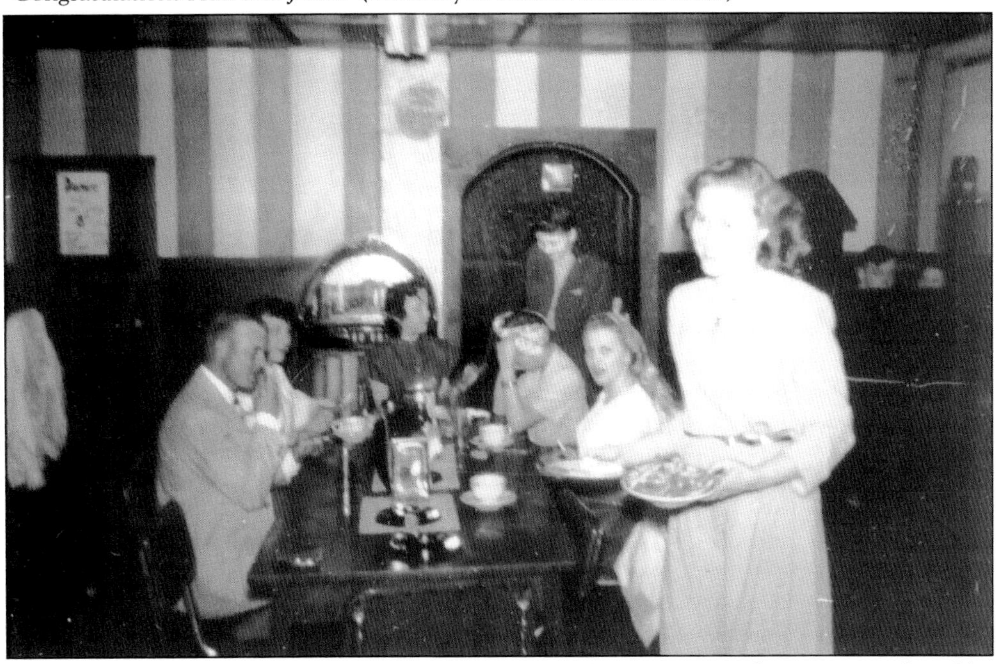

Some interior remodeling resulted in the addition of a dining room with more space for tables and booths. The walls of the dining room were painted in bright red and white vertical stripes, the University of Wisconsin school colors. The old jukebox is partially visible behind the diners in this photograph. (Courtesy of Ida and Richard Lenz.)

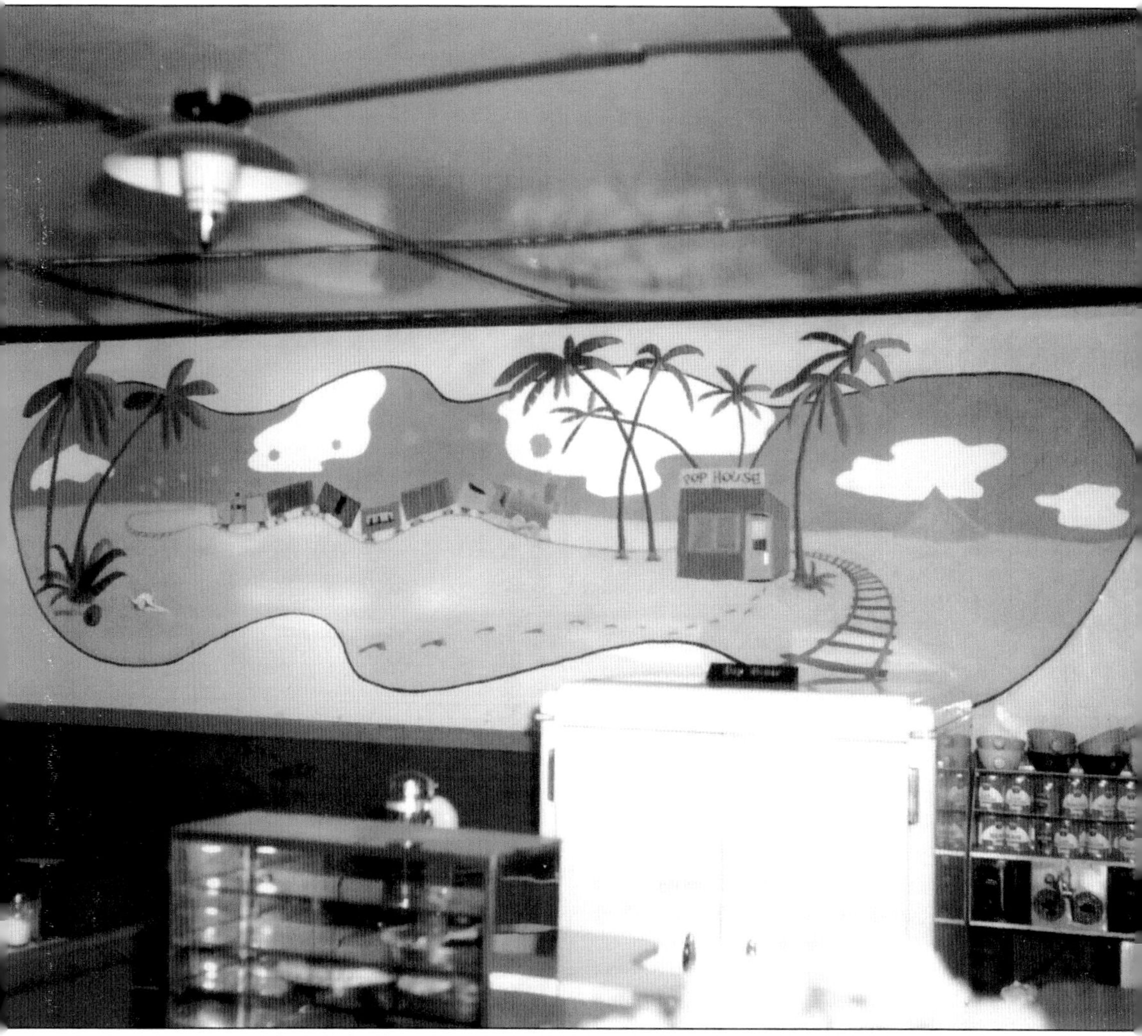

Pop House members helped out by contributing their time and talent in creative ways, whether lending a hand with construction projects or manning the grill. Some used an artistic flair to liven up the interior decoration. Shortly after the Pop House reopened in 1946, two murals were painted. The mural shown here was painted above the lunch counter by Dave Driesbach, a student at Beloit College. Although done in watercolors, it remained there for more than 30 years. (Courtesy of the Pop House collection.)

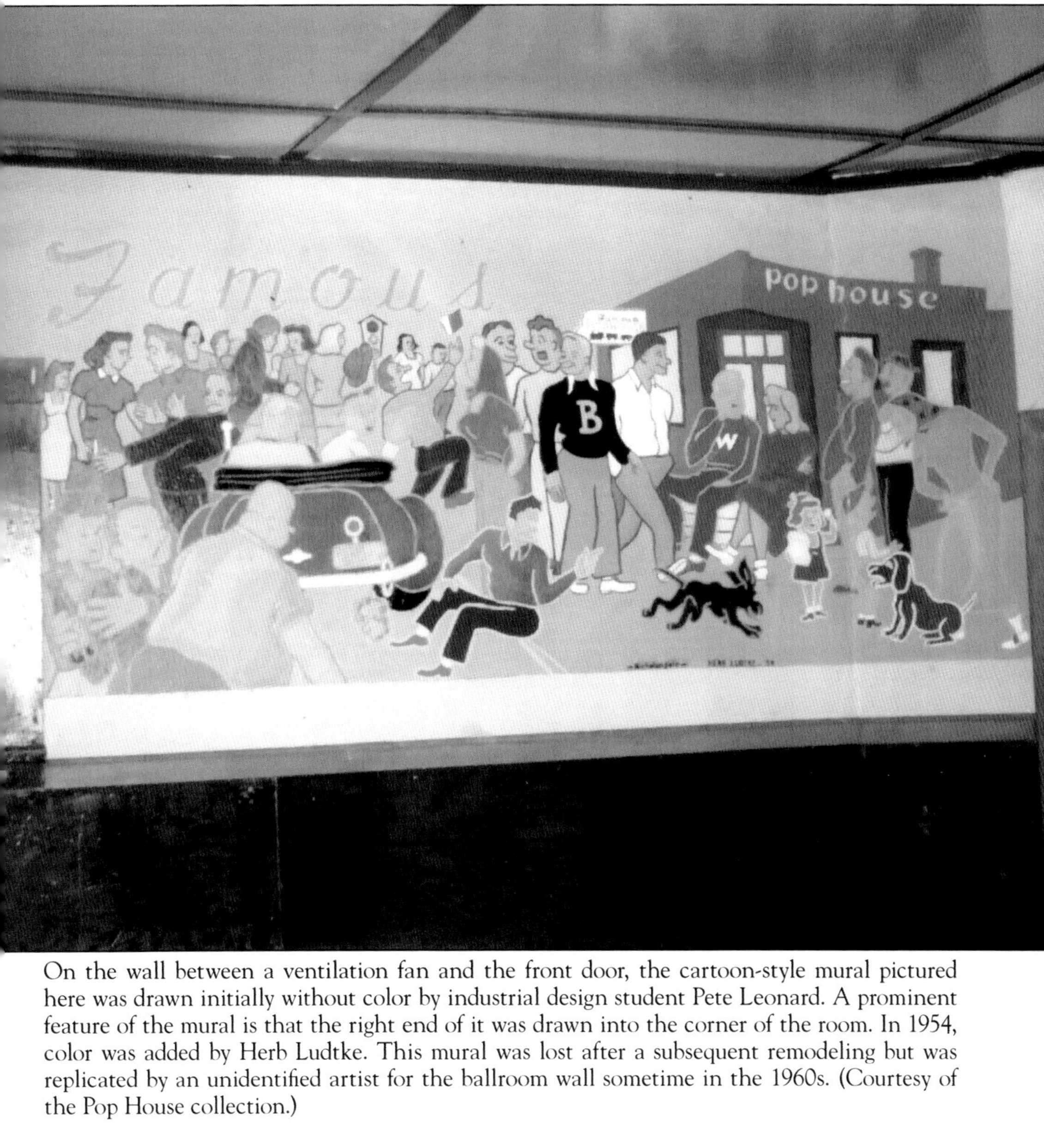

On the wall between a ventilation fan and the front door, the cartoon-style mural pictured here was drawn initially without color by industrial design student Pete Leonard. A prominent feature of the mural is that the right end of it was drawn into the corner of the room. In 1954, color was added by Herb Ludtke. This mural was lost after a subsequent remodeling but was replicated by an unidentified artist for the ballroom wall sometime in the 1960s. (Courtesy of the Pop House collection.)

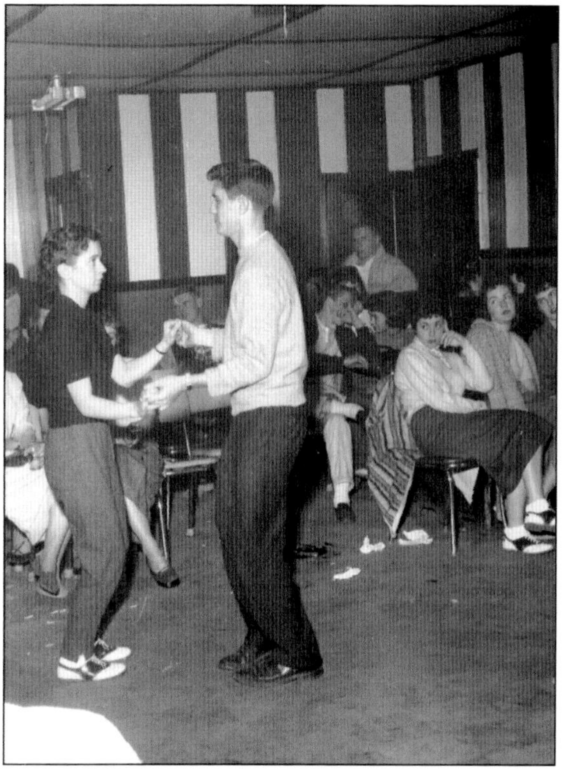

Additional remodeling was done that allowed tables and chairs to be pushed aside to make room for dancing, whether to music from the jukebox, a record hop, or a swing band. No other footwear characterizes the 1950s quite like saddle shoes. Pictured above is a couple dancing in the main dining room of the Pop House. Music was fast becoming a big draw, and George Stankewitz responded by hiring bands on a regular basis to provide entertainment for a growing number of appreciative kids. Music by Jack Farina (drums) and his band, Jam Session, often were heard there. A Beloit native, Farina graduated with a degree in instrumental music from Beloit College. He taught music at Beloit Catholic and Beloit Turner High Schools while also leading the Jack Farina Big Band for many years. (Courtesy of the Pop House collection.)

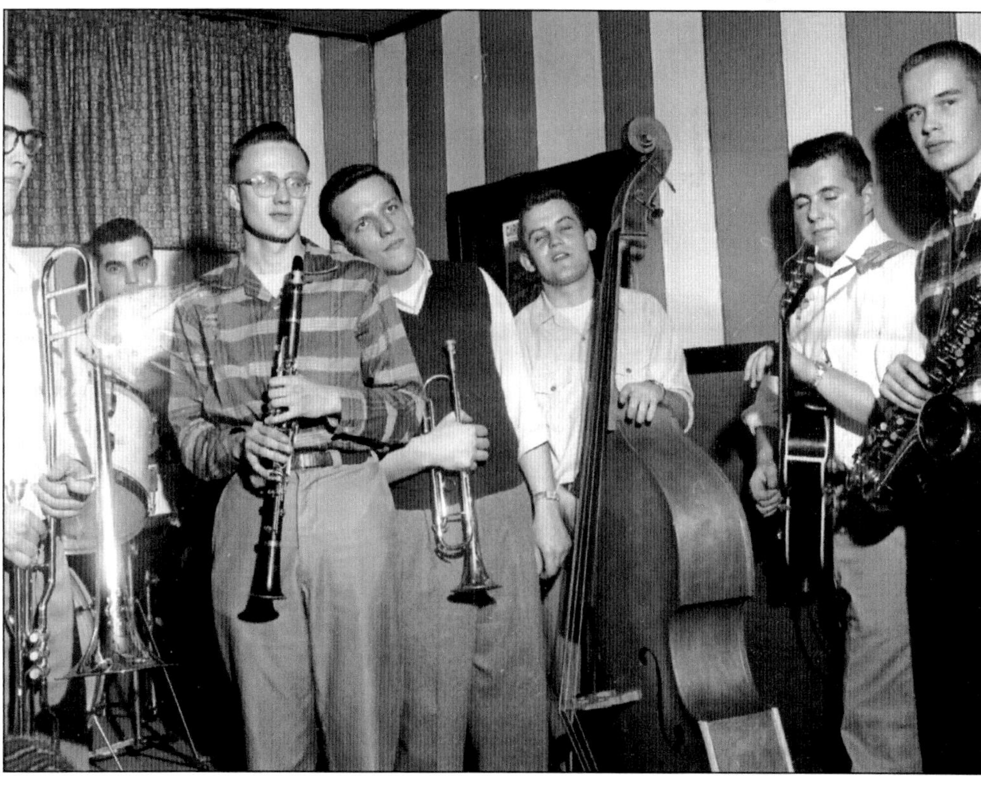

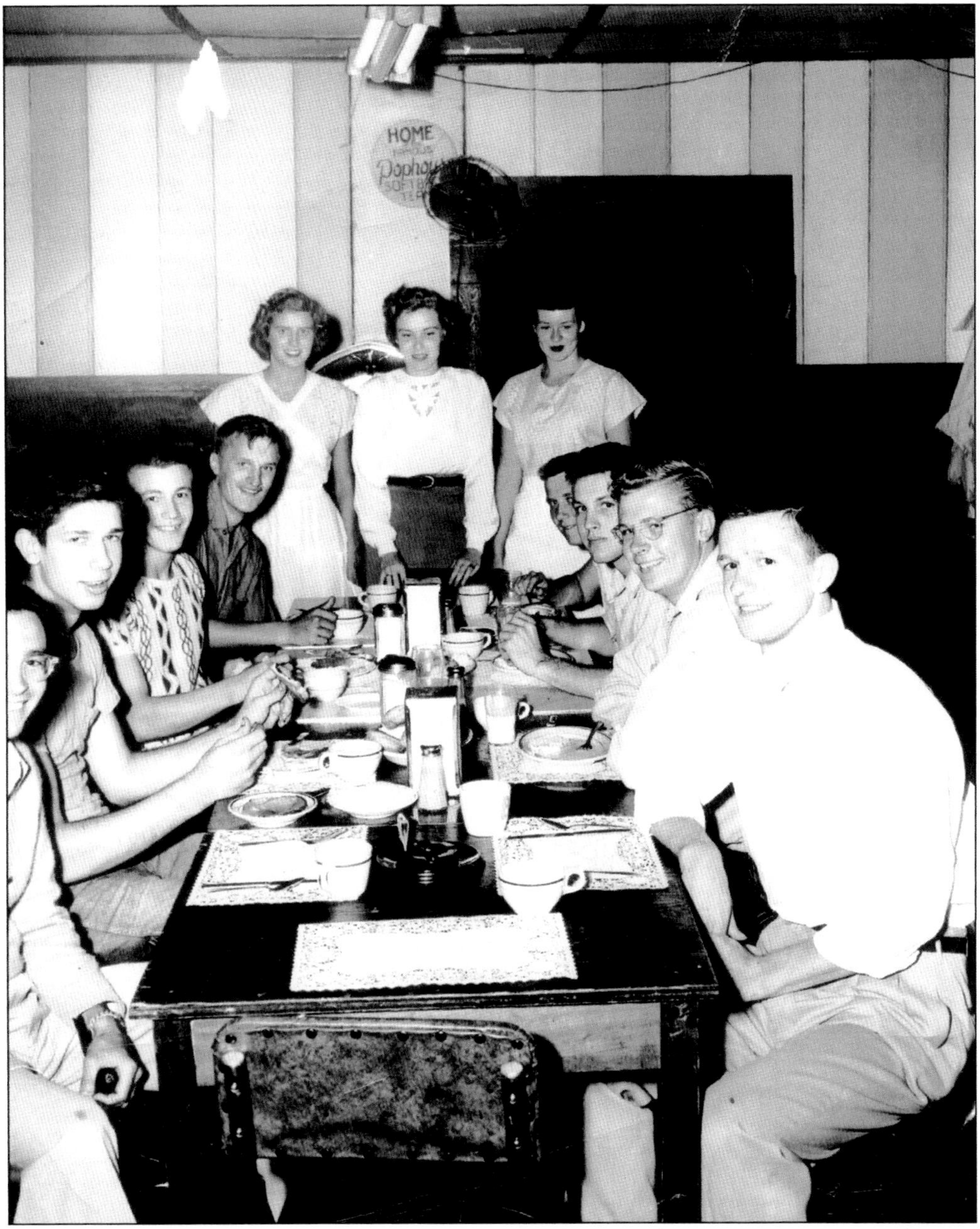

Softball was popular in the summer. In the 1940s and 1950s, the Pop House sponsored teams in city leagues. Twelve games into the 1949 season, the Pop House team was at the bottom of the rankings. Always a showman, George Stankewitz organized a homecoming celebration that included breakfast, a homecoming court, and a parade to the game. On the morning of the big game, August 3, 1949, the team began its homecoming celebration with a victory breakfast at the Pop House. Standing in the photograph above are, from left to right, Marie Johnson, queen Frances Bjorklund, and Margie Enking. Seated at the table are, from left to right, team members Dick Sharp, Vince Stankewitz, Bill Merkle, Bob McDowell, Buzz Gunderson, Fritz Wright, Don Tamulis, and manager Stankewitz. A hand-drawn sign on the back wall reads, "Home of the Famous Pop House Softball Team." (Courtesy of the Pop House collection.)

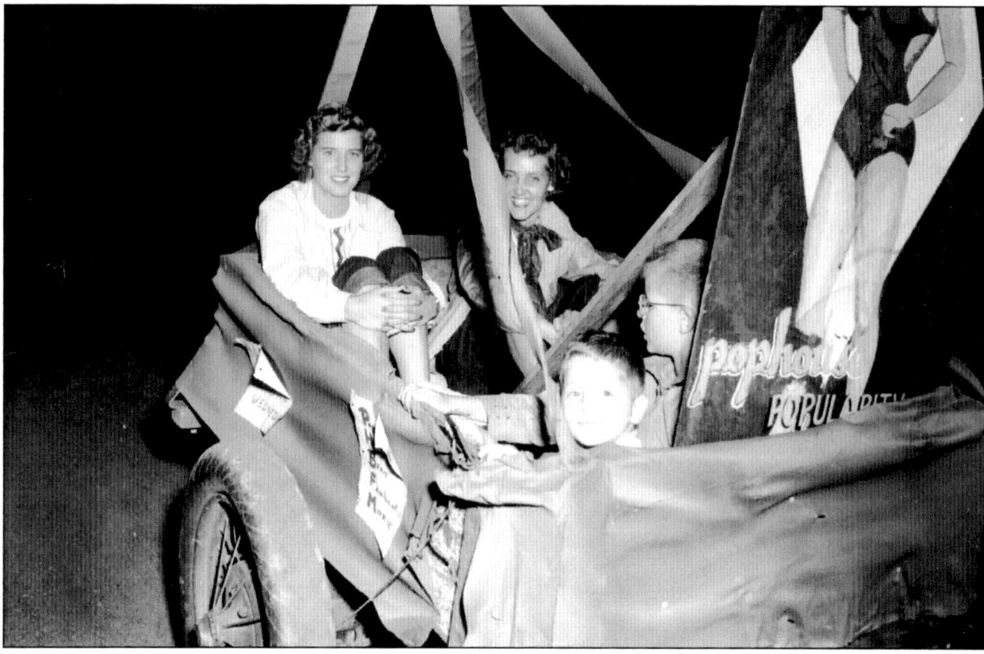

The homecoming celebration included a parade through Beloit with decorated floats and handmade signs. Two members of the homecoming court pictured above are Marie Johnson (left) and Eleanor Simenson. Others on the court that year were Jean Worthington, Betty Lusby, Judy Keefer, Margie Enking, and Virginia Melcher. The trailer sported crepe paper–draped boards that supported a hand-painted poster. A sign on the trailer reads, "Pop House Beat Fairbanks-Morse." The Fairbanks-Morse Fairies were the city league champions. The theme of the parade as it made its way to the Roosevelt Junior High playing field that evening was "Gobble Garbe," seen painted on the side of the vehicle pictured below. The name of the Fairies' pitcher was John "Pops" Garbe, who ended up delivering a one-hit shutout to defeat the Pop House 3-0. (Courtesy of the Pop House collection.)

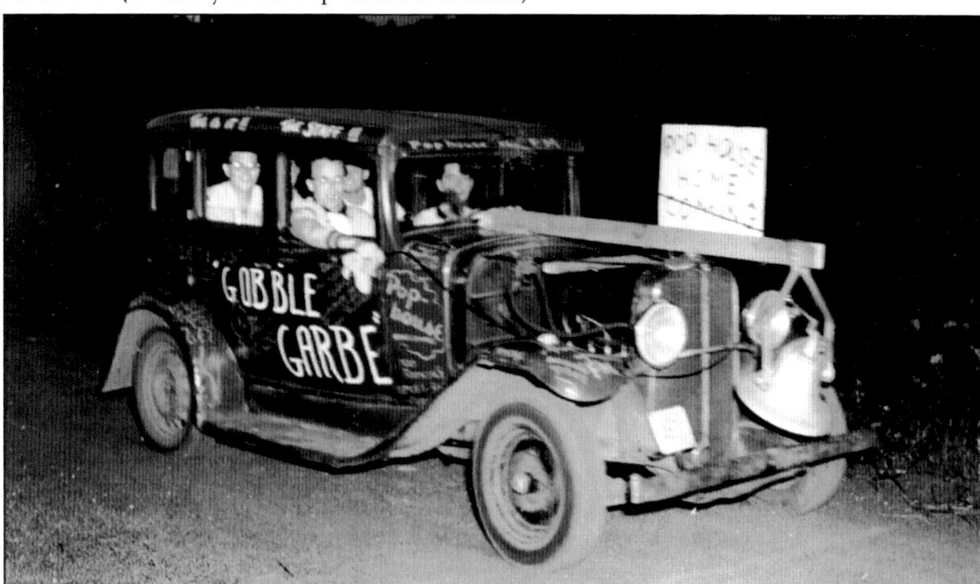

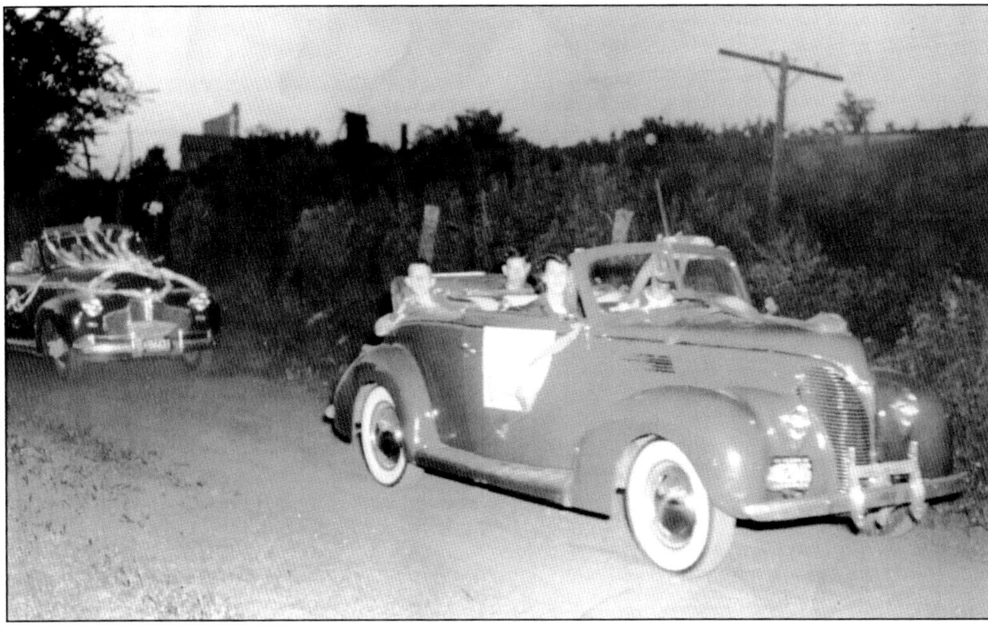

The parade left from the Pop House and wound its way through town before arriving at Roosevelt Field for the 7:30 p.m. game. The photograph above shows two decorated cars in the parade with members of the club's board of directors leading. As noted in the *Beloit Daily News*, the Pop House was the only known restaurant in the city league with a student body and an alumni association that made such amusing events possible. Finishing last in the league that year, the 1949 Pop House softball team is pictured below. Pictured are, from left to right, (first row) Buzz Gunderson, Fritz Wright, Don Kocen, Bill Merkle, and Marv Mauel; (second row) Dick Sharp, Trev Porter, Vince Stankewitz, Don Tamulis, Bob Mauel, and manager George Stankewitz. Not pictured is pitcher Roger Nielson. (Courtesy of the Pop House collection.)

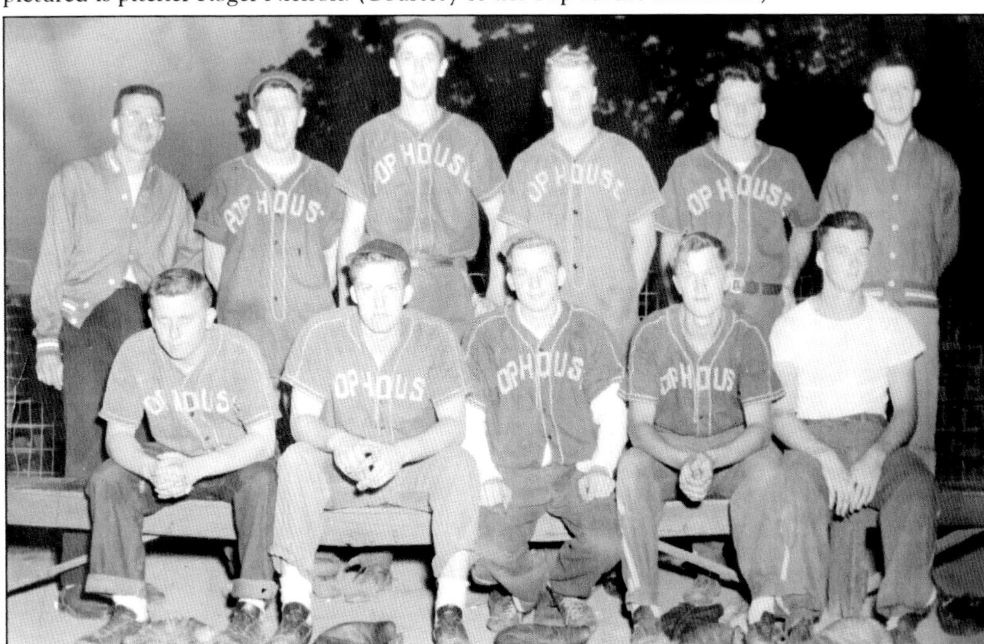

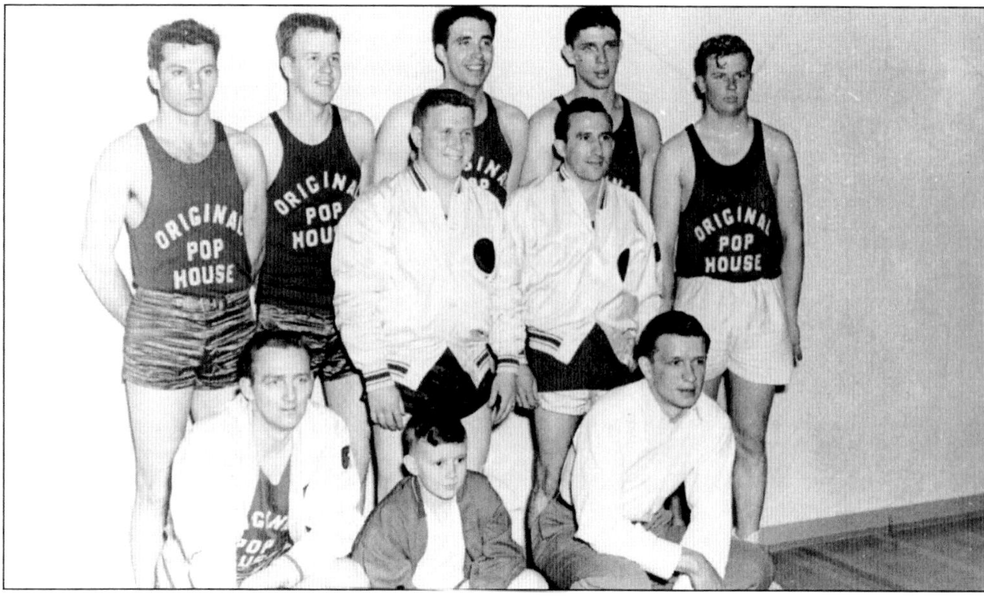

Although the softball teams struggled, the Pop House basketball teams of the 1940s and 1950s earned several championships. In a 1951 game, center Vince Stankewitz scored 39 points to lead the Pop House team to a 76-68 victory. The win gave the team the National League title in city competition. It captured the State Tournament of Champions crown that same year. Stankewitz is identified in the back row of this team photograph, fourth from the left. (Courtesy of the Beloit College Archives.)

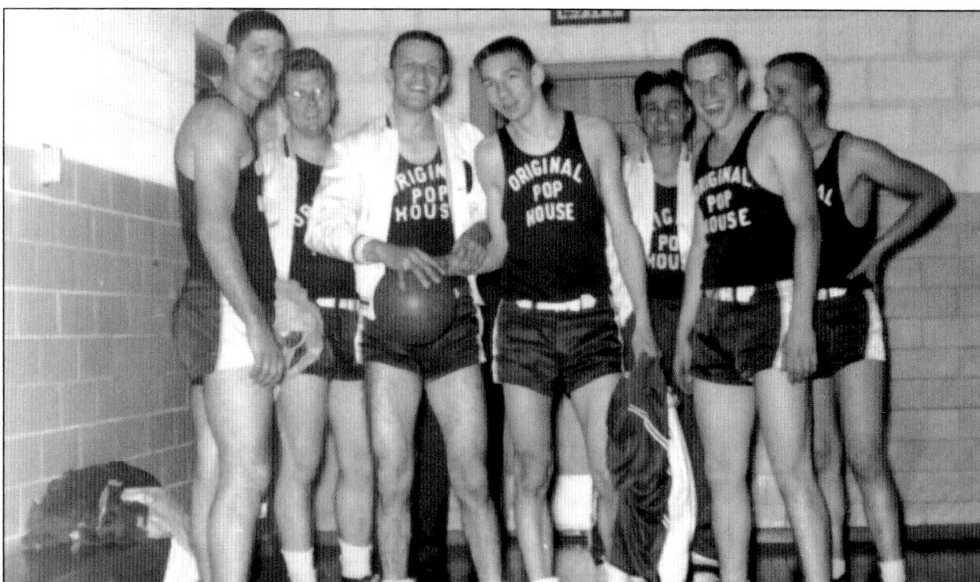

Pop House squads played traveling professional teams like the Broadway Clowns and the Texas Cowgirls. One team drove to a Western State all-star tour in a hearse. Occasionally a ringer from Beloit College would play with the Pop House under an assumed name. Pop House basketball teams won 12 city tournaments in 20 years. Some players pictured here are Vince Stankewitz, Don "Goose" Tamulis, George Stankewitz, Bill "Ace" Hanewall, and Bill Watson. (Courtesy of Ida and Richard Lenz.)

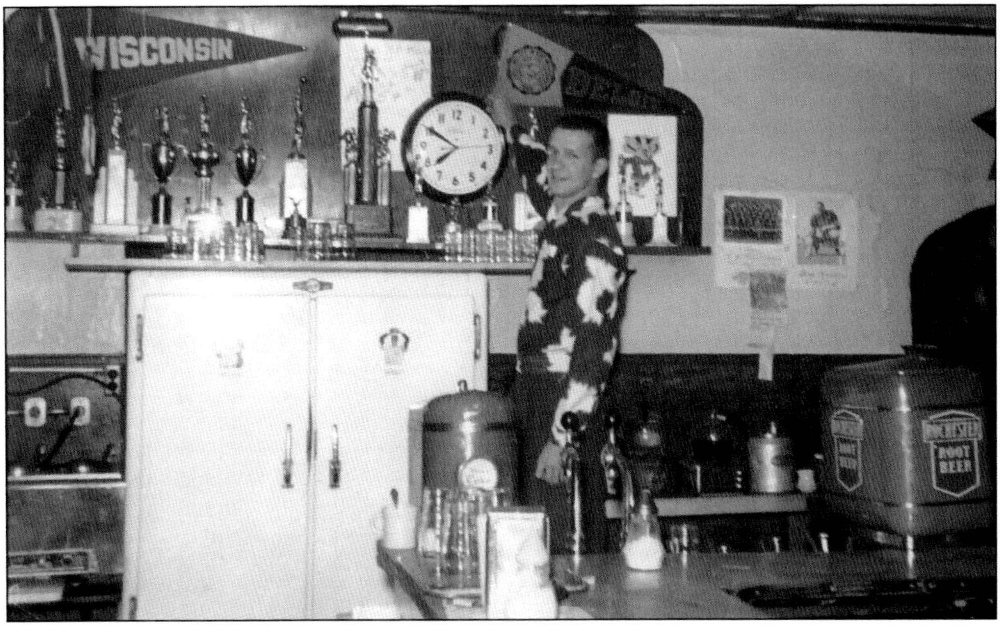

Pop House teams earned numerous trophies, which were displayed with other souvenirs and gifts. In this photograph from Christmas 1953, George Stankewitz is hanging a wall clock, a gift from the Beloit High School senior class, in the original Pop House. The photograph was used for an advertisement in the 1954 *Beloiter* yearbook with a caption that read, "Congratulations to the Class of '54." (Courtesy of Dr. William Fitzgerald.)

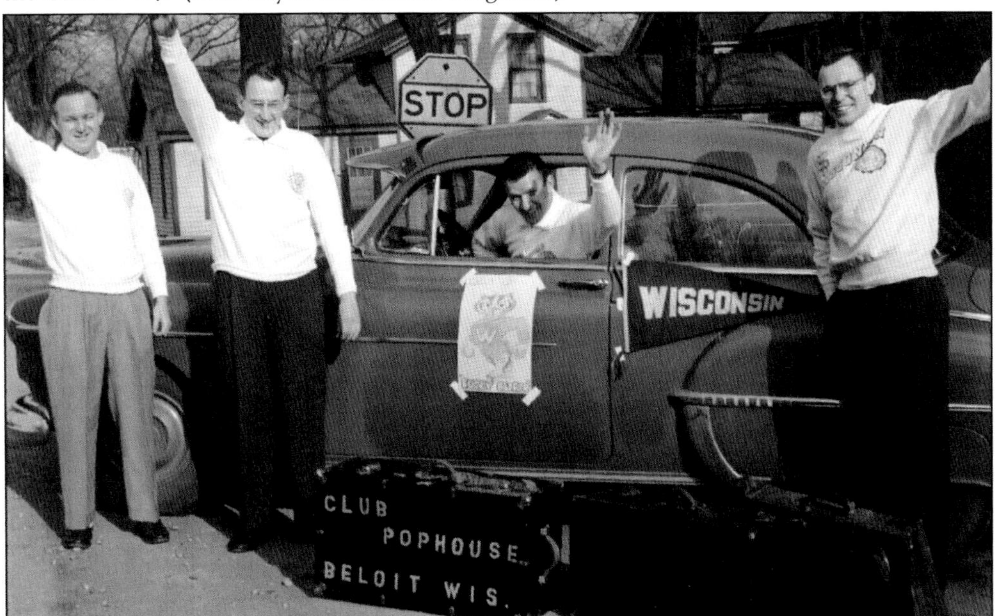

An avid University of Wisconsin football fan, Stankewitz took many bus trips to Badger games. He also attended games of Beloit teams to cheer on the Purple Knights, the Crusaders, and the Bucs. On Christmas Day 1952, he left by car for Pasadena with Bill Lockwood, Jim Osgood, and Alex Naidenovich to watch the Badgers play the University of Southern California in the 1953 Rose Bowl. The Badgers lost 0-7. (Courtesy of the Pop House collection.)

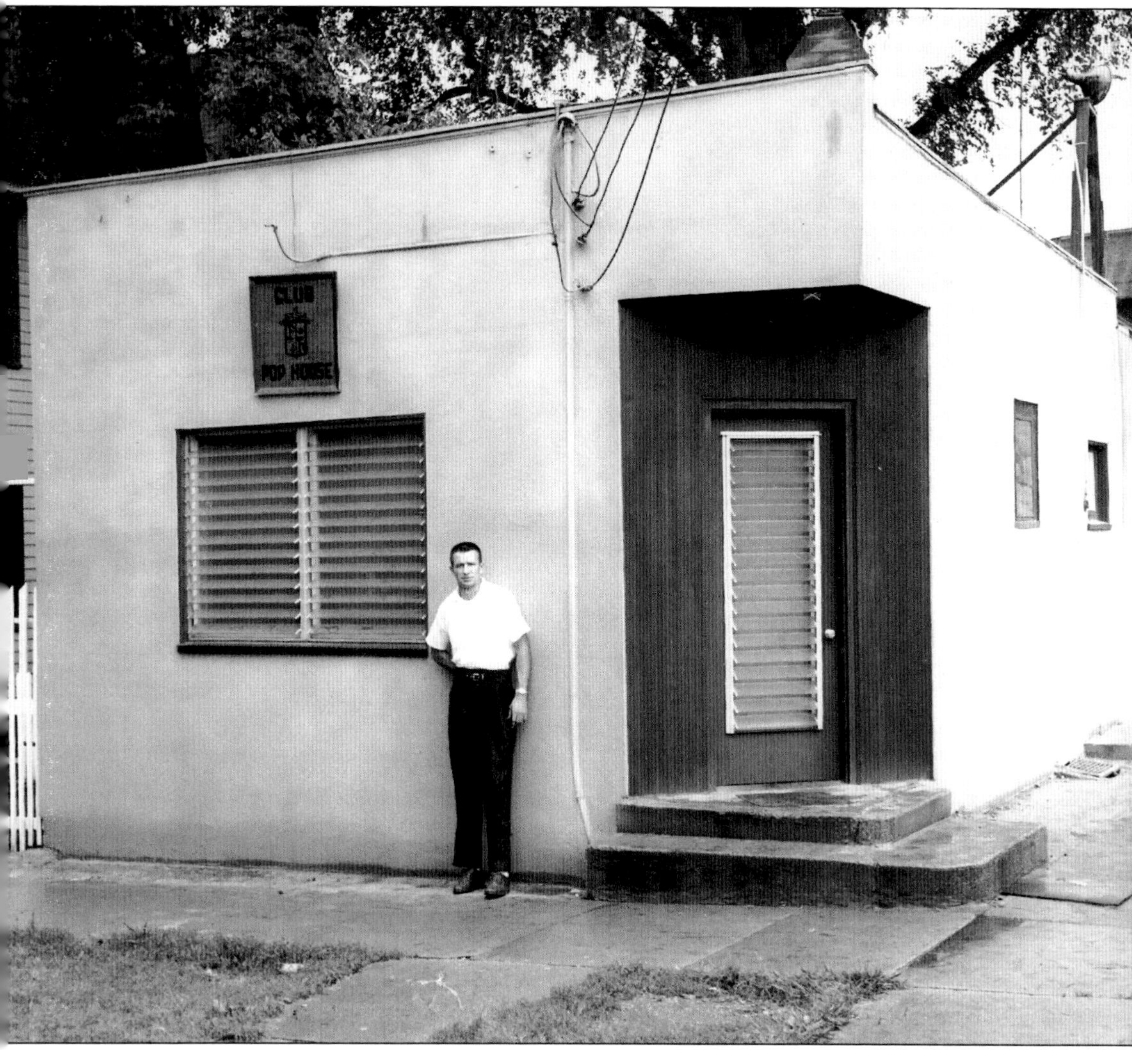

The first major renovation of the Pop House in 1954 created a new entryway in the northwest corner of the building, the installation of jalousie windows, and a fresh exterior. The Pop House logo painted on a piece of plywood was affixed to the front of the building. George Stankewitz poses for this picture in the summer of 1954, shortly after completion of the remodeling. (Courtesy of the Beloit College Archives.)

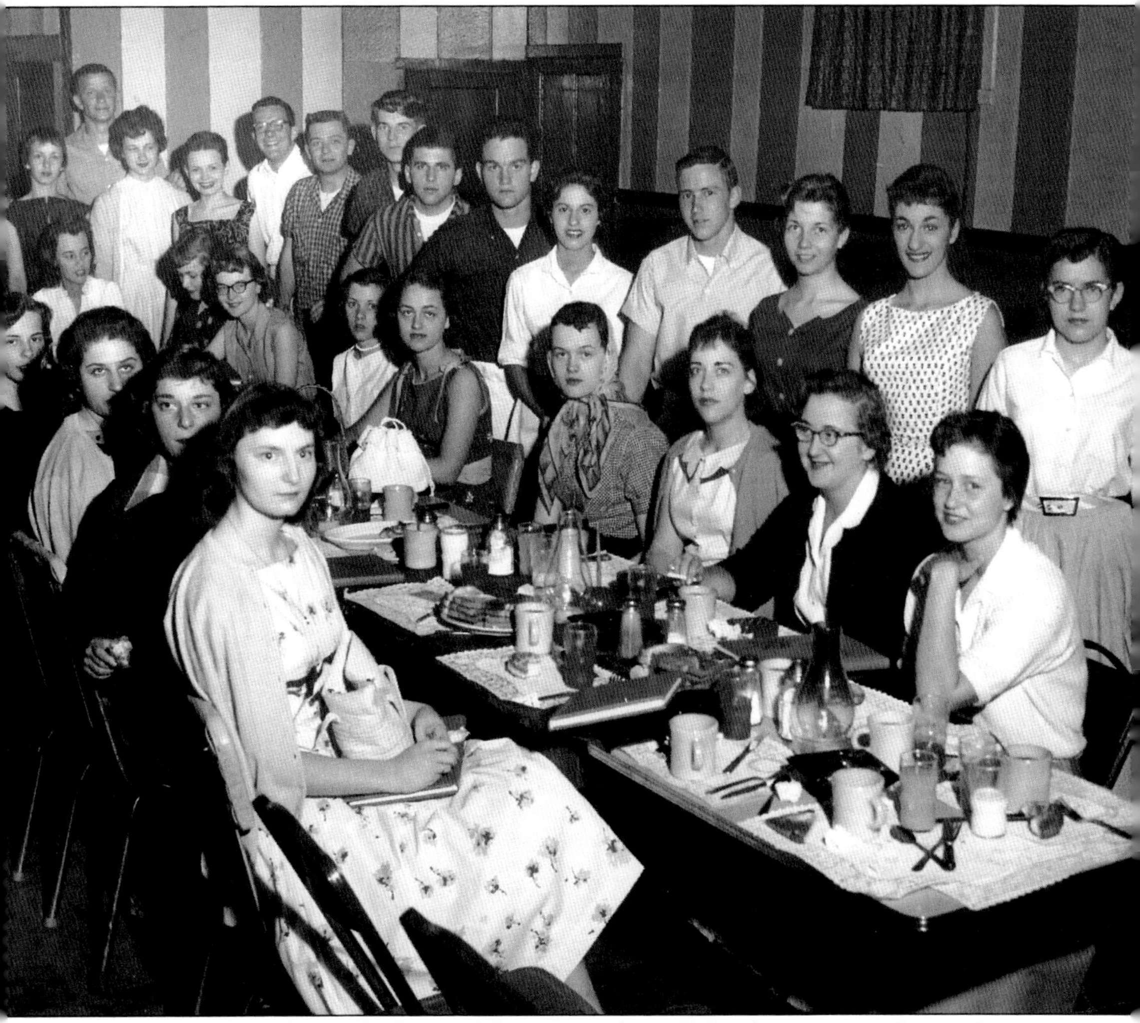

The 1954 renovation also resulted in modifications to the grill, lunch counter, and main dining area. Now there was more room for events such as the senior girls' breakfast. Each May, Stankewitz would serve rolls, juice, toast, and coffee to the graduating senior girls from Beloit High School, as seen in this photograph taken after the remodeling. (Courtesy of the Pop House collection.)

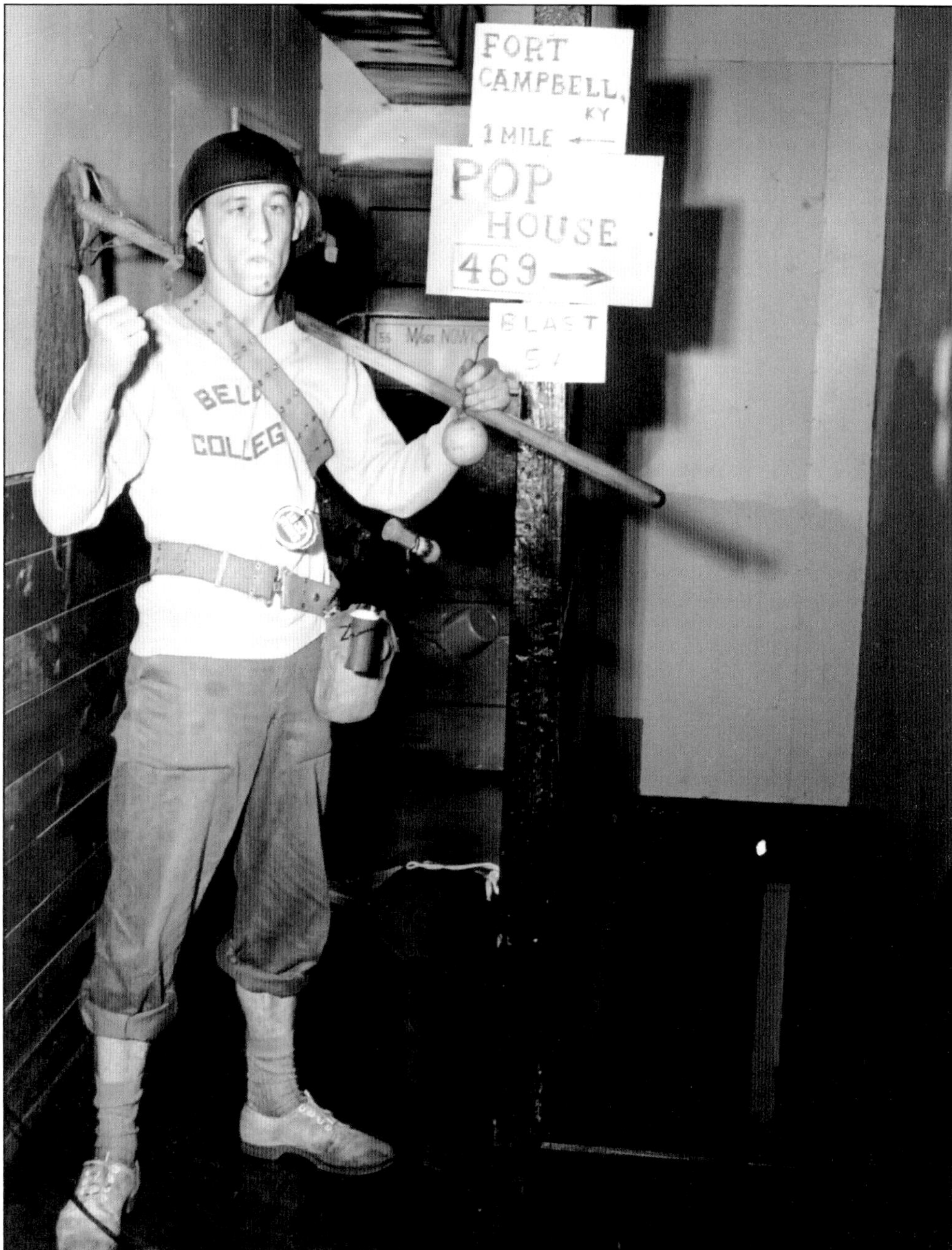

The Pop House had such a great impact on its customers that some carried those impressions with them on their travels. For the amusement of friends back home, a few even took the time to photograph themselves in faraway places, accompanied by some quirky reminder of their present location in relation to where they would rather be. The photograph here illustrates how a soldier at Fort Campbell, Kentucky, could be craving a cup of Blast, a reference to Pop House coffee. (Courtesy of the Pop House collection.)

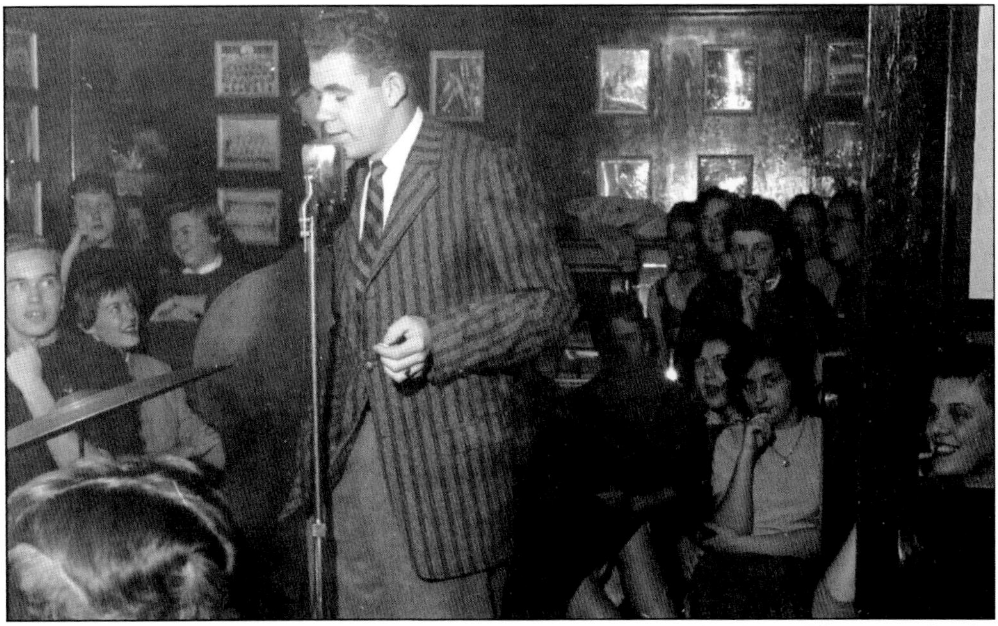

In the Walnut Room, Beloit radio personality Bob Gregory reveals who will be queen for the chili festival, an annual fall event. Toward the end of November, George Stankewitz would cook up the season's first batch of chili. The affair was accompanied by the election of a chili queen from a slate of senior high school girls nominated by the Pop House Activity Board. (Courtesy of the Pop House collection.)

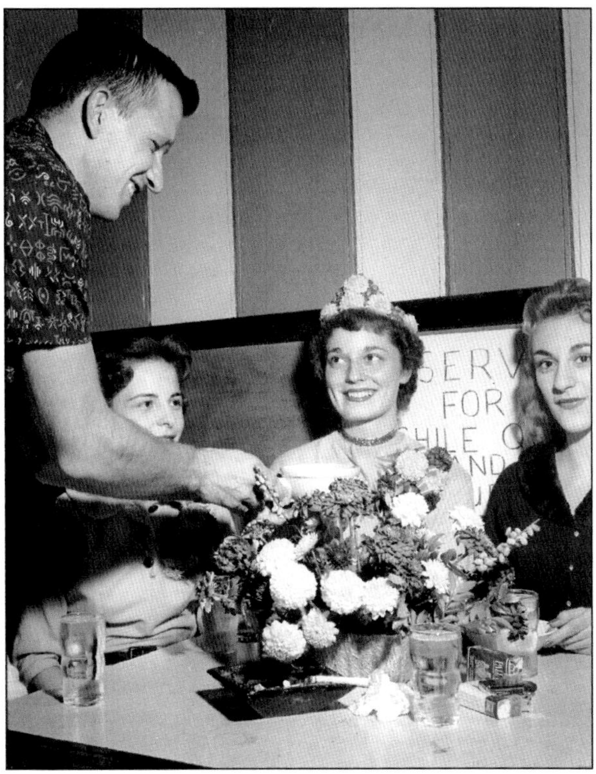

Chili queen candidates were seated at a table of honor. A radio was tuned to a local station where the balloting results were announced. Upon coronation by an appropriate dignitary and a parade through downtown Beloit, Stankewitz officially presented the first bowl of chili to the queen. Here Crystal (Cris) Pearson won the title for 1956. (Courtesy of the Pop House collection.)

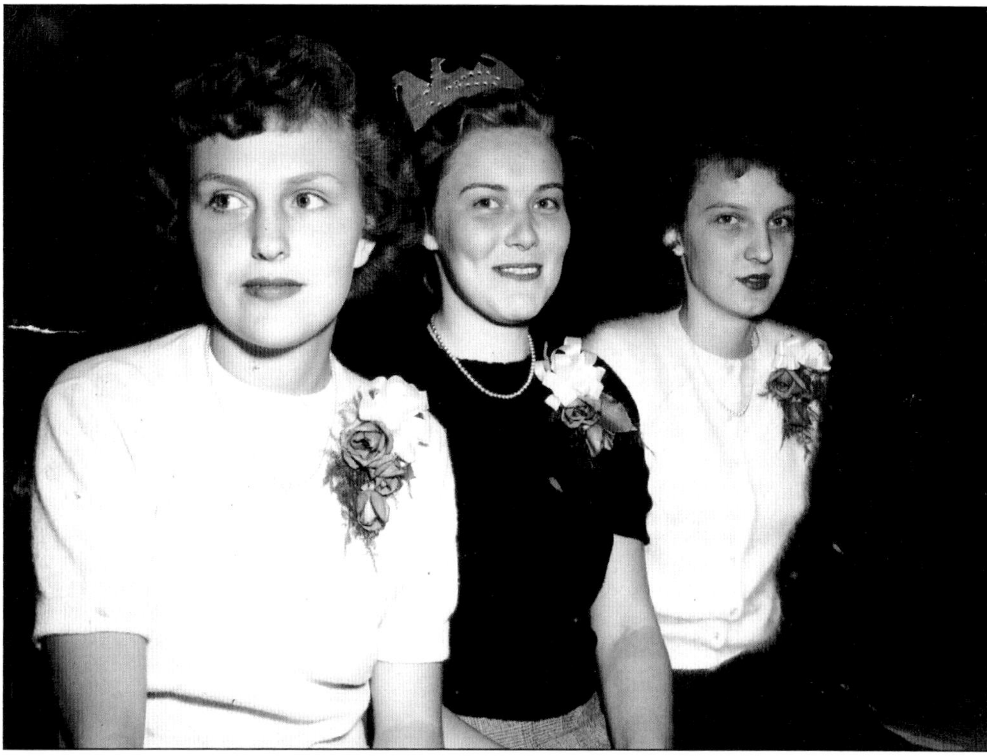

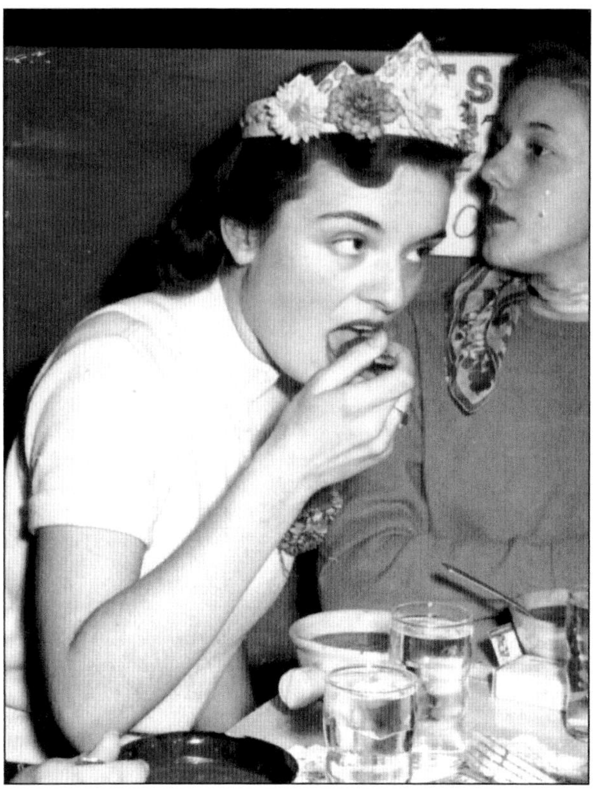

Prior chili queen titleholders included Beverly "Toots" Tuttle, Virginia (Ginny) Jacobson, and Mary Alice "Mimi" Winger. The 1953 chili queen, Tuttle is pictured in the photograph above with two members of her court. In the photograph at left, chili queen Winger is seen having the first spoonful of chili at the 1955 festival. (Courtesy of the Pop House collection.)

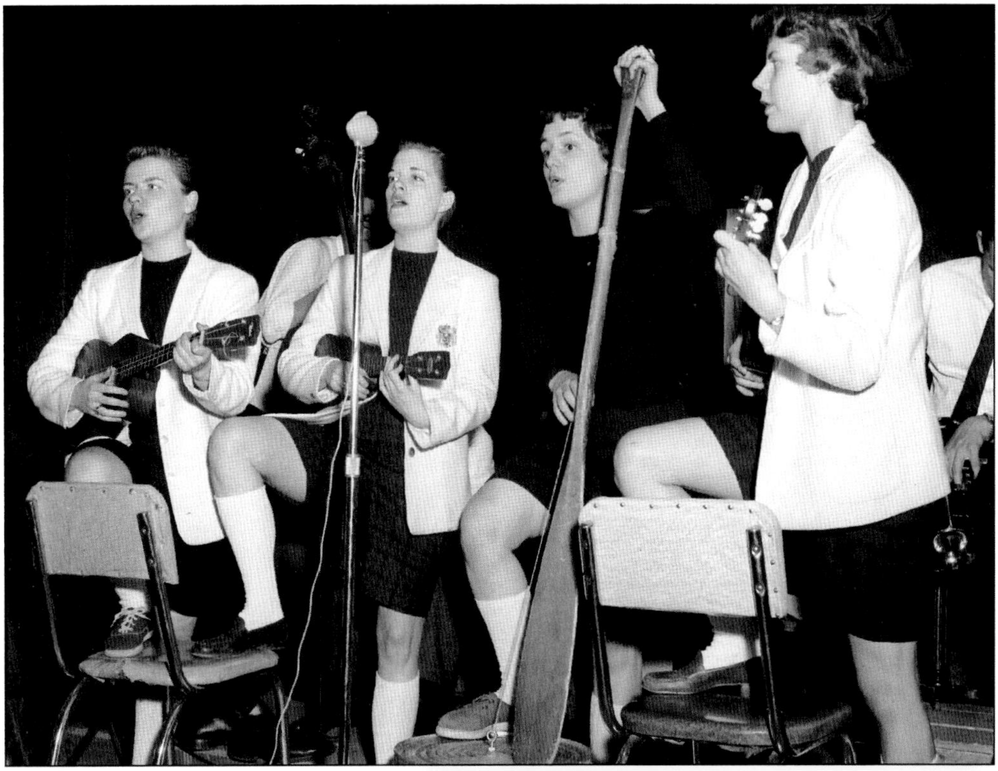

A 1956 variety show was staged that attracted both college and high school participants. A special stage was built for the show, and performers included dancing acts, vocal groups, and soloists. The photograph above shows a group of Beloit College girls singing while accompanying themselves with ukuleles and a homemade washtub bass. One of the highlights of the show was an Elvis impersonator, seen in the photograph at right. To accommodate a large crowd, two shows were presented. When the first show ended, audience members were directed to exit out the back door while a new crowd filed in through the front door. (Courtesy of the Pop House collection.)

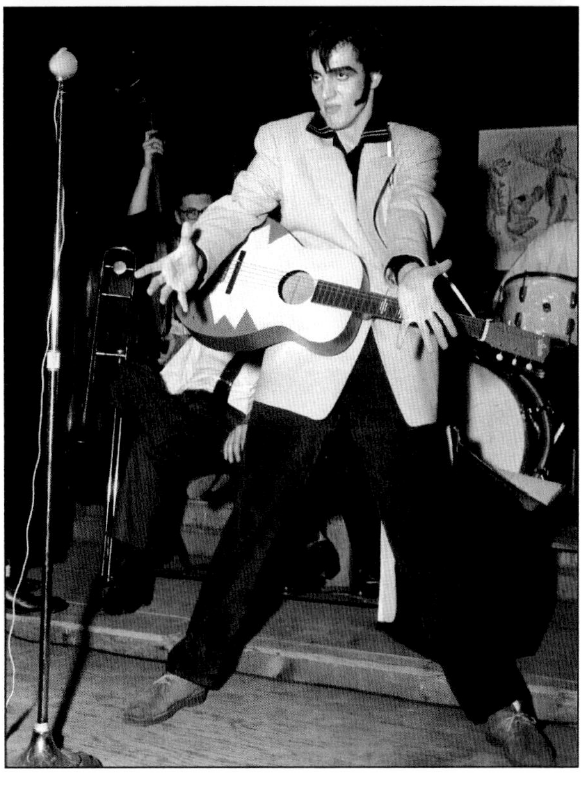

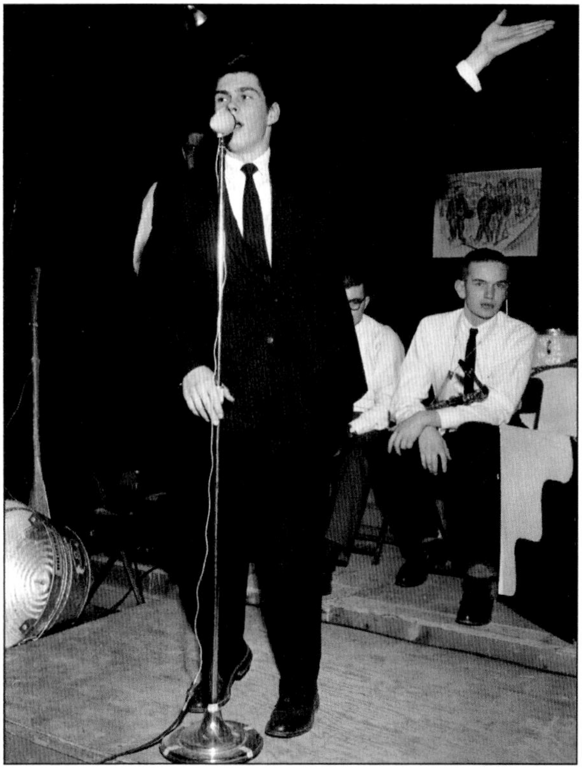

The idea for a variety show was suggested by Pop House regular Gerald Werle, who organized the production and served as emcee for the show. The show proved to be successful, and it also served to further demonstrate not only the popularity of live entertainment but the need for more space to accommodate it. (Courtesy of the Pop House collection.)

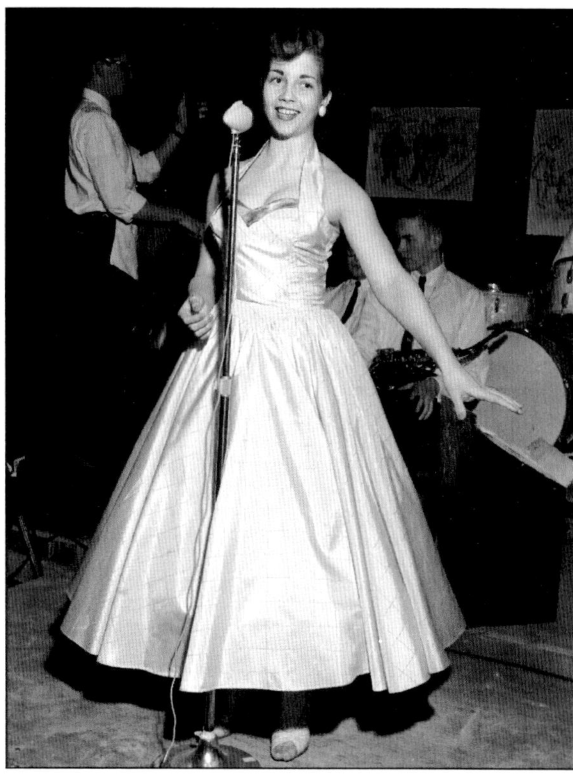

A popular television series in 1956 was *Your Hit Parade*, and it is likely that the Pop House show was based partly on that program. On the television show, Dorothy Collins and Gisèle MacKenzie were two of the vocalists whose songs may have been performed by this unidentified vocalist decked out in her evening gown. A swing band provided backing music for the show. (Courtesy of the Pop House collection.)

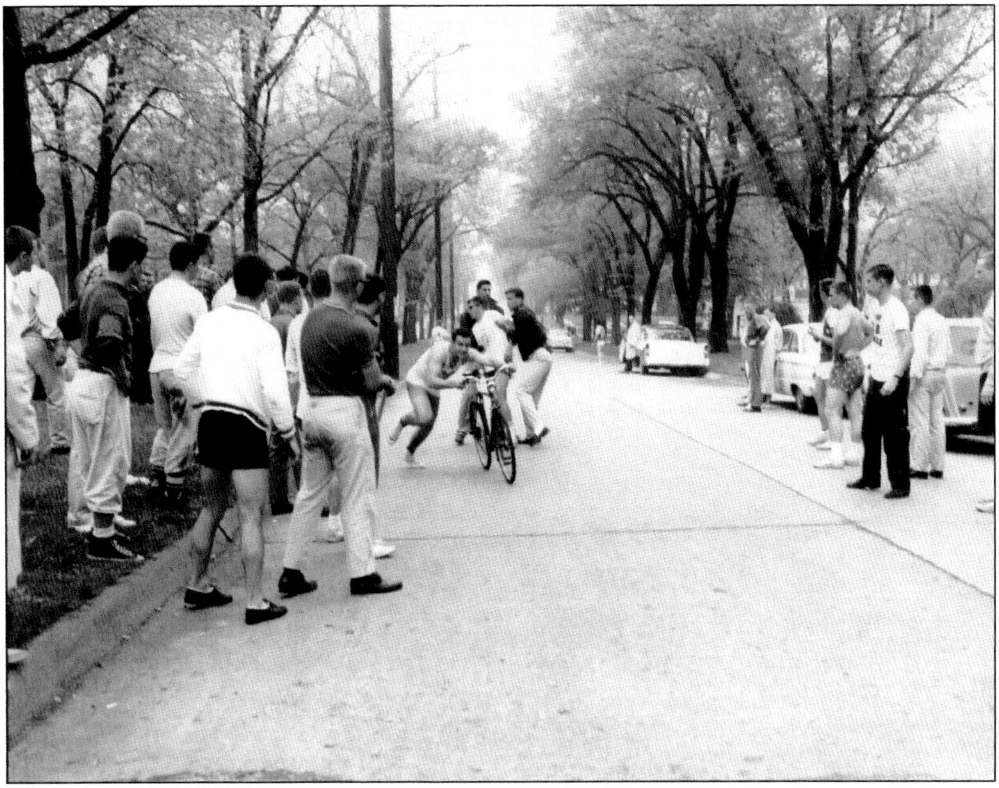

The college kids needled George Stankewitz about having beaten the Pop House softball team for two years running, so he challenged them to participate in a selection of sports the following spring. It became an annual event known as the Pop House Collegiate Olympics, pitting high school and Beloit College students against each other in softball, basketball, tennis, golf, canoeing, and bicycle racing. A nine-mile bike relay race from 1957 is shown in the photograph above. One event in 1953 became known as the great water fight. Hundreds were involved. The battle started with squirt guns and progressed to buckets, hoses, and a final stand on the banks of the Rock River only to be quelled by a police tear gas bomb. Below, a *Beloit Daily News* account of the melee was published on May 19, 1953. (Courtesy of the Pop House collection.)

College Squirt Gun 'Commandos' Stage Clean Fight but Tear Gas Forces Truce

By Dave Mason

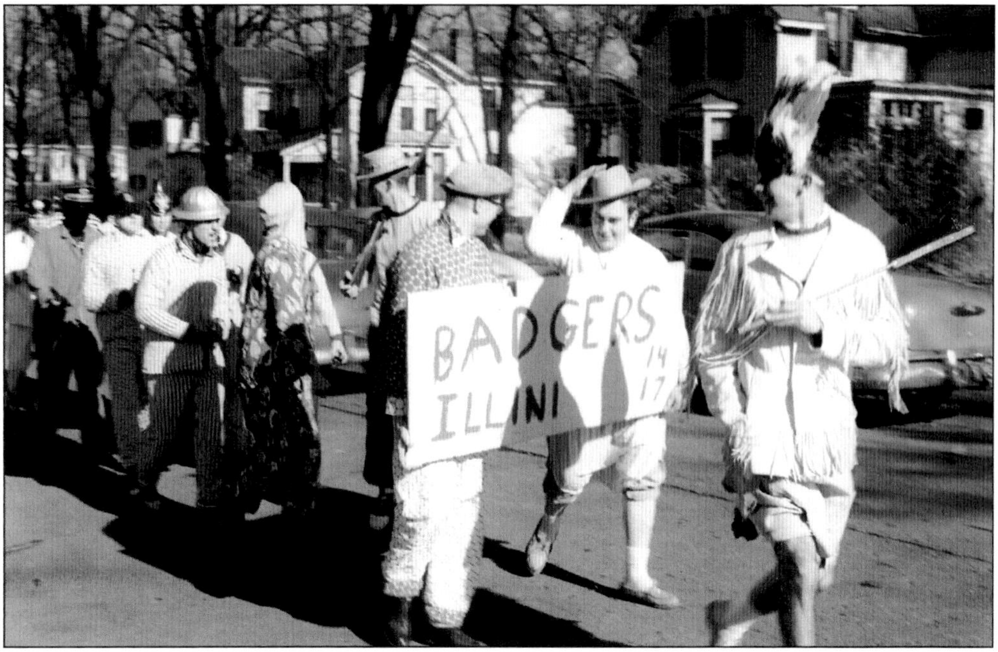

The pajama parade was a ritual that involved Badger football fans who were Pop House regulars. When the Badgers lost to the Fighting Illini in 1955, the cadre of fans was required to dress in pajamas and follow George Stankewitz (also in pajamas) down College Street in shame with a banner displaying the final score. (Courtesy of the Pop House collection.)

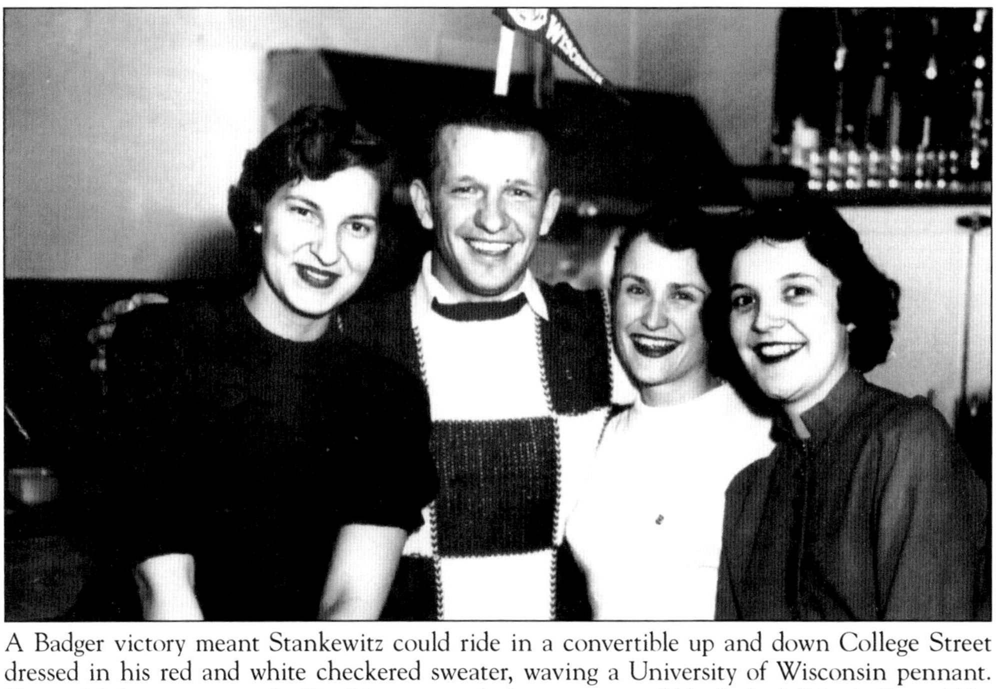

A Badger victory meant Stankewitz could ride in a convertible up and down College Street dressed in his red and white checkered sweater, waving a University of Wisconsin pennant. He would then return to the Pop House crowd where arms would be linked, "Varsity" would be sung, and cheeseburgers would be served. This photograph of Stankewitz wearing his sweater appeared in the 1954 *Gold* Beloit College yearbook. (Courtesy of the Beloit College Archives.)

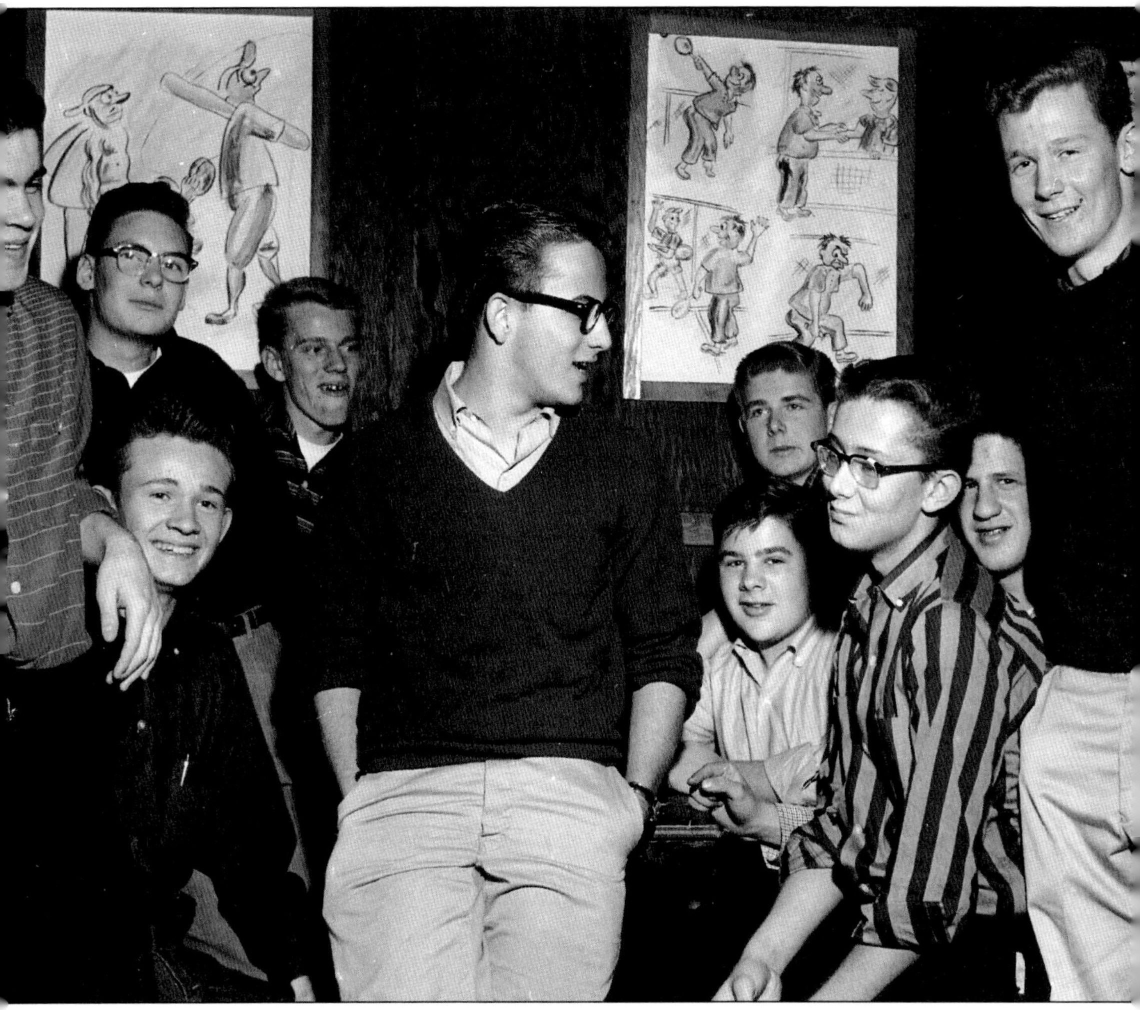

Shown here is a scene from the original Pop House. In front of the hand-drawn posters are 1959 seniors Les "Chub" Helgeson, Terry Christiansen, Mike Dane, Ron Nelson, Jerry Pate, Phil Spielmacher, Jerry Koopman, Jerry Gunning, Pete Springberg, and Jeff Stanley, son of Beloit College basketball coach Dolph Stanley whose teams won 40 straight Midwest Conference games and six consecutive titles. (Courtesy of the Pop House collection.)

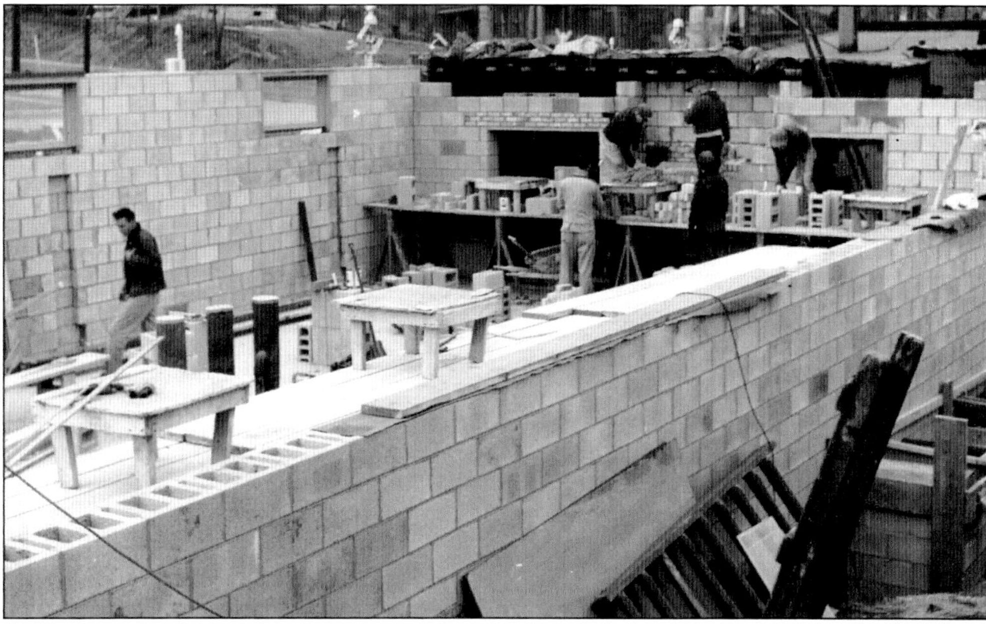

With a growing clientele and greater space demands for entertainment, a major expansion of the Pop House was undertaken. Work on a 1,400-square-foot addition to the original building was started in 1957. Looking southwest, the exterior walls are underway and workers are focused on the chimney of the fireplace that would dominate the south wall of the new dining room. (Courtesy of the Pop House collection.)

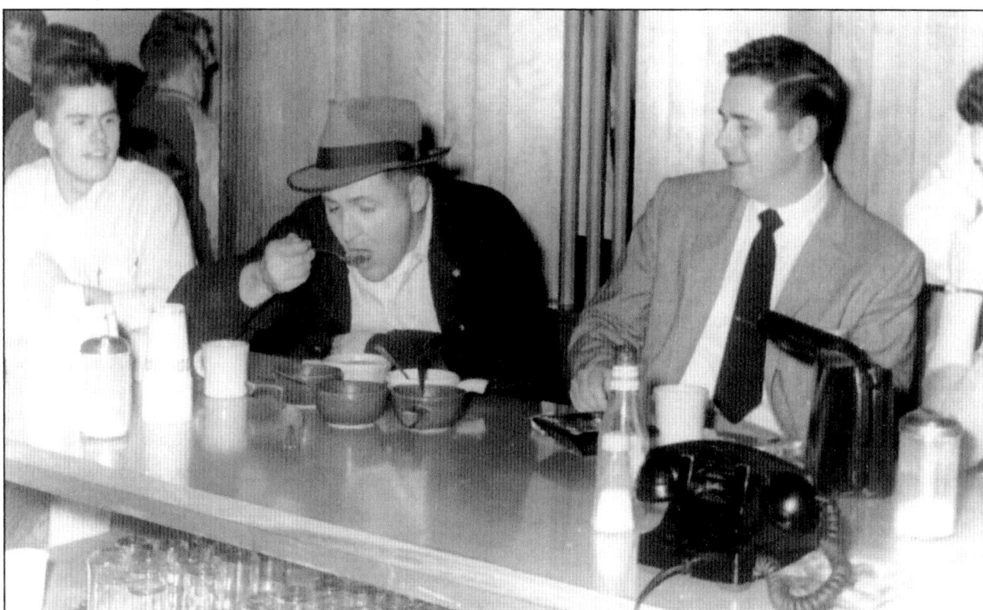

The addition was built with the help of customers, sometimes for just a few hamburgers. Here bricklayer John Clark takes a break with a bowl of chili. A dozen firms were involved with the construction project, including masonry contractors Clark, Ernie Champlin, and Dean Phelps. Young customers also helped out on Saturdays by picking up debris and sweeping the sidewalks. (Courtesy of Ida and Richard Lenz.)

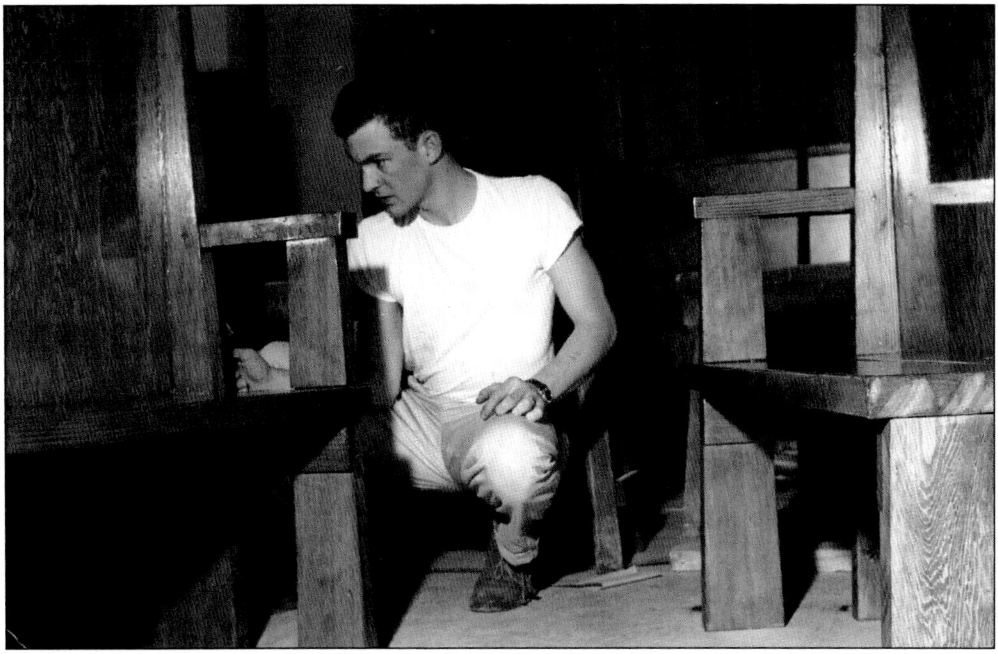

Changes to the interior included the addition of booths along the east and west walls of the new dining room. New booths and tables were stained and varnished in dark tones. The dining room would also feature a large brick fireplace at the south end and a new Wurlitzer jukebox on the opposite wall. (Courtesy of the Pop House collection.)

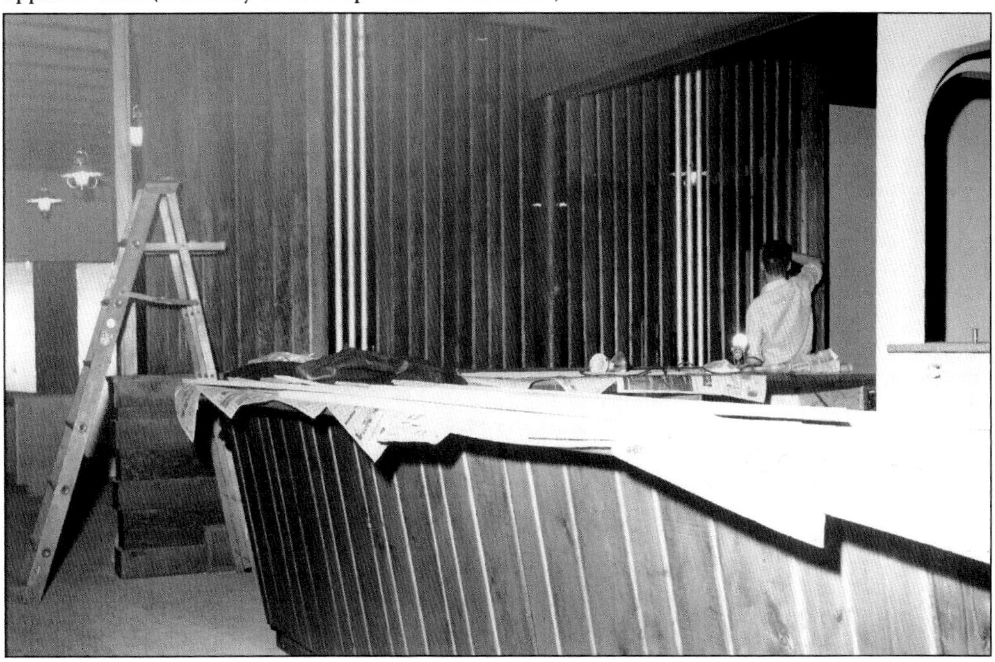

A new lunch counter would become the focal point upon entering the club through the relocated main door in the northwest corner of the addition. On the other side of the arched pass-through was a new kitchen and grill. A partition separated the lunch counter from the main dining room. (Courtesy of the Pop House collection.)

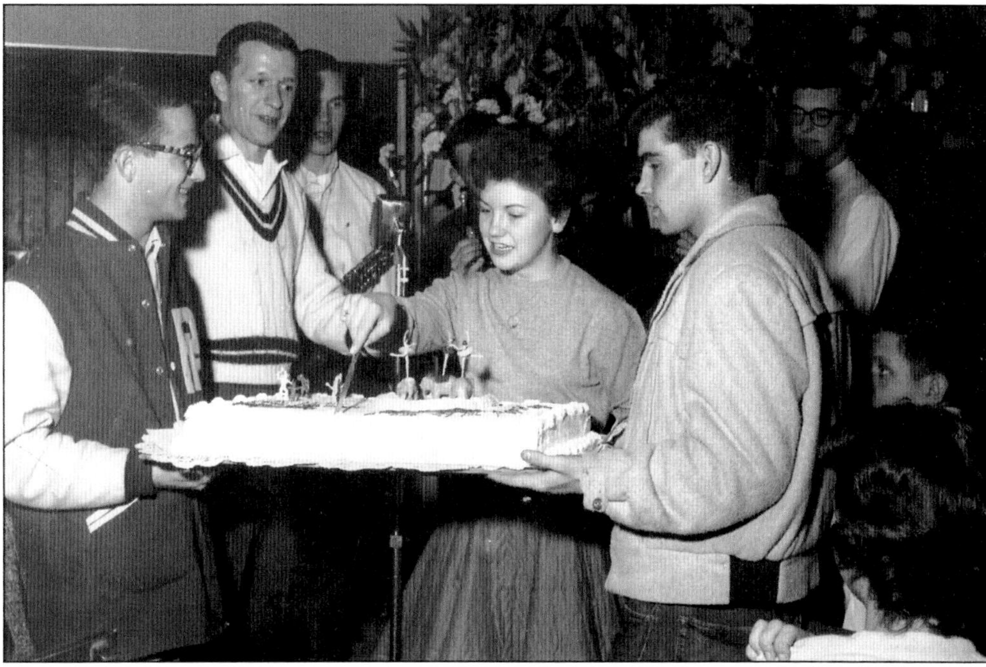

The grand opening of the new Club Pop House was celebrated on March 12, 1958. Jerry Pate (left in Pop House jacket) and Les "Chub" Helgeson hold the cake as 1957 chili queen Carol Maryott cuts it. George Stankewitz, in the V-neck sweater, oversees the ceremony. The festivity also marked the opening of a new sport shop adjacent to the original building at 158 Portland Avenue. (Courtesy of the Pop House collection.)

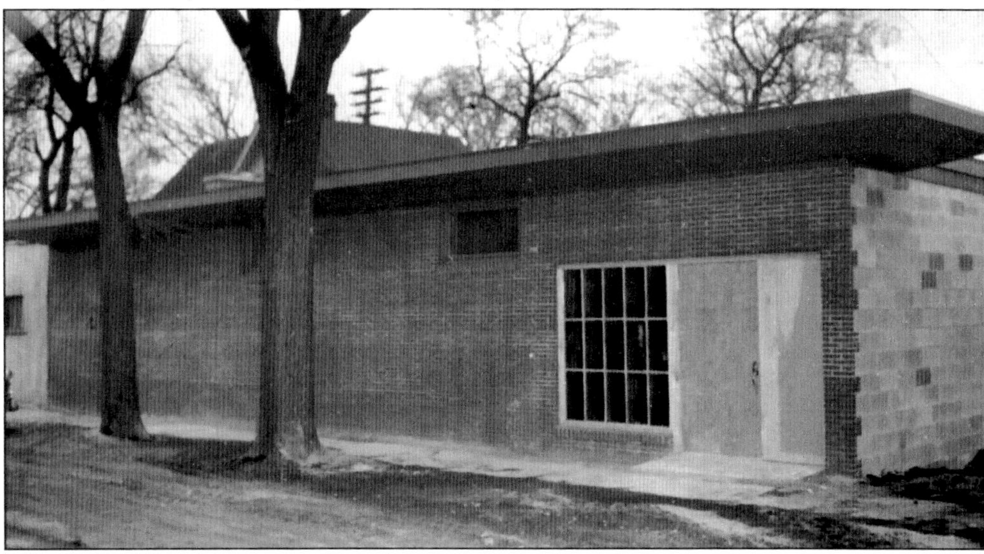

A photograph of the completed addition was featured in a half-page advertisement announcing the grand opening of the new Club Pop House. The advertisement appeared in the March 12, 1958, issue of the *Beloit Daily News*. Speculation is that the two trees in the foreground were not part of the original landscape on Fifth Street. Trick photography may have been used to insert them. Note the original building partially visible on the left. (Courtesy of the Pop House collection.)

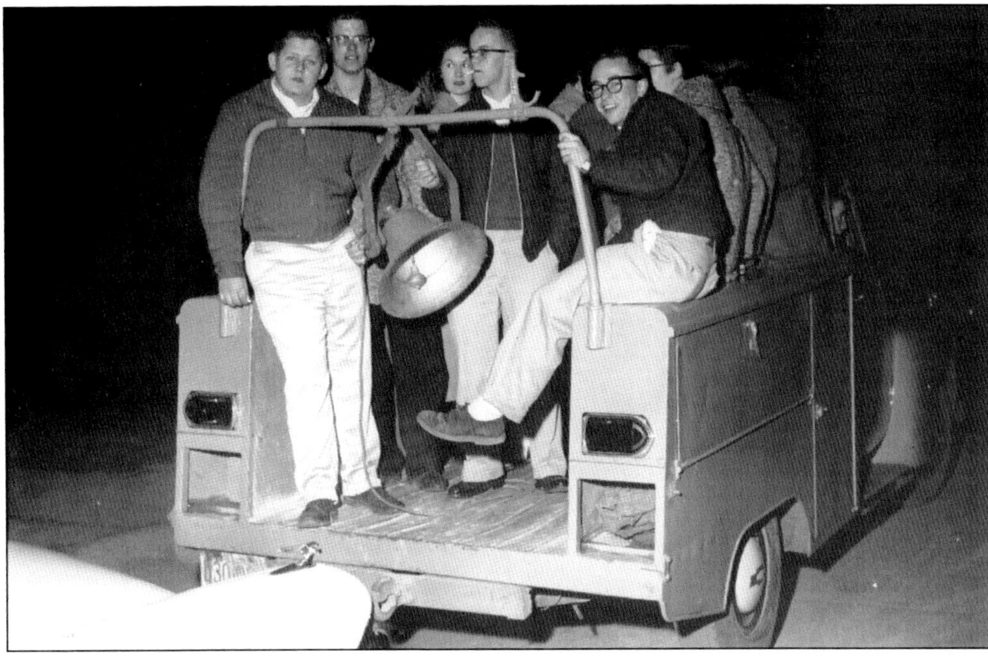

No Pop House event would have been complete without a parade. This truck was outfitted with the old school bell that had been used for celebrations going back a decade, including the 1949 softball homecoming parade. Revelers and dignitaries paraded through downtown streets ringing in a new era for the Pop House. (Courtesy of the Pop House collection.)

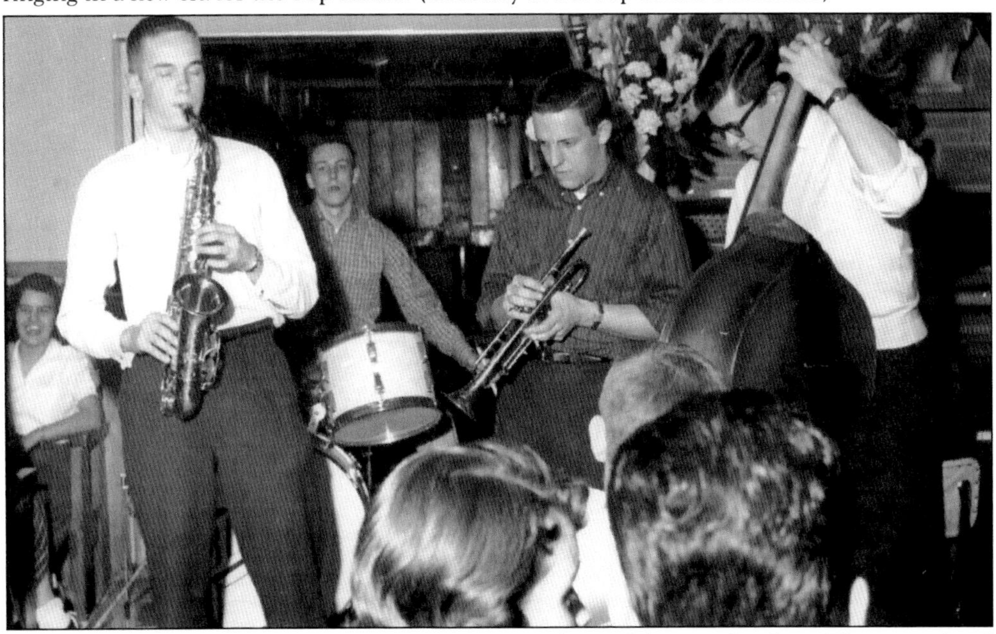

With more space available, musicians could set up in front of the new fireplace. This swing band played for the grand opening. By 1958, swing music had become less popular as rock and roll was gaining more radio airplay. Some rock-and-roll artists still included a few swing-era standards in their repertoires, but musical preferences leaned more toward folk music and rock and roll. (Courtesy of the Pop House collection.)

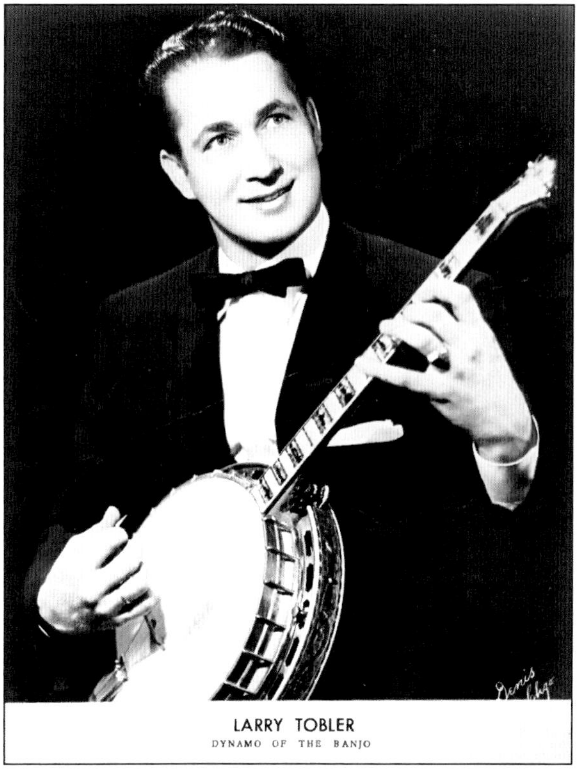

Billed as the "Dynamo of the Banjo," Larry Tobler was in demand at school assemblies around the country. His appearance at the Pop House included an educational presentation about the banjo's place in the history of American music. The banjo stands as the only truly American instrument, and Tobler would trace its history from its origin in the 1840s through the Stephen Foster era. Foster was the first composer to recognize and write specifically for the banjo, and Tobler would play selections of those compositions. The program would include a discussion about the instrument's place in minstrel shows, the westward migration, and in the development of Dixieland music. The show would close with classic selections, novelty tunes, and trick playing methods. Tobler was still playing banjo into the 1990s. (Courtesy of the Pop House collection.)

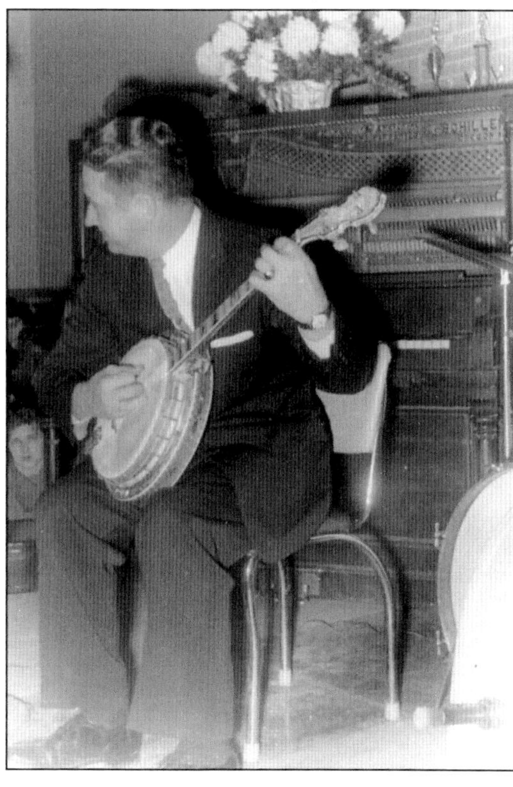

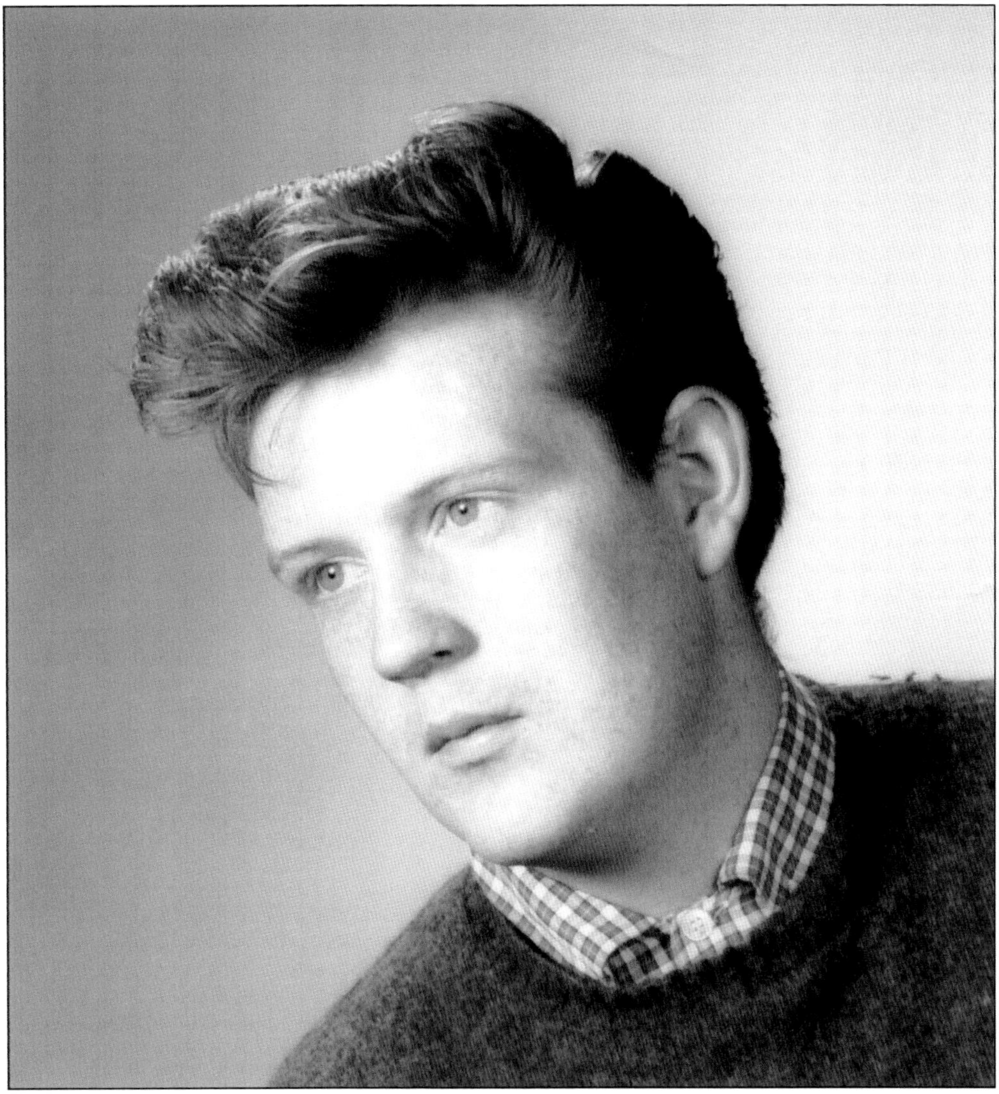

Jerry Martin and the Sounds recorded Iowa's first rock-and-roll record, *Janet*, on the Fredlo label. Their appearance at the Pop House in 1958 marked the first time a rock-and-roll act performed there. About the venue Martin recalls, "The Pop House was one of my finest memories. . . . It had a spirit all its own. I really loved that place. I once had a Pop House jacket, but I wore it out." (Courtesy of the Pop House collection.)

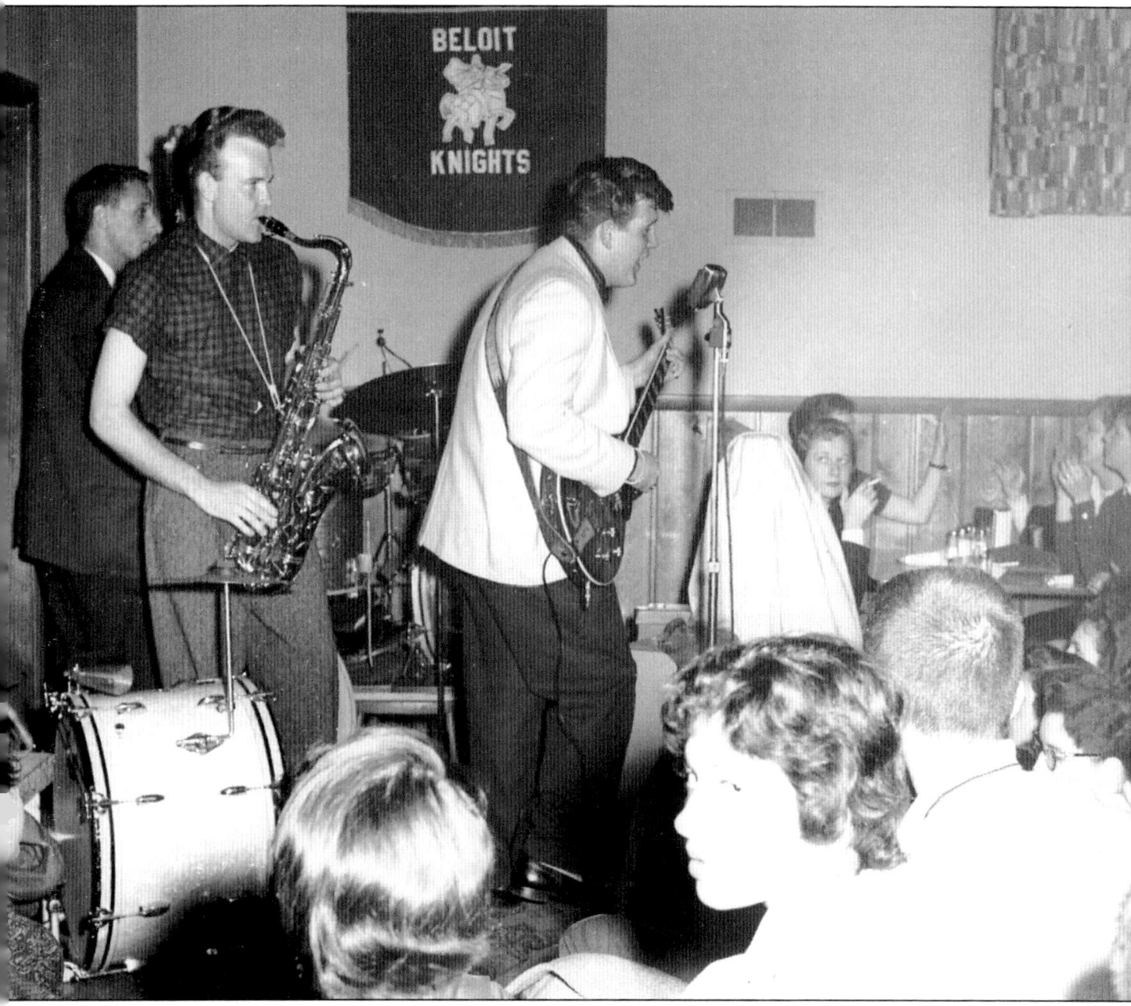

Club member Linda Jensen remembers inviting Jerry Martin to her home after the show. He played guitar in the living room, waking her parents, who wondered what was happening. Martin returned to the Pop House in 1960 before hanging up his guitar and becoming Layton "King" Zbornik, a noted radio personality. He was inducted into the Iowa Rock and Roll Music Association Hall of Fame in 1998. Today Zbornik continues to teach, write, and perform as Jerry Martin. (Courtesy of the Pop House collection.)

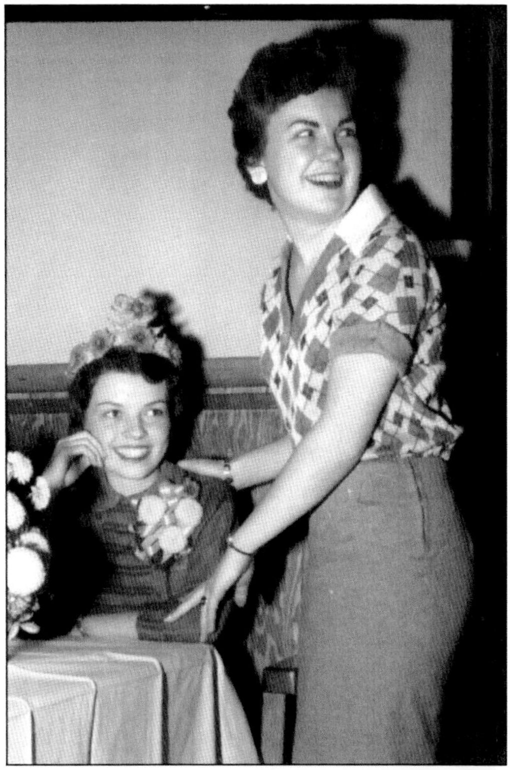

Karen Durben, 1958 chili queen, is congratulated here by past queen Carol Maryott in the new Pop House. Durben was the first chili queen to be crowned in the new building. In the photograph below, Christine Laage is congratulated by her court upon winning the title of chili queen for 1959. (Courtesy of the Pop House collection.)

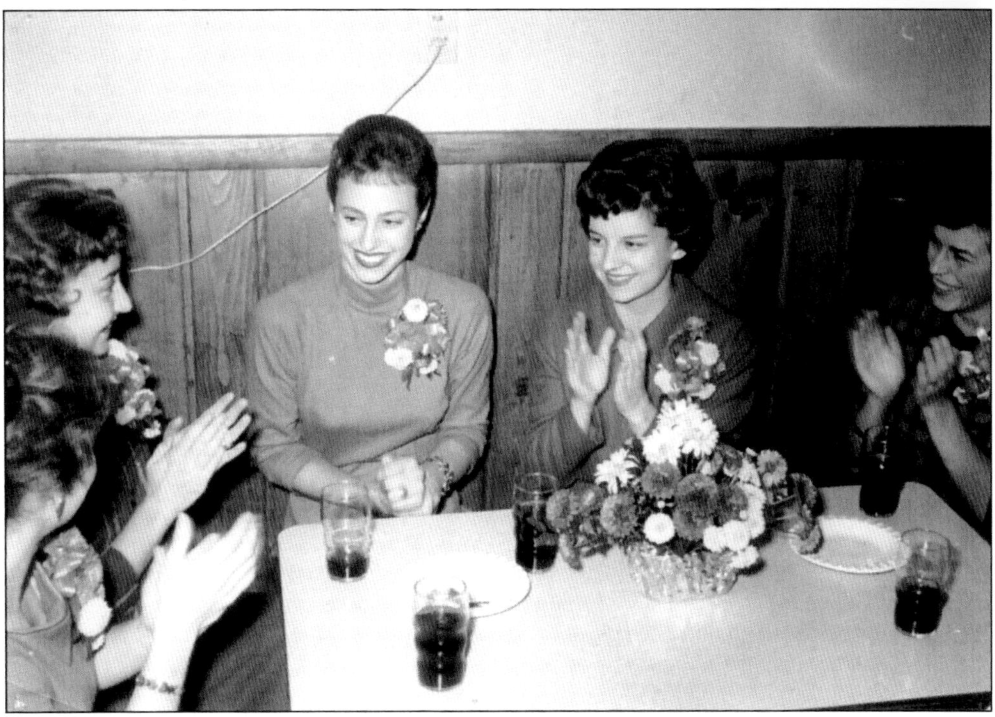

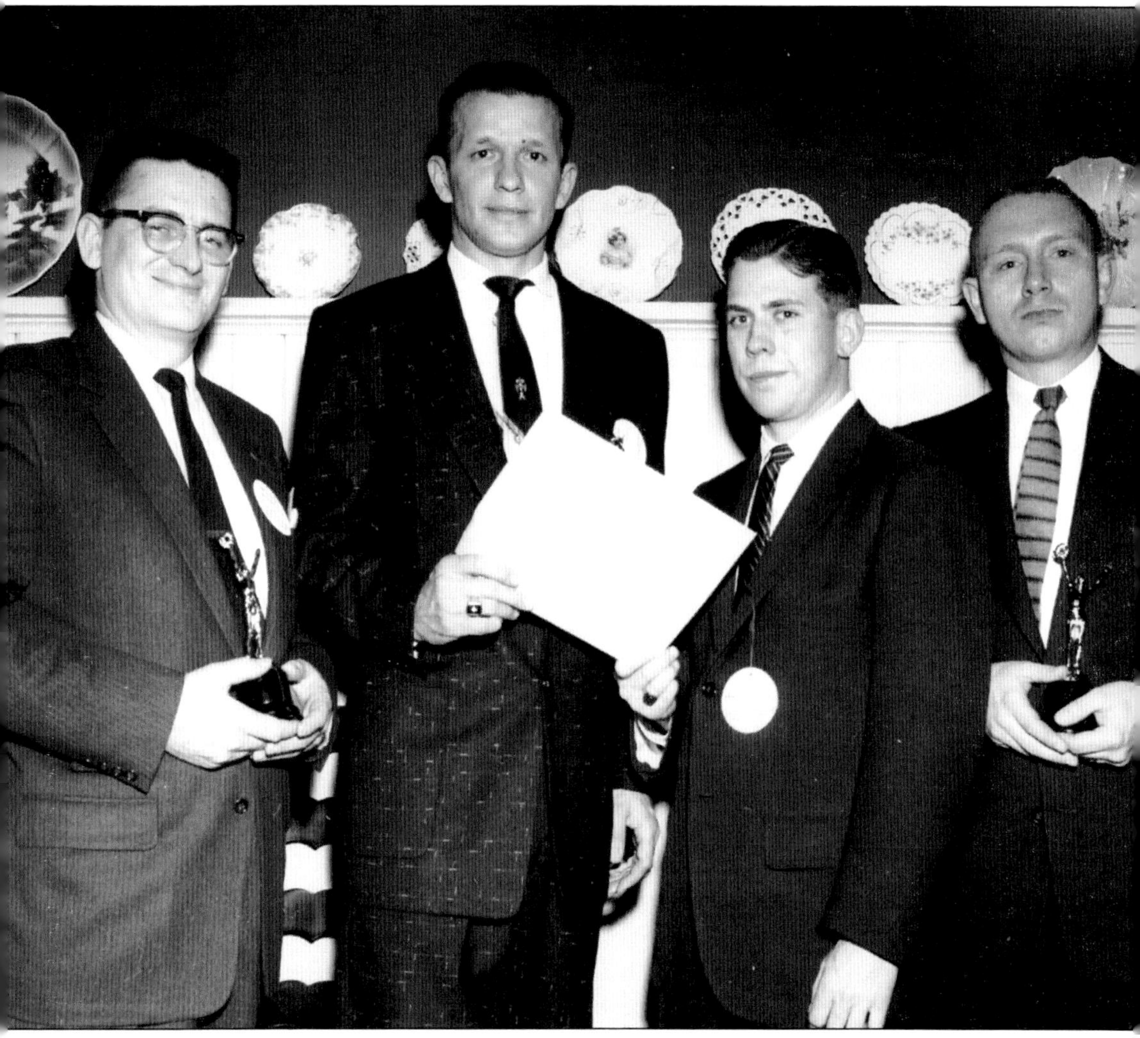

In 1958, the Beloit Junior Chamber of Commerce honored George Stankewitz as the community's outstanding citizen of the year. Selected for his service to humanity and the community, he was presented with a certificate from Peter Halverson, Jaycee president. The award was presented during the 10th annual "Bosses' Night" program at the Wagon Wheel restaurant. Also pictured are Russell Ratzlaff, outstanding chairman for 1957, and Richard Pfeil, outstanding member. Other community honors bestowed on Stankewitz over the years were the Outstanding Beloiter Award in 1966 and Beloit Booster Award in 1970. He was named parade marshal for the Beloit Catholic High School festival Saderfest in 1987. In May 1989, about 500 friends and business associates roasted Stankewitz at a celebration in his honor. His high school classmates dedicated their 50th anniversary book to his memory. (Courtesy of the Pop House collection.)

Two

THE PLACE TO BE

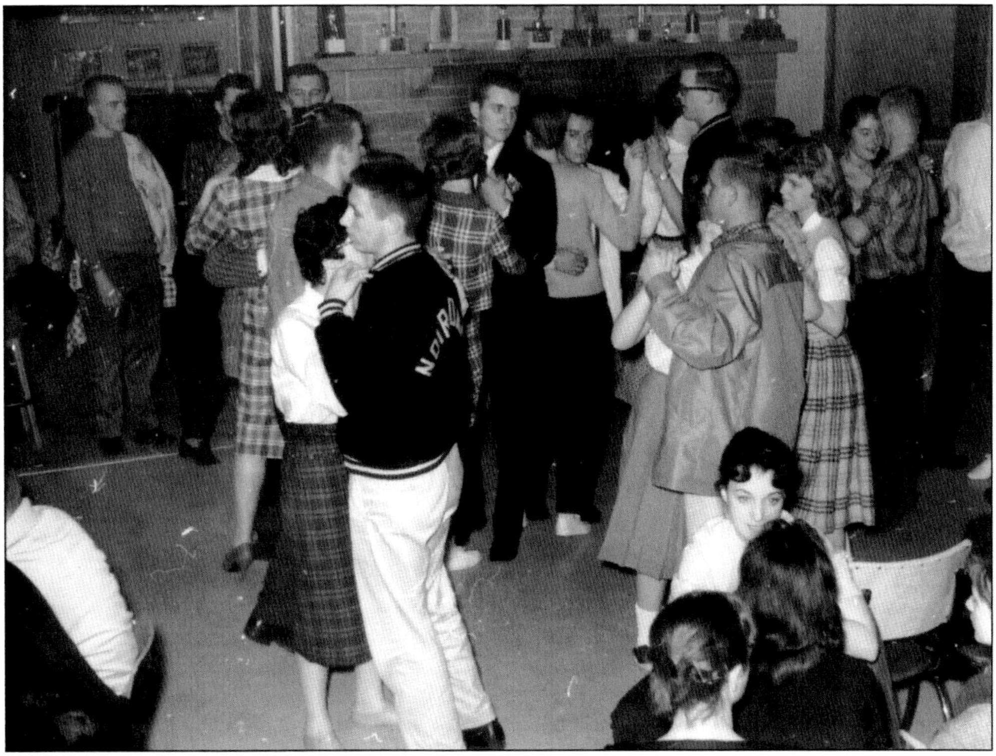

With a new building completed and a new decade approaching, Club Pop House experienced unprecedented growth as new classes of high school sophomores clamored to become members. As the 1950s came to a close, dancing, record jams, and live music had become the norm. Numerous musical acts, including more than two dozen national artists, were presented during the coming years. (Courtesy of the Pop House collection.)

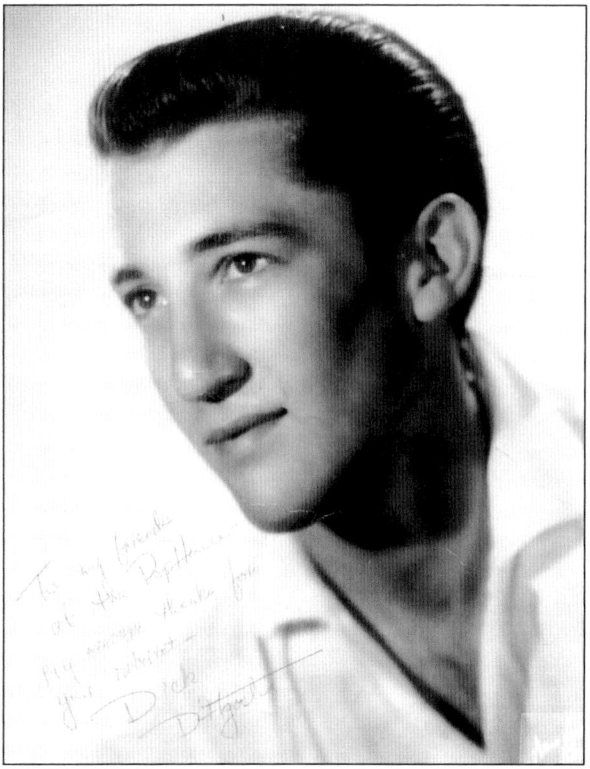

Dick D'Agostin and the Swingers were among the early national acts to get the nod. They were a Los Angeles rockabilly band with a song called "Nancy Lynne" that had become a minor hit in 1958. D'Agostin, who played piano and guitar, and his band, the Swingers, were also known for backing rocker Eddie Cochran on recordings and tours in the late 1950s. (Courtesy of the Pop House collection.)

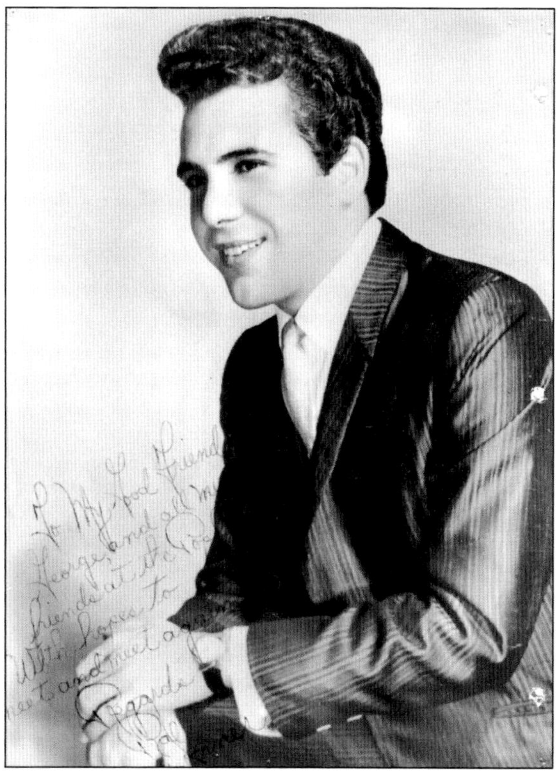

Ral Donner's career caught fire with his Elvis Presley–style vocals. His biggest hit, "You Don't Know What You Got," reached number four on the *Billboard* charts in 1961. He performed at the Pop House in the early 1960s when he signed this photograph, "To My Good Friend George, and all my friends at the Pophouse. With hopes to meet and meet again." (Courtesy of the Pop House collection.)

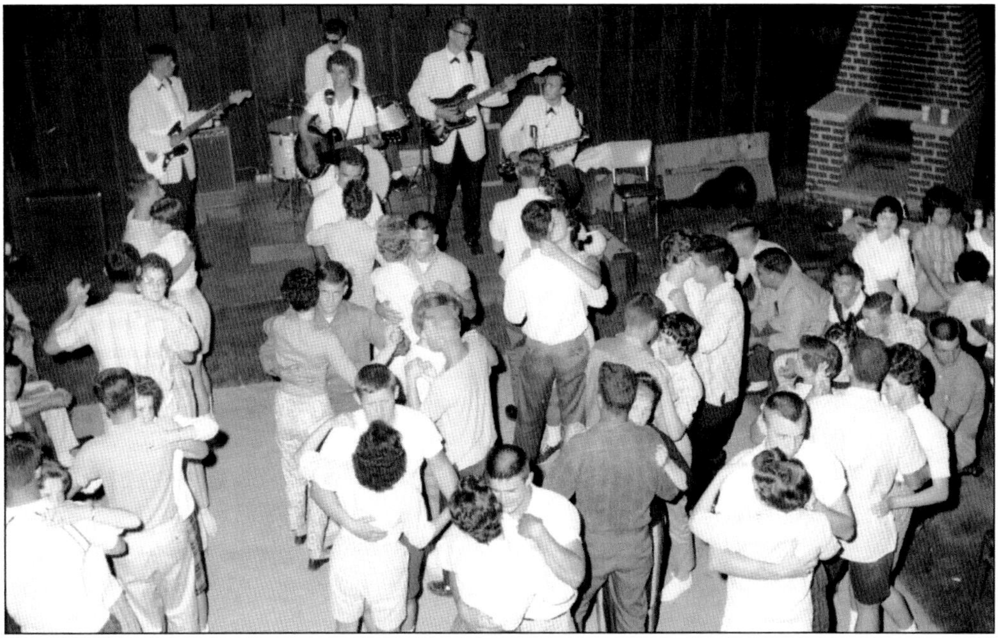

No longer needed, the original Pop House building was demolished to make room for a patio area featuring a dance floor, a stage, and a brick barbecue grill. Above, summer weekends on the Pop House patio were filled with music and dancing. George Stankewitz hired a number of big-name bands through the 1960s for which he often lost money or only broke even. According to Stankewitz, the Pop House was usually good for a pickup date when stars toured the Midwest. Eventually the stage was covered to offer some degree of protection for the musicians. Below, Jack Isaacson and the Corduroy Clowns perform on the covered stage. (Above, courtesy of the Pop House collection, photograph by Edwin Sweet; below, courtesy of the Pop House collection.)

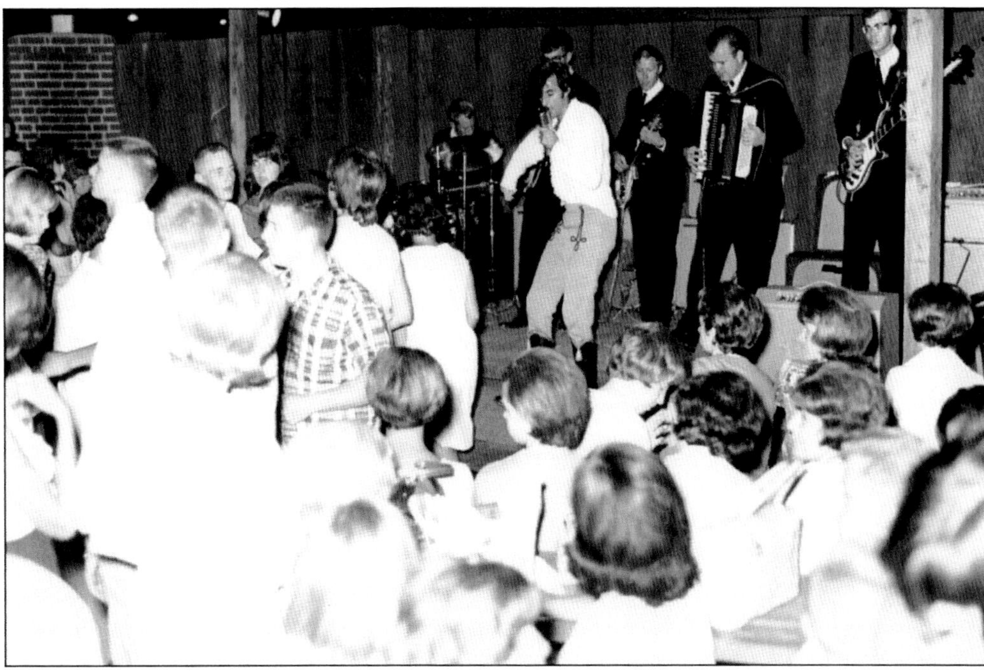

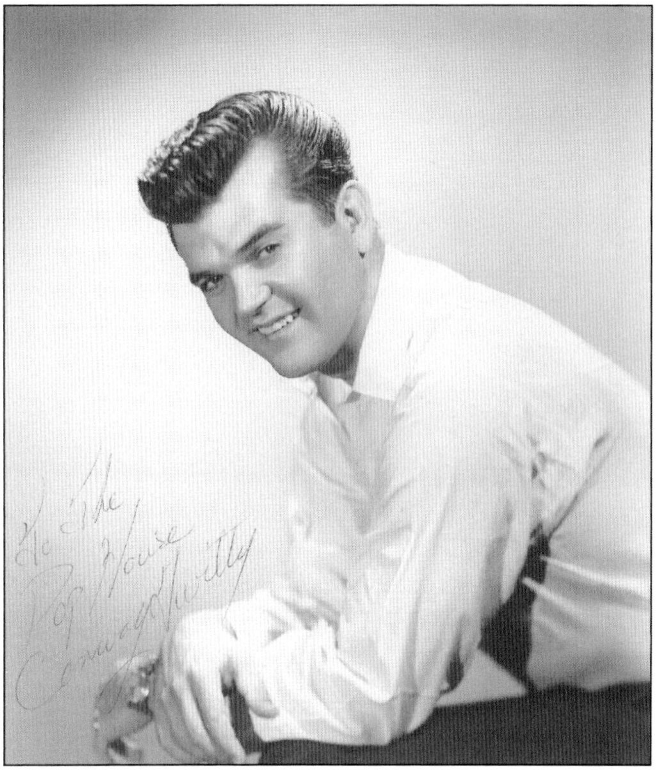

Before country music stardom, Conway Twitty enjoyed success in rock and roll. In 1958, his song "It's Only Make Believe" reached number one. He scored another top-10 hit with "Lonely Blue Boy." Twitty's performance at the Pop House in the early 1960s was one of his many appearances at dance halls and sock hops all over the country. (Courtesy of the Pop House collection.)

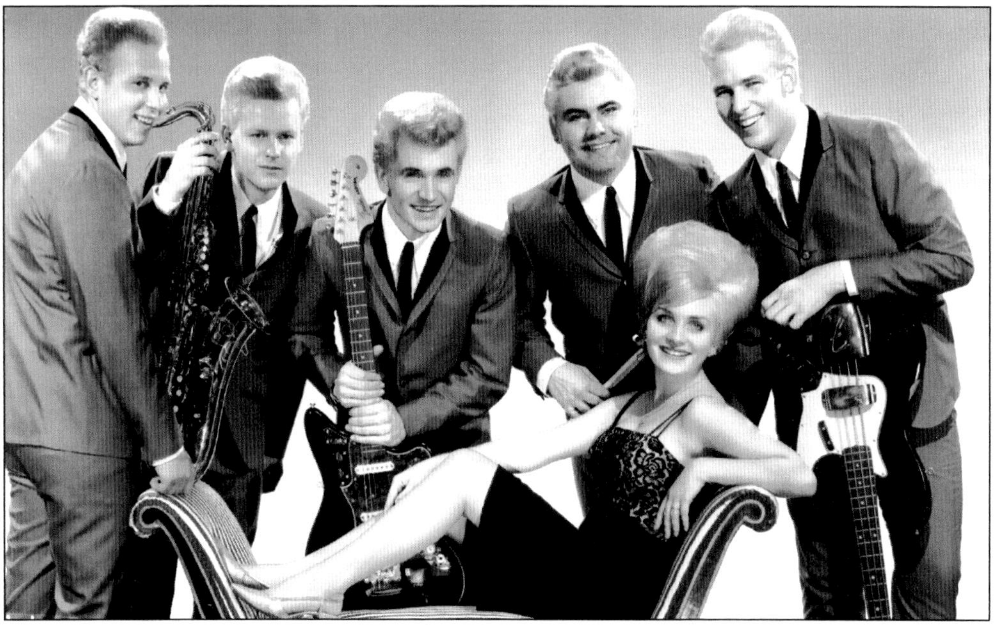

A 1960s favorite, Johnny Green and the Greenmen dyed their hair green, highlighted by overhead black lights, resulting in one of the first light shows. Fire-eating was also part of the band's act. The Greenmen appeared in a 1964 *Batman* television episode and scored a hit song with the "Batman Theme," recorded with the Billy May Orchestra. Johnny Green was still touring in the early 21st century. (Courtesy of the Pop House collection.)

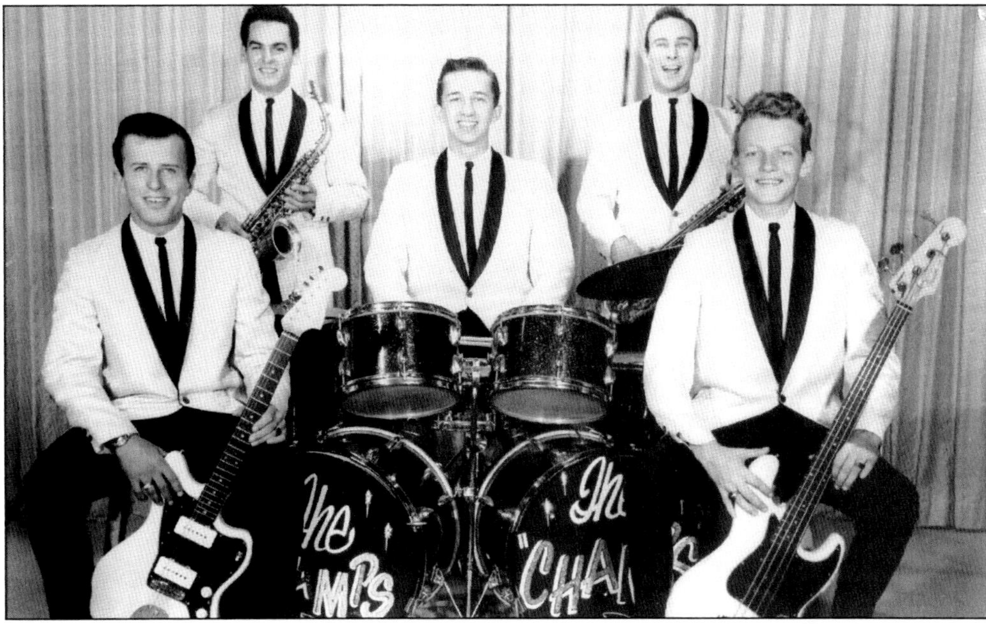

The Champs were famous for their 1958 number one instrumental hit "Tequila." Personnel included Jim Seals (saxophone) and Dash Crofts (drums) who, some years after the band's breakup in 1965, reunited as the successful recording duo Seals and Crofts. Seals began his career as a saxophonist and also played violin. Crofts started as a drummer and pianist. Both play guitar and mandolin. (Courtesy of the Pop House collection.)

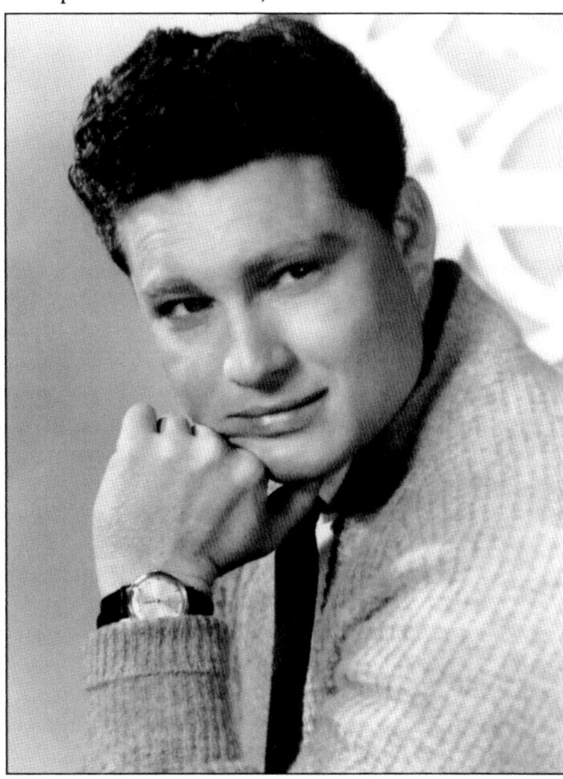

Promoting his 1962 hit song "Hey! Baby," Bruce Channel made the Pop House a stop on his national tour. Channel also toured England where the Beatles, still unknown at the time, opened for Channel. It is believed that Channel's harmonica player, Delbert McClinton, inspired John Lennon's playing harmonica on the Beatles' single "Love Me Do." Channel continues to work in the Nashville music scene. (Courtesy of the Pop House collection.)

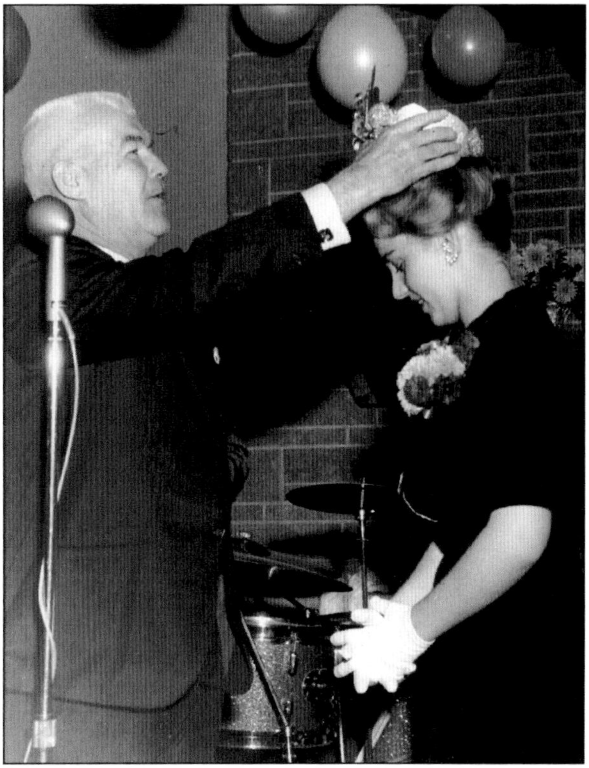

Chili festivals continued into the 1960s and became a much-anticipated event every fall. Here 1960 chili queen Mary Lynn Poole is crowned by Tom Schuler, executive director of the Greater Beloit Association of Commerce. Each year, a local dignitary was invited to be guest of honor and to conduct the coronation. (Courtesy of the Pop House collection.)

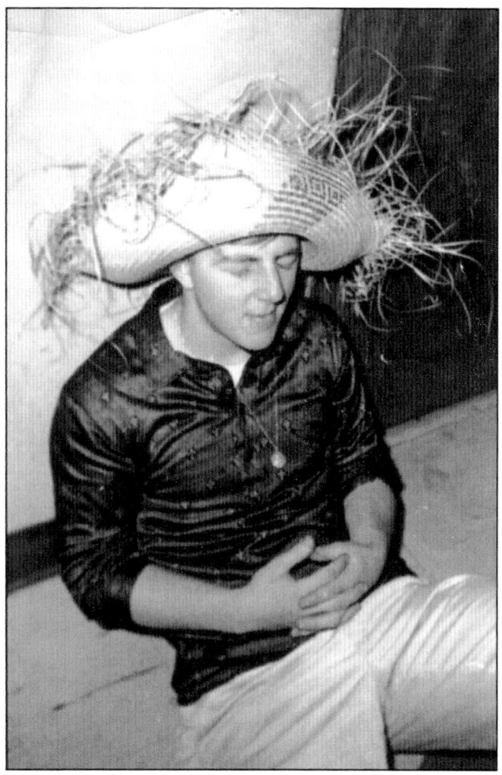

Pop House grillmen were called upon to work behind the scenes for the chili festival and were on hand to guard the chili until it was ready to be served, first to the queen and then to the rest of the crowd. Here grillman Bob Harrer is caught taking a siesta while on guard duty at the 1960 festival. (Courtesy of Bob Harrer.)

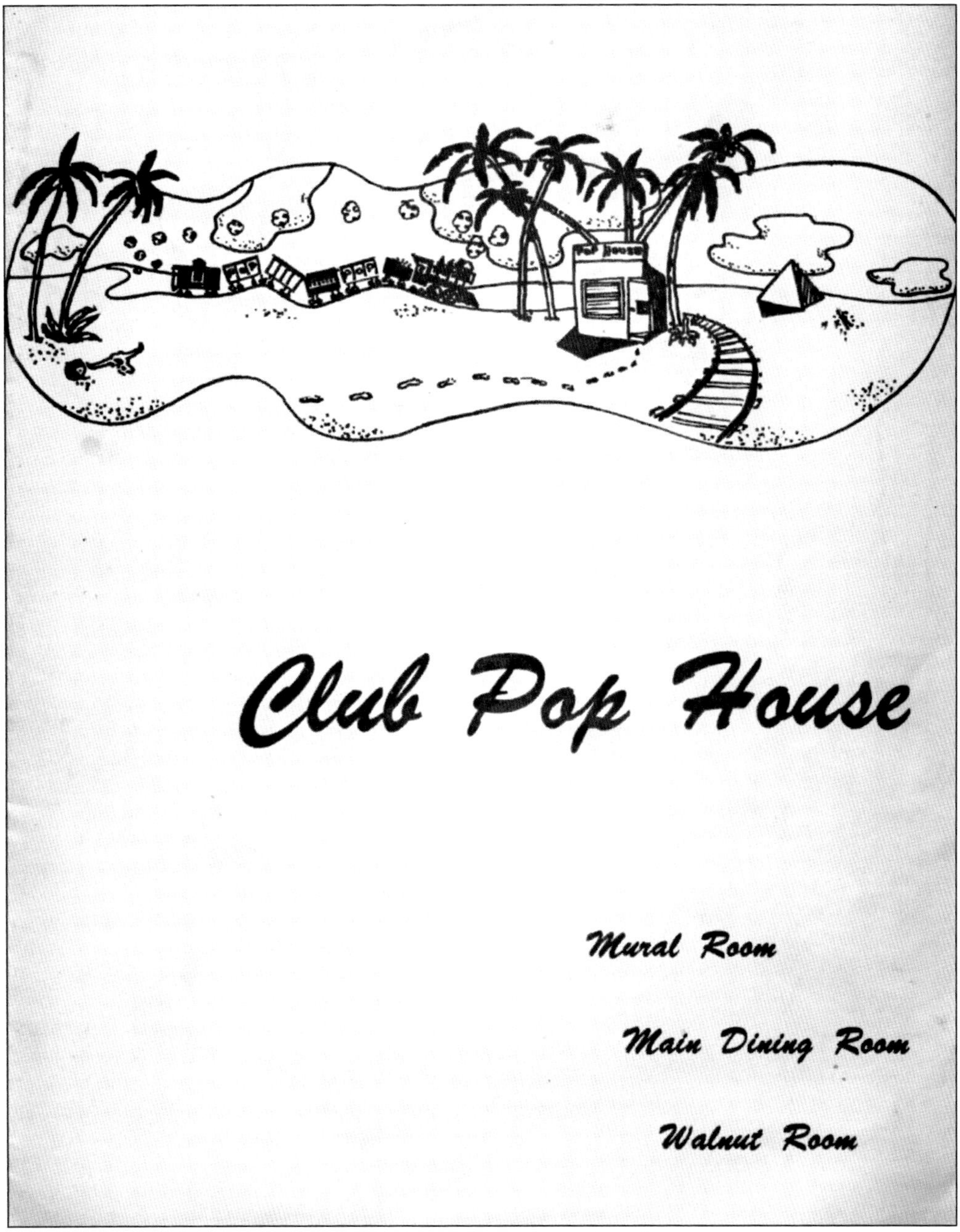

From the time Club Pop House opened its doors as a student hangout, it was popular for the hamburgers it served. George Stankewitz dished up the food his young customers wanted to eat at an affordable price. He used to say, "Where else could you get two hamburgers, fries, and a soft drink or milk for 45 cents?" Hamburgers started out at 15¢ until the early 1950s, when the price went up to 20¢. The menu expanded over the years to feature complete steak dinners that included salad, fries, bread, and a drink. Although prices increased with the times, food continued to remain affordable for student pocketbooks. The Club Pop House menu cover featured an image of the Dave Driesbach mural that had been moved from the original building to the wall above the new lunch counter. (Courtesy of the Pop House collection.)

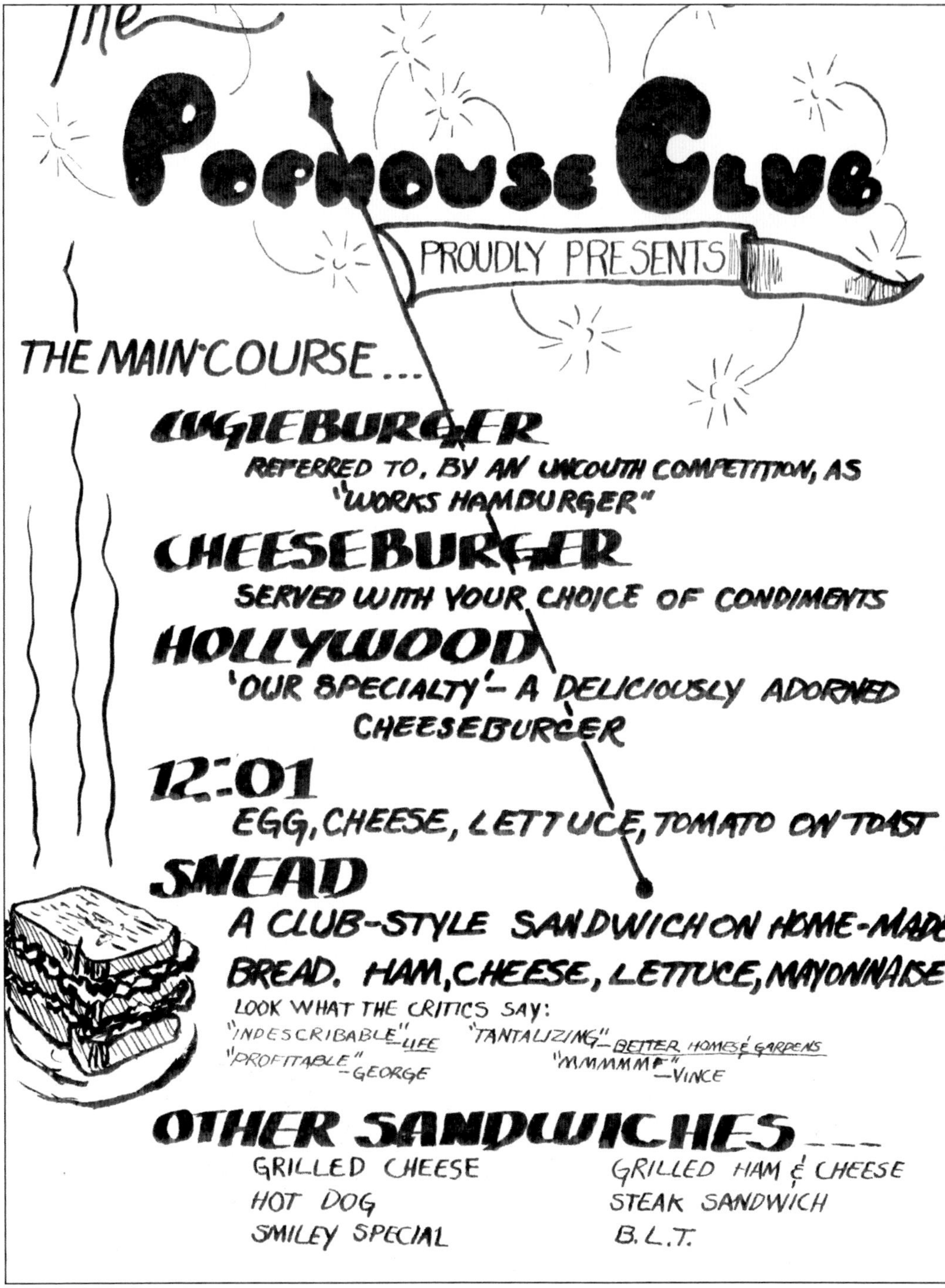

The menu contained entertaining descriptions of sandwiches, including the Lugie, short for Lithuanian hamburger. The Hollywood was a cheeseburger with lettuce, tomato, and mayonnaise. The Smiley Special was simply cheese with lettuce and tomato. There was also the 12:01, a fried egg, cheese, lettuce, and tomato. Its name came from the requirement that Catholics give up meat on Fridays. The granddaddy of all sandwiches was the Snead, a towering combination of

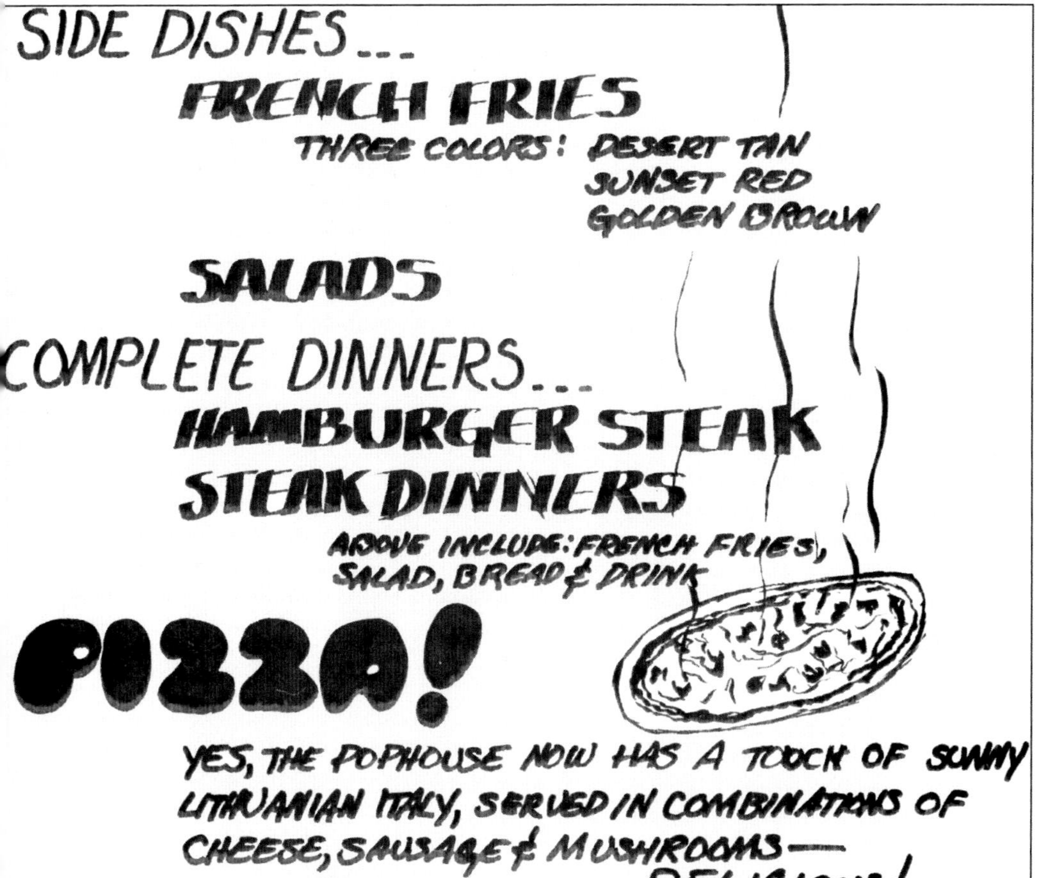

a cheeseburger with lettuce and tomato and ham with more lettuce and tomato, all in between three layers of toast. French fries came in three colors—desert tan, sunset red, and golden brown. Pizza offered "a touch of sunny Lithuanian Italy." Blast was "brewed 53 times" and "laughingly called 'coffee.'" One customer purportedly won a Blast-drinking contest by downing 24 cups in a half hour. (Courtesy of the Pop House collection.)

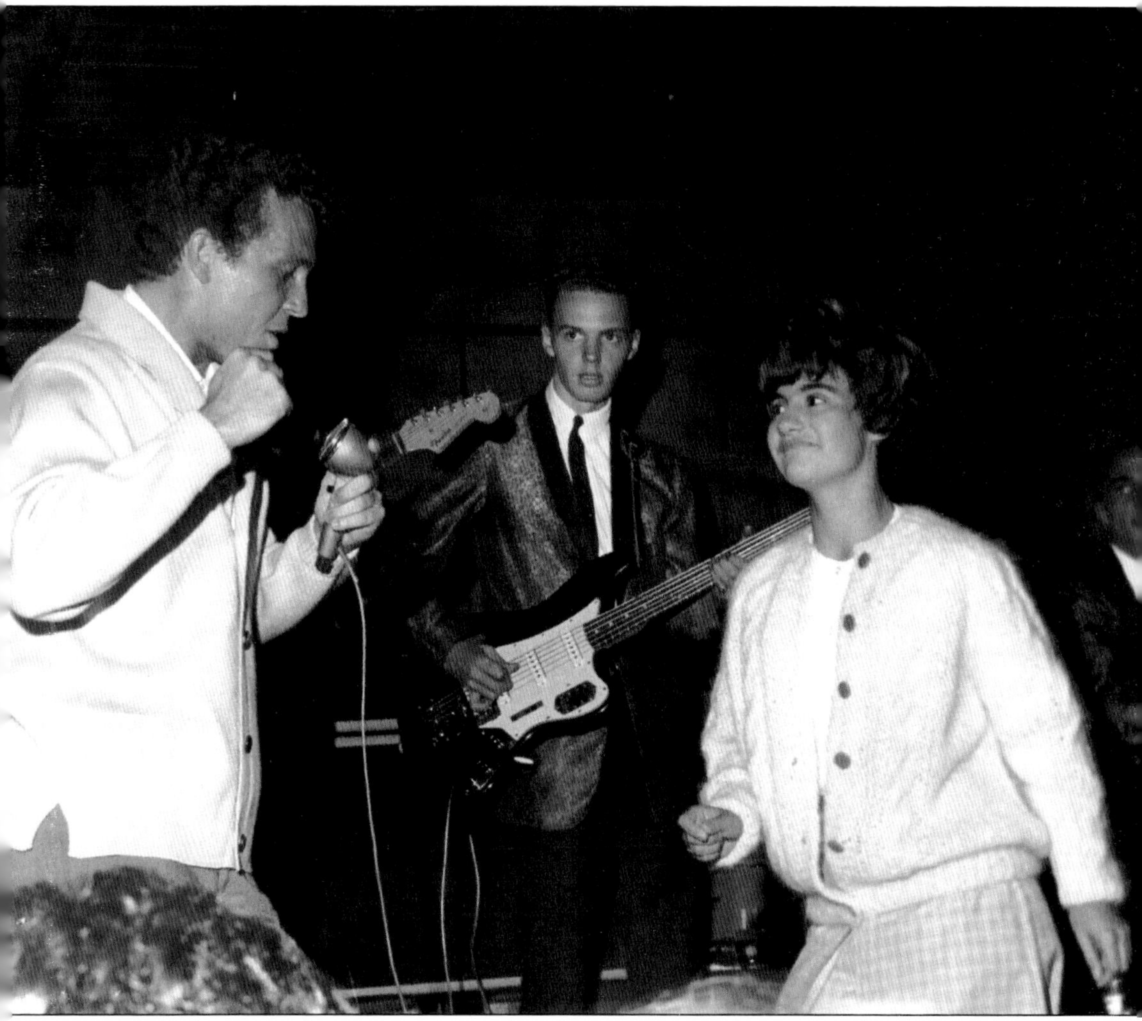

Of all the national acts that appeared at the Pop House, George Stankewitz would say years later that Bobby Vinton was the finest entertainer among them. Vinton had topped the charts in 1962 with "Roses Are Red (My Love)" and was about to do the same with "Blue Velvet." He is captured in this photograph singing to fan Joanne Anastasi on a cool evening on the patio stage. (Courtesy of the Pop House collection.)

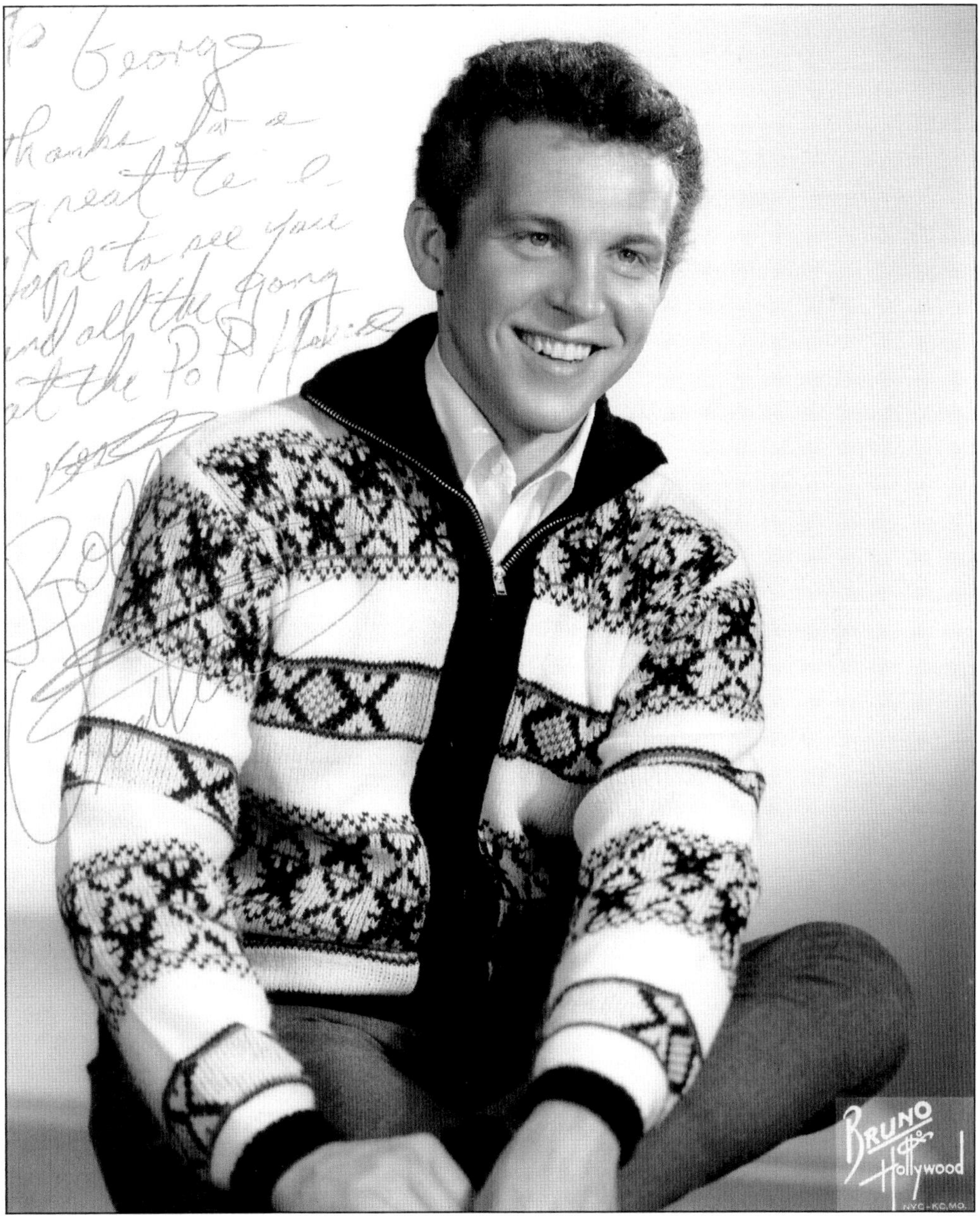

Performers and their agents would send publicity stills to the Pop House for promotional use. Stankewitz tacked them to the bulletin board and at times would ask artists to autograph them. The message on this Vinton photograph reads, "To George, Thanks for a great time. Hope to see you and all the gang at the Pop House." Vinton continued to have big hit records during the British Invasion while many other major artists of the early 1960s struggled. A consummate entertainer, Vinton still plays to full houses into the early 21st century. (Courtesy of the Pop House collection.)

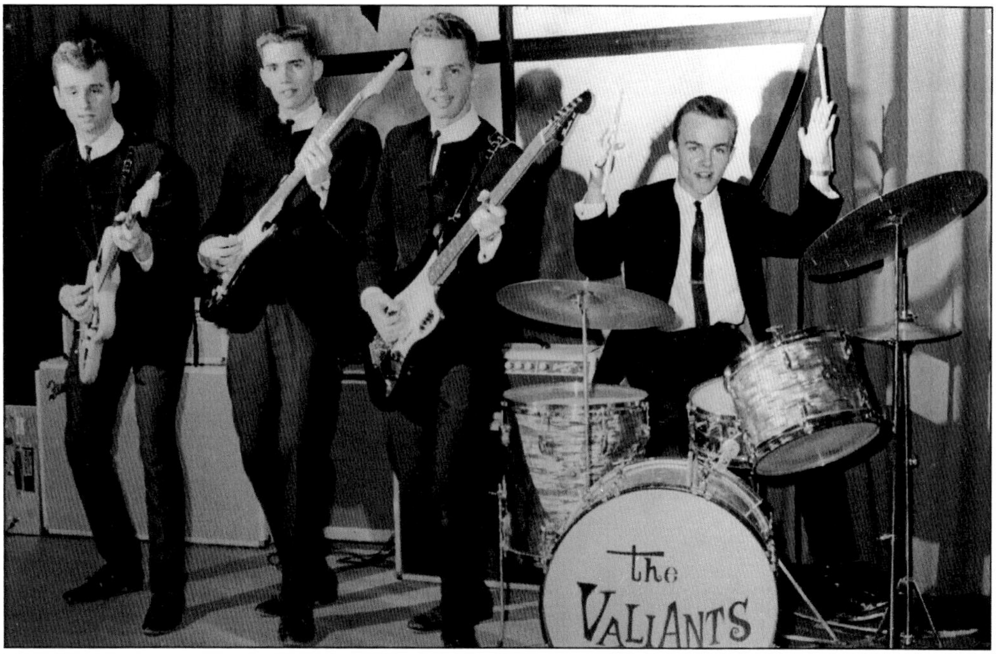

For many solo performers, a contract rider would state that the employer agreed to furnish a backing band. For Bobby Vinton and other solo acts appearing at the Pop House, George Stankewitz hired a band from Rockford called the Valiants because, as he put it, "they were close-by and good." (Courtesy of the Pop House collection.)

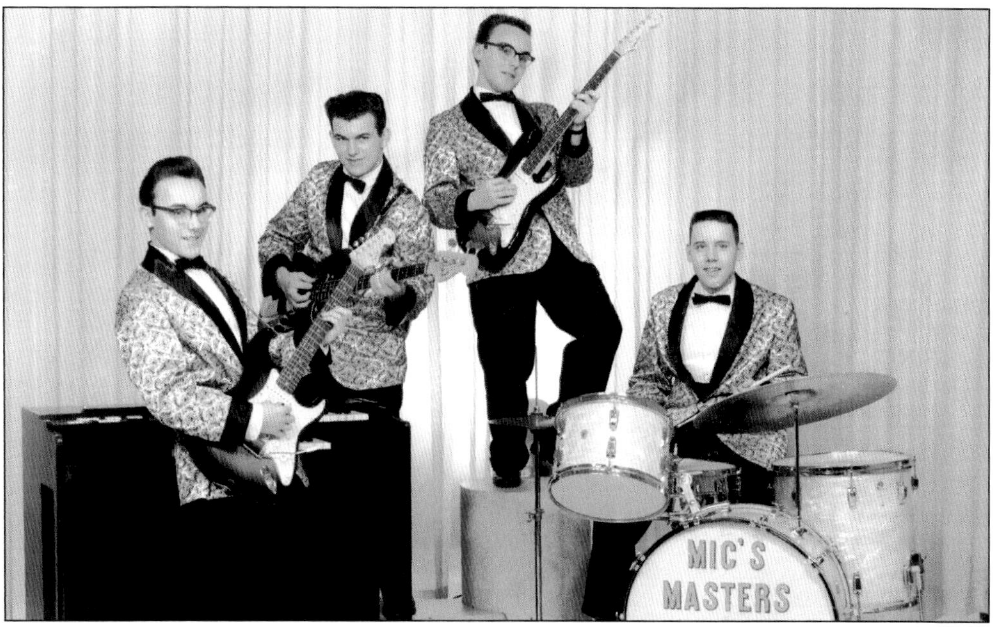

A favorite local band was Mic's Masters. Twin brothers Bob and Roger Mickey, Chuck Voss, and Jim Rogers were among the first Beloit rock and rollers to record on Leaf Records, a studio near Janesville used by many area bands, in 1963. The A side was an instrumental originally by Johnny and the Hurricanes called "Sand Storm." The B side, "Rock-N-Round," was written by Roger Mickey. (Courtesy of the Pop House collection.)

Chili festivals and chili queen coronations had become a much-anticipated annual event into the 1960s. In the photograph at right, Sally Bua is crowned by Beloit city councilman Bob Tilley at the chili festival in 1961. Below, chili festival queen Barb Conry is pictured with her court in 1962. (Courtesy of the Pop House collection.)

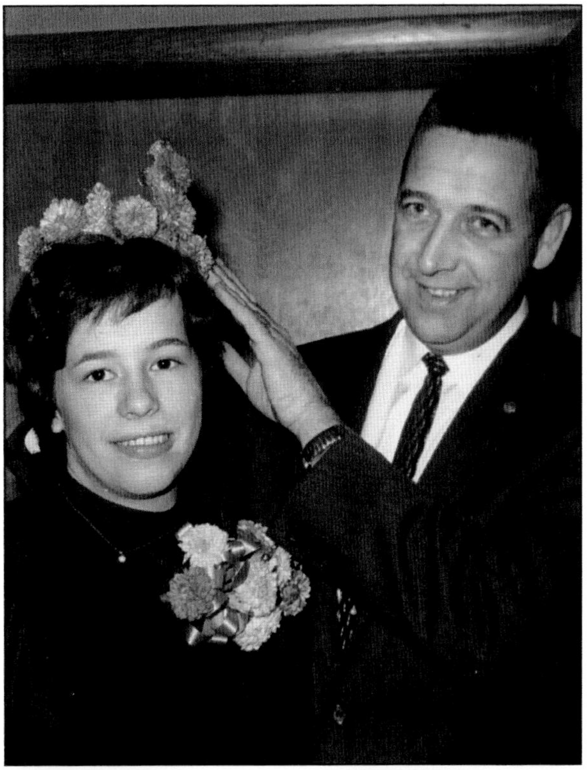

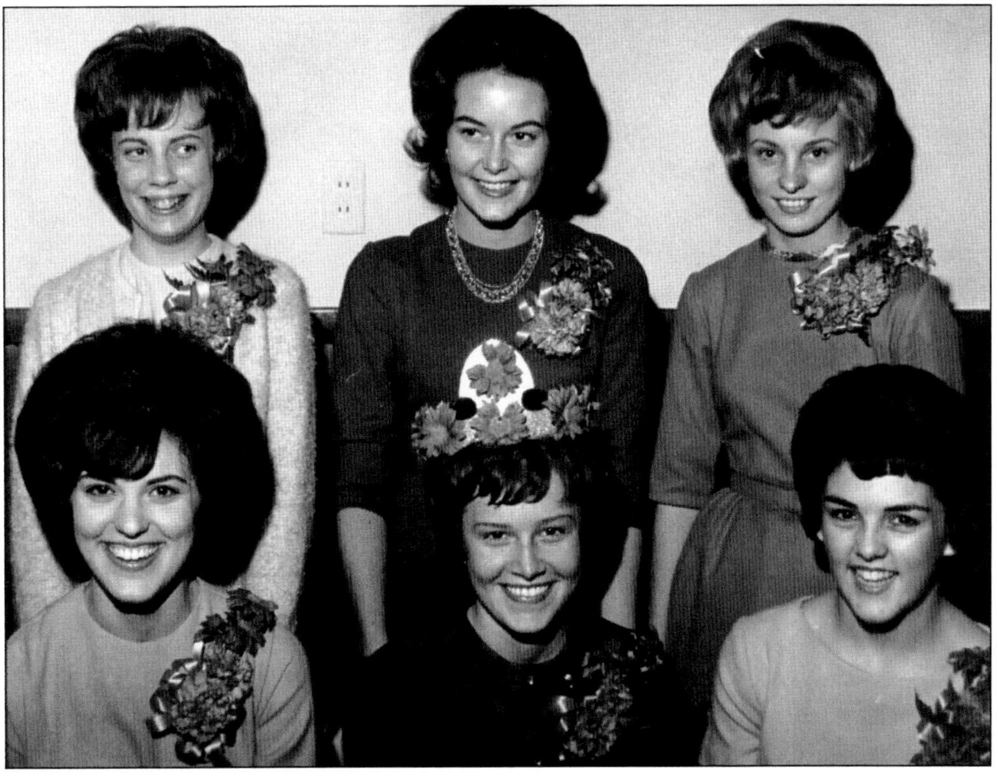

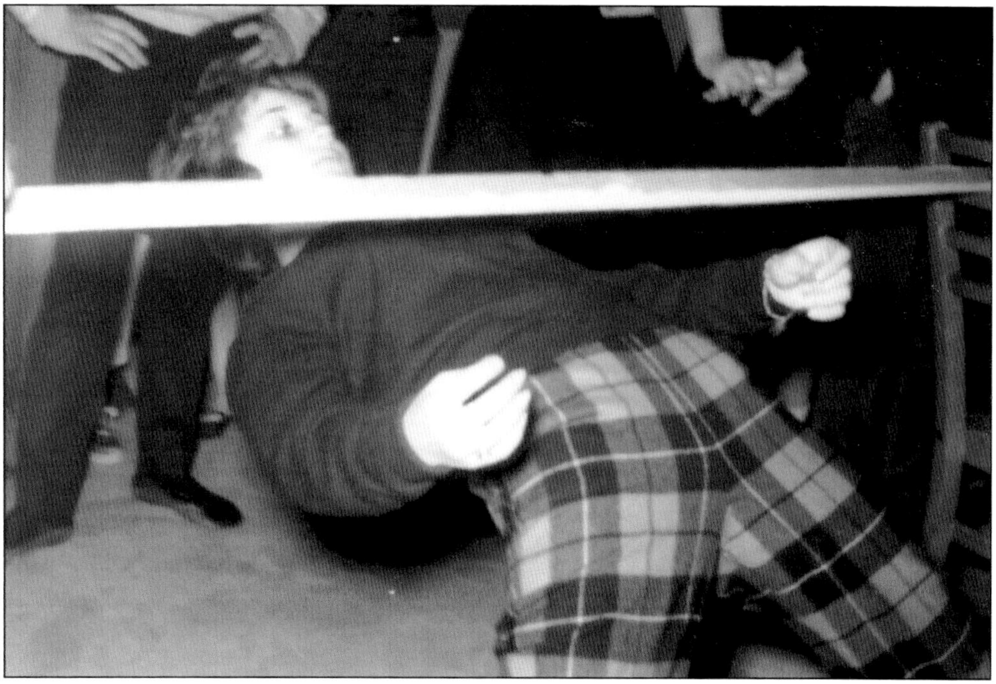

Chubby Checker released the song "Limbo Rock" in 1962, and by the following year, the limbo dance had become all the rage. For the limbo, a dancer moves forward to a Caribbean rhythm, then leans backward and dances under a horizontal stick without touching it. Upon touching it or falling backward, the dancer is out. When several dancers compete, they move in single file and the stick is gradually lowered until only one dancer who has not touched either the stick or the floor remains. The limbo dance was sometimes used as a social icebreaker. (Courtesy of Ida and Richard Lenz.)

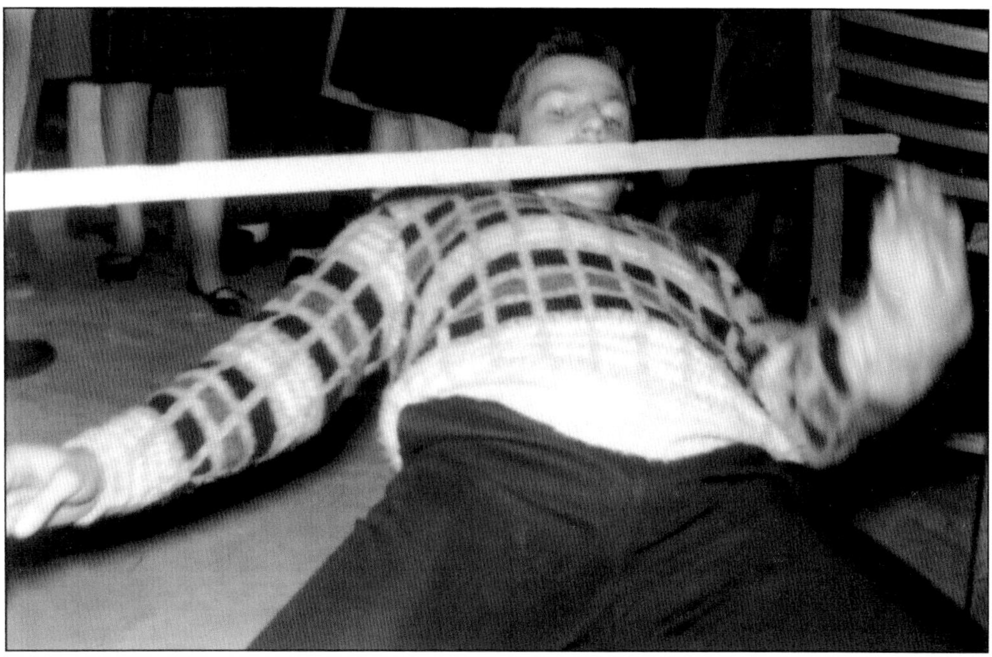

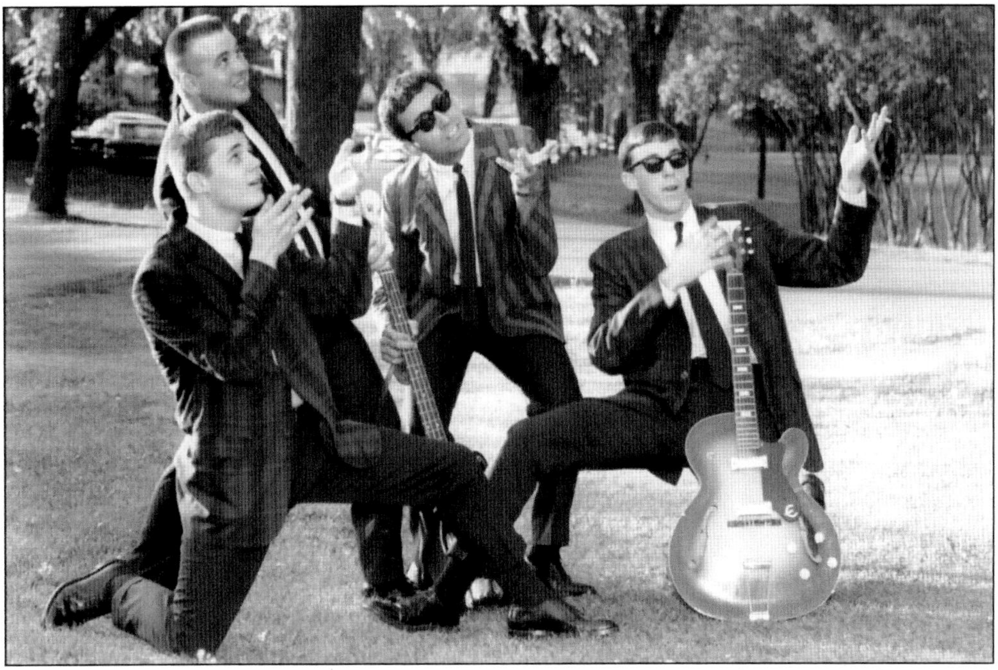

The KnighTranes featured Ron Boyer (standing left) on drums, Ken Adamany (standing center) on organ, Steve Miller (kneeling left) on guitar, and William "Boz" Scaggs (kneeling right) on bass. The band formed while they were students at the University of Wisconsin–Madison. Although their personnel sometimes changed based on musician availability, this lineup featuring Miller and Scaggs appeared many times at the Pop House in the early 1960s. Miller and Scaggs became international stars. Ken Adamany began a successful career as a booking agent. In the note below, Adamany provides George Stankewitz with an offer to schedule some "package deals" for the summer. He eventually represented over 100 bands and booked many of them at the Pop House, including a number of national acts. (Courtesy of Ken Adamany.)

January 29, 1963

Mr. George Stankowitz
Pop House
Beloit, Wisconsin

Dear George:

Well it's about that time when we start thinking of our summer schedules.

I hope you had good luck with the "Crossfires" last week.

Please keep us in mind when making out your schedule, as I am in a position to offer you a "package deal" for the groups you want.

Ken

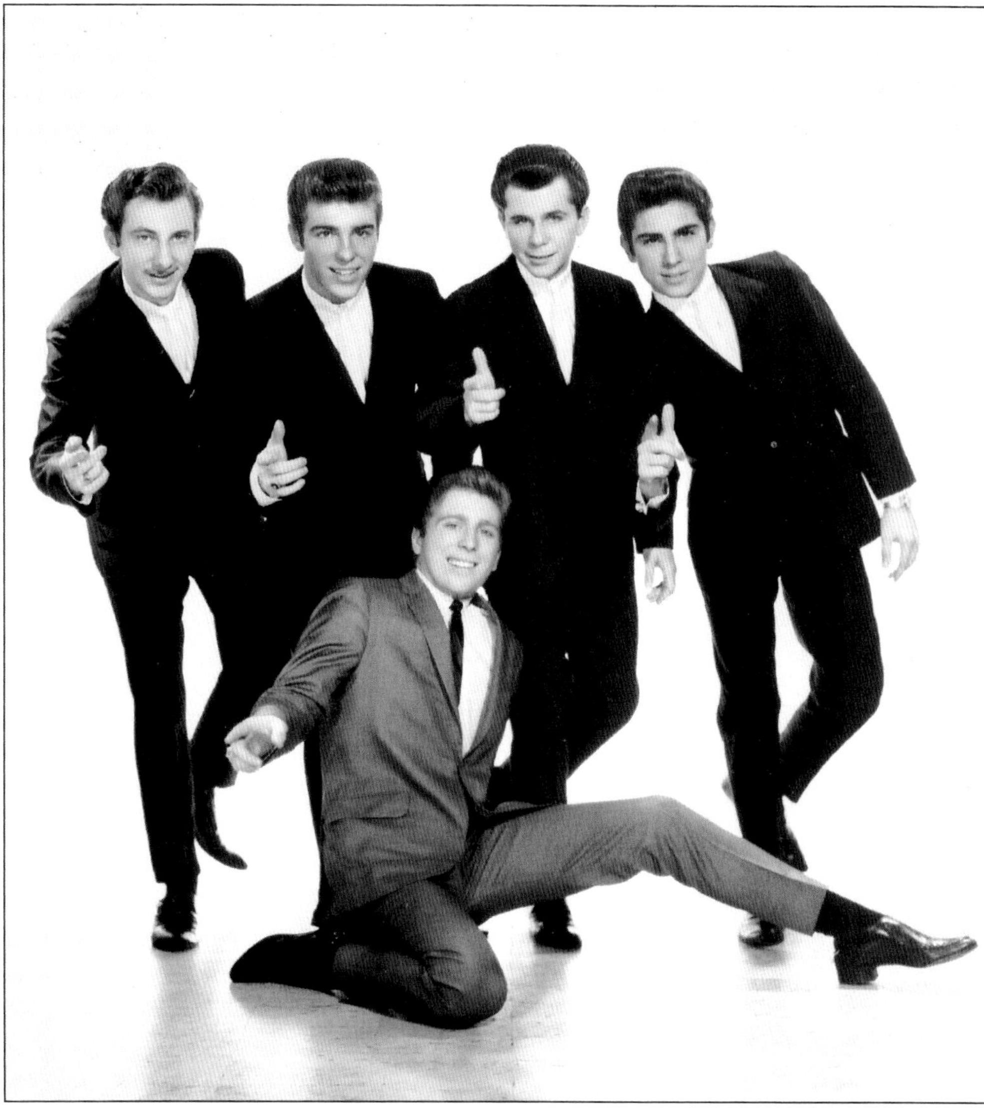

Appearing at the Pop House in 1963 as Dee Robb and the Starliners, this band from Oconomowoc also performed as Dee Robb and the Robbins. Some years later as the Robbs, they released a self-titled album of songs on the Mercury label, one of which was the familiar "Race with the Wind." They also became the house band for Dick Clark's television show *Where the Action Is*. The Robbs are also known for placing the most singles (six) on *Billboard*'s Bubbling Under charts, a designation for records that failed to enter the Hot 100. The Robb brothers—Dee, Bruce, and Joe—founded Cherokee Studios near Los Angeles in 1971 where they cut records for many top artists, including David Bowie, Cheap Trick, Al Green, Diana Ross, and Frank Sinatra, among others. (Courtesy of the Pop House collection.)

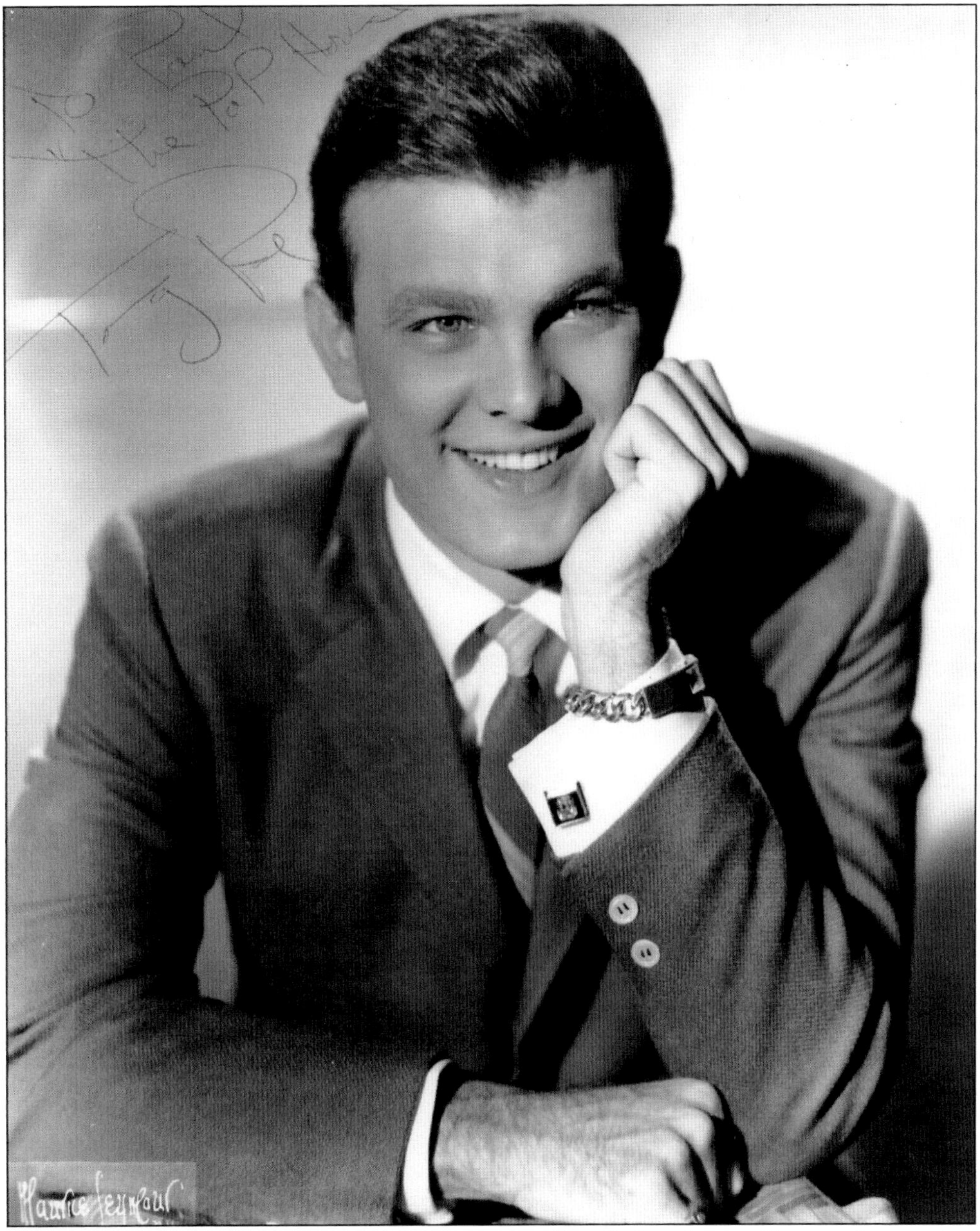

Tommy Roe's show at the Pop House in the 1960s followed the release of his number-one hits "Sheila" (1961) and "Everybody" (1963). At that time, Roe was backed by his band, the Roemans, who later split with him but continued to tour on its own. In 1969, his song "Dizzy" went to number one. His final top-10 single, "Jam Up and Jelly Tight," was released in 1970. Roe was inducted into the Georgia Music Hall of Fame in 1986 and continues to write music and perform at a variety of concert venues. (Courtesy of the Pop House collection.)

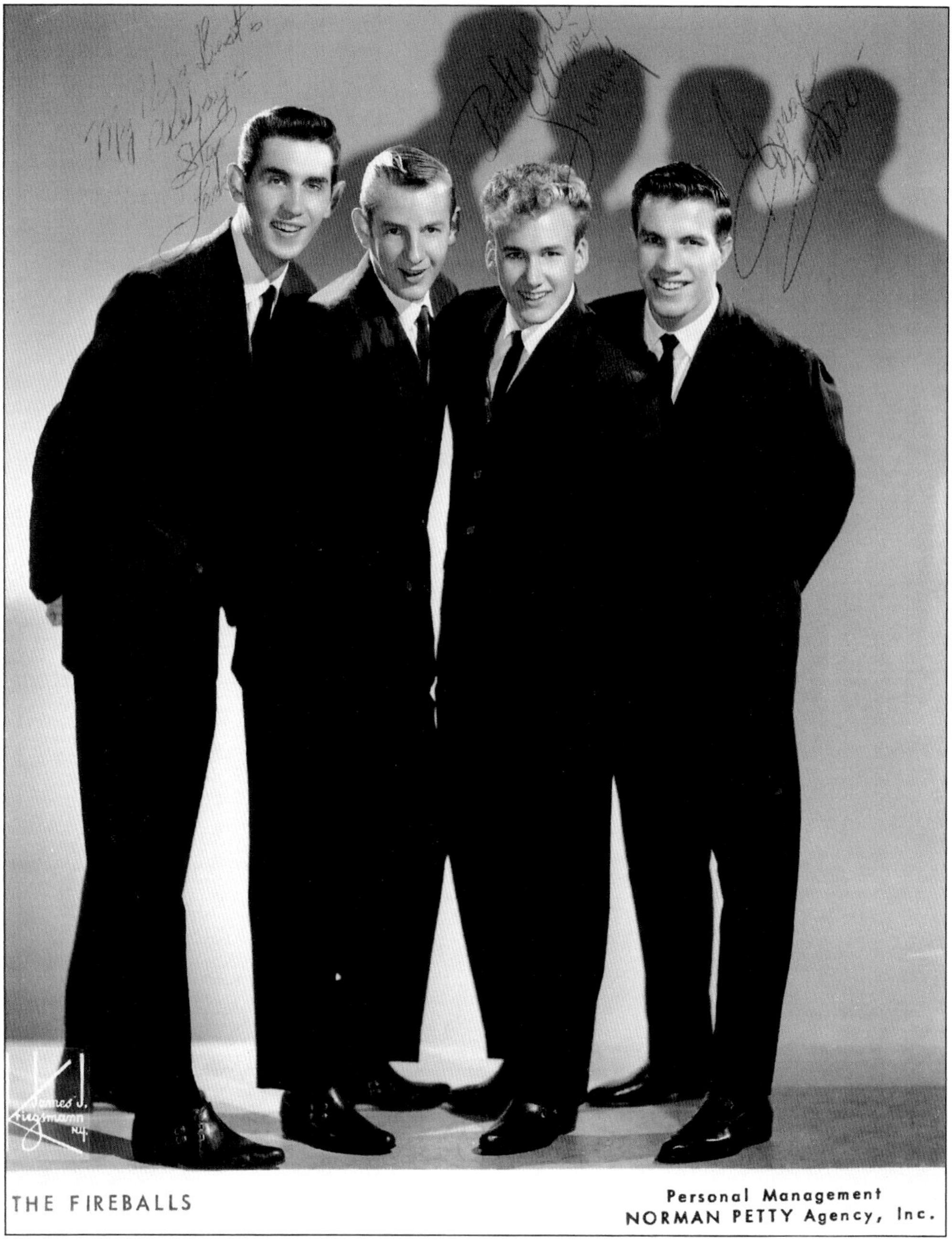

Jimmy Gilmer and the Fireballs had a number-one hit in 1963 with the song "Sugar Shack" and appeared at the Pop House on their subsequent tour. Agent Ken Adamany booked the show in cooperation with Fireballs representative Norman Petty. The autographed photograph above includes Stan Lark, Eric Budd, Jimmy Gilmer, and George Tomsco. When the Fireballs played the Pop House, Budd had already left the band and was replaced by Doug Roberts. (Courtesy of the Pop House collection.)

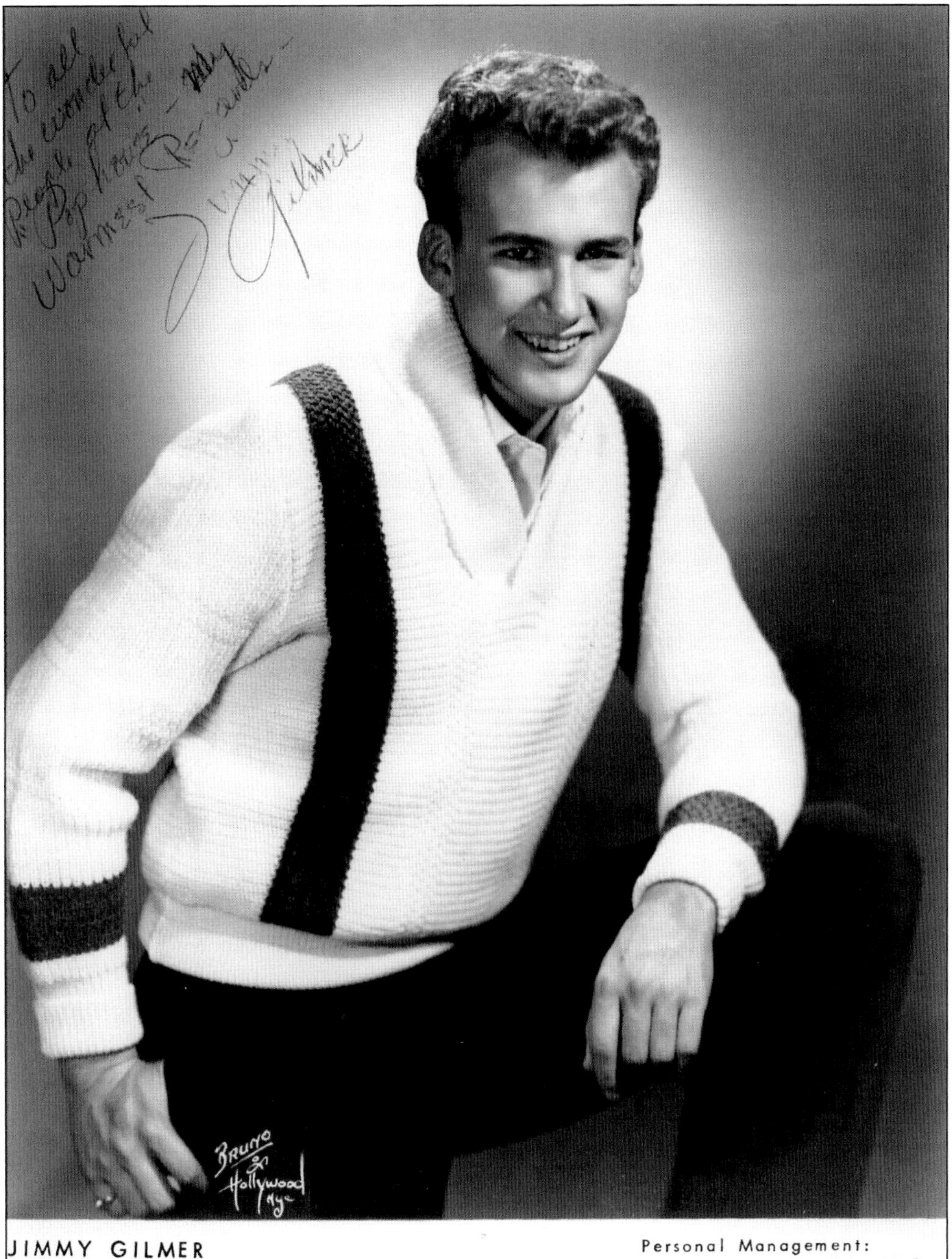

In later years, George Stankewitz mentioned the Fireballs whenever he was interviewed about the Pop House. Jimmy Gilmer wrote on his photograph above, "To all the wonderful people at the Pop House — My warmest regards." Gilmer left the group in 1969 to pursue a career in artist management and production in Nashville. The Fireballs, with original members Tomsco and Lark, continued to perform into the 21st century, occasionally joined by Gilmer. (Courtesy of the Pop House collection.)

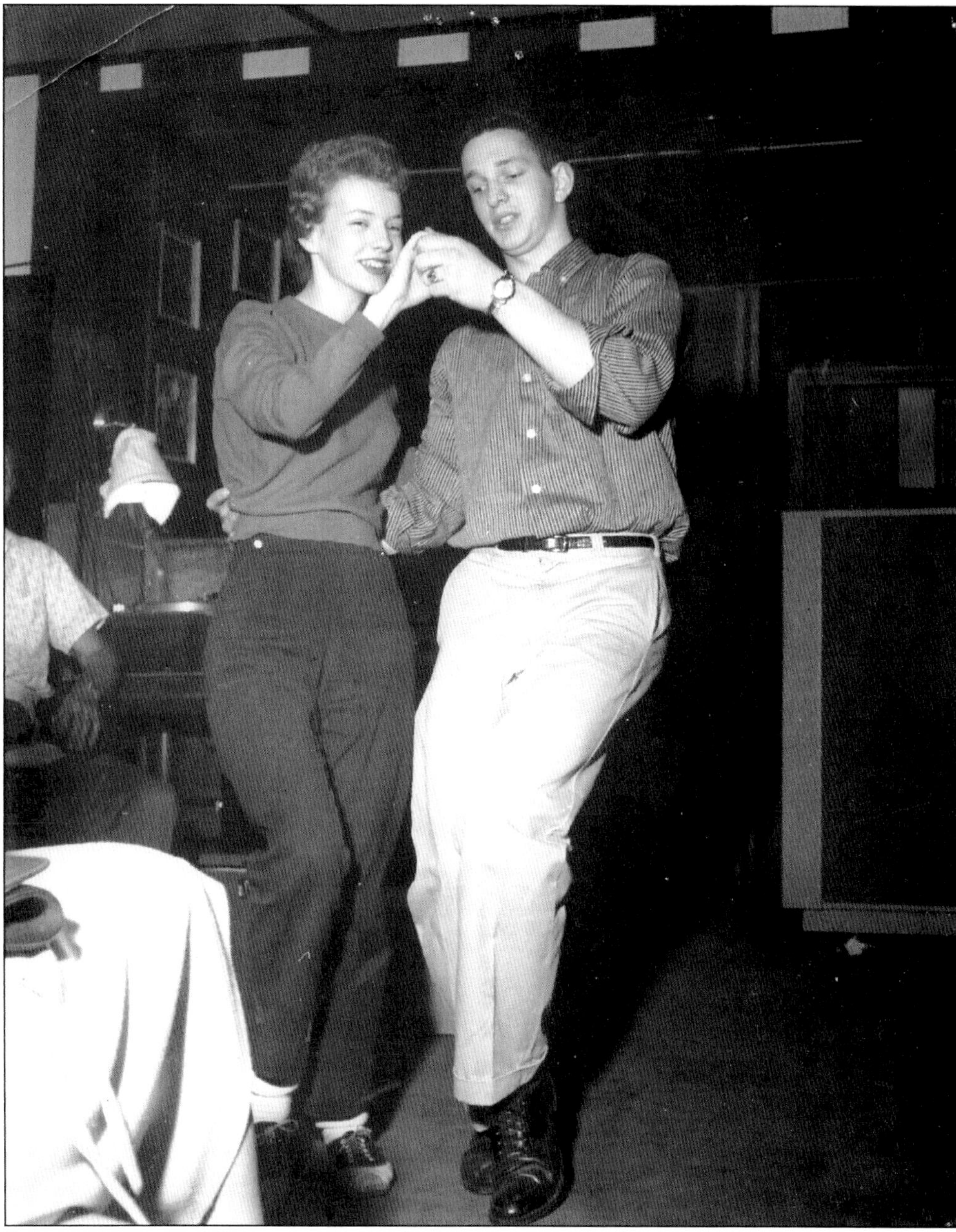

Dancing was one of the attractions at the Pop House. Whether it was a record jam or a band, the dance floor was the place to try out new steps. In the original Pop House, the tables would be pushed aside and couples would dance the jitterbug or the Lindy, as this couple is doing. Over the years, rock-and-roll music spawned new dance crazes. Teens watched Dick Clark's *American Bandstand* to keep up on the latest dance styles. From the mid-1960s on, couples moved further away from each other on the dance floor so they were no longer touching while doing the twist, the Watusi, the mashed potatoes, the pony, the swim, the monkey, the jerk, and many more. (Courtesy of the Pop House collection.)

The annual chili festivals continued to be a much-anticipated event each fall. Here George Stankewitz, in his customary sombrero, is presenting the first bowl to 1963 chili queen Maureen Griffin. The recipe for Pop House chili was a closely guarded secret. One year, Stankewitz even posted a policeman at the grill to guard the pot of chili. (Courtesy of the Pop House collection.)

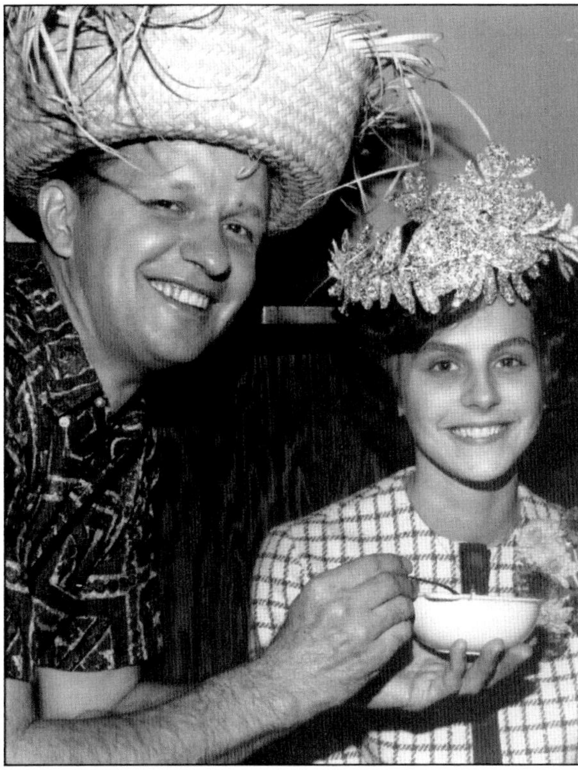

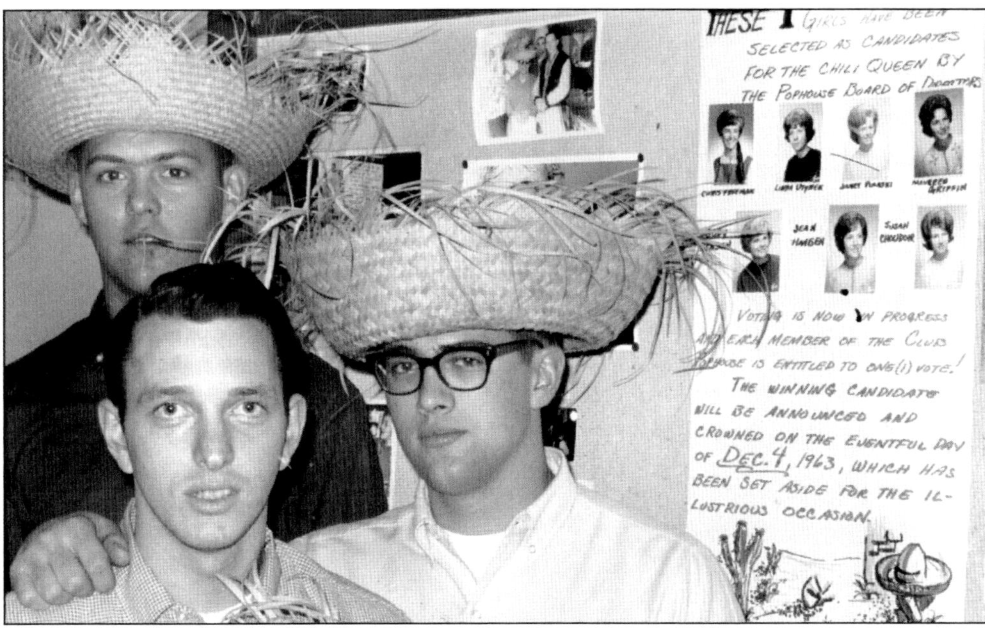

It was never difficult to find grillmen to help out with the chili festival work assignments that ranged from minding the lunch counter to serving tables. Pictured here are grillmen Steve Amend, John Maloney (center), and Steve Eichman (right). Photographs of the nominees for festival queen are posted on the bulletin board promoting the date December 4, 1963, "set aside for the illustrious occasion." (Courtesy of the Pop House collection.)

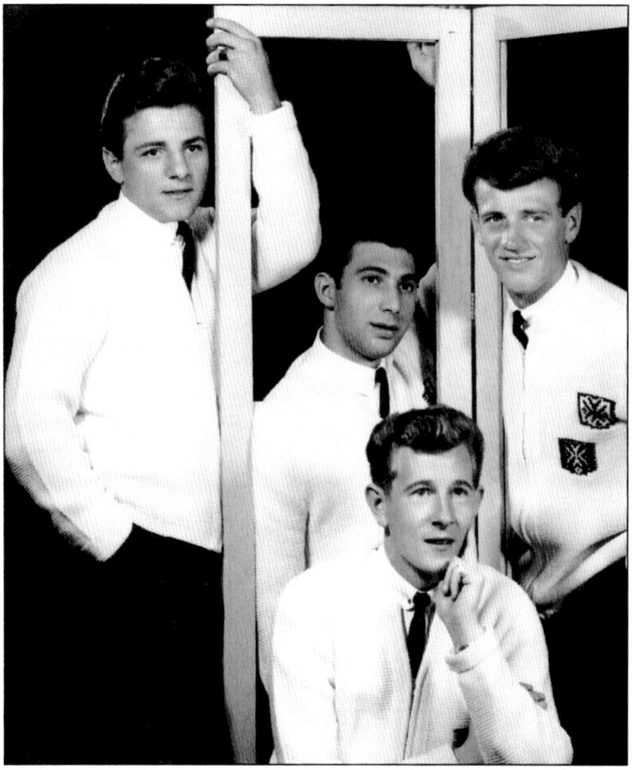

The Reflections had one hit single in 1964 called "Just Like Romeo and Juliet" on Golden World Records that reached the top 10. The original Reflections included Tony Micale, Ray Steinberg, Dan Bennie, Phil Castrodale, and John Dean. Their appearance at the Pop House in 1964 came toward the peak of their success. Original members Micale and Dean continue to perform as the Reflections. (Courtesy of the Pop House collection.)

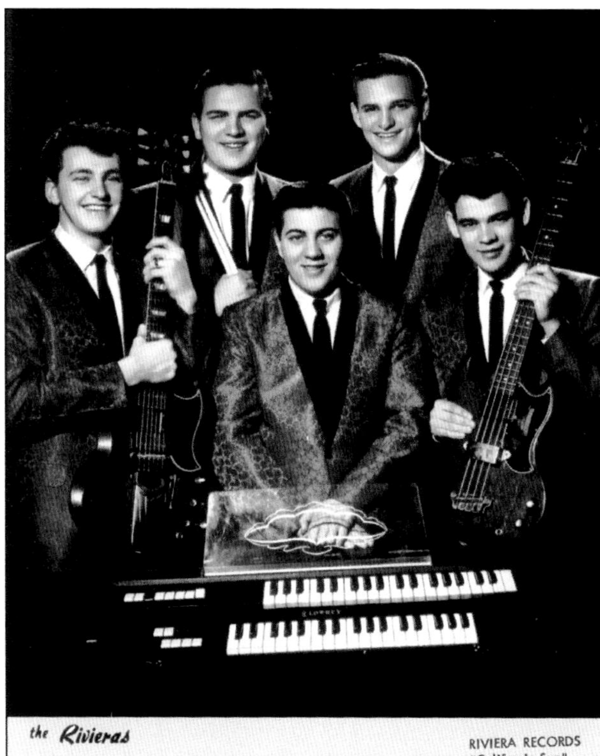

The Rivieras, from South Bend, Indiana, were one-hit wonders with the 1964 dance song "California Sun." Although it charted nationally in the top 10, the Rivieras never actually performed the song in California, even after its great success. They remained a popular band in dance halls around the Midwest, and the Pop House was no exception. By 1966, the band had broken up. (Courtesy of the Pop House collection.)

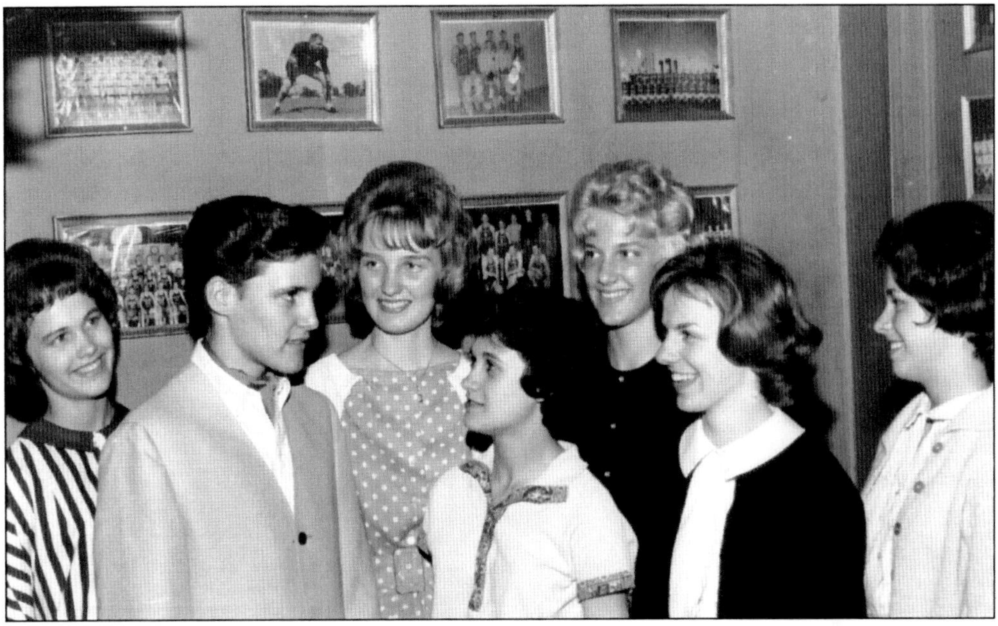

The Pop House provided a place for kids to socialize and meet new friends. It did not matter which high school one attended or which side of town one was from. Once inside teens could relax and feel at home with one another. Here, from left to right, Marilyn Peterson, Karen Chamberlain, Mary Parrinello, Kathy Meyer, Kathy Gorychka, and Connie Guelzow are pictured chatting with Russ Mackie. (Courtesy of the Pop House collection.)

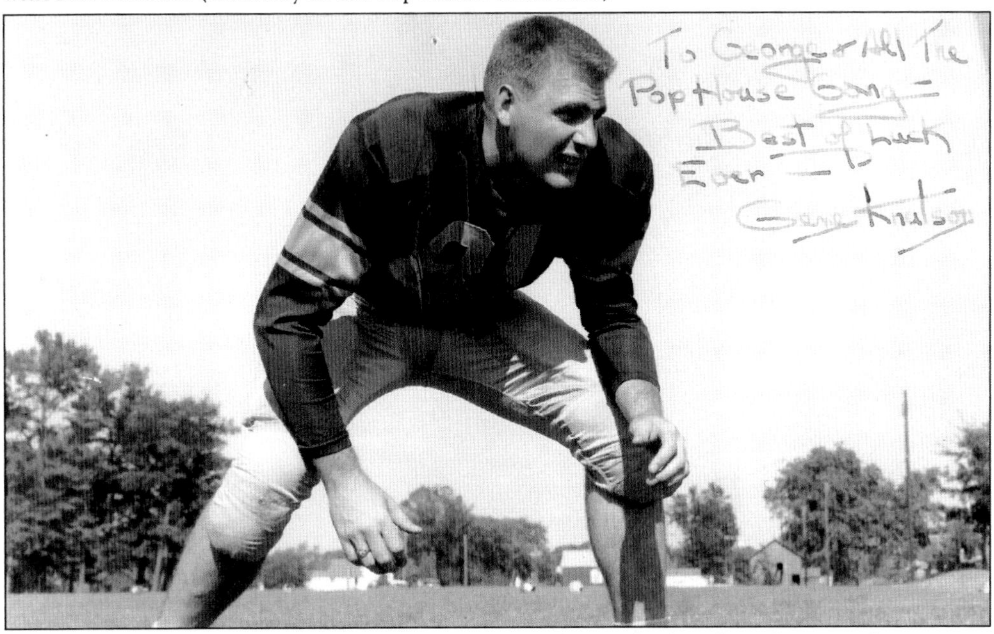

Visible in the top image are framed photographs of athletes displayed on the main dining room wall, including this one of Gene Knutson. Knutson was a 1950 graduate of Beloit High School, where he excelled in football. He attended the University of Michigan and then played for the Green Bay Packers in 1954 and 1956. Knutson also was an early Turkey Bowl participant. (Courtesy of the Pop House collection, photograph by LeFebvre-Luebke Commercial Photographers.)

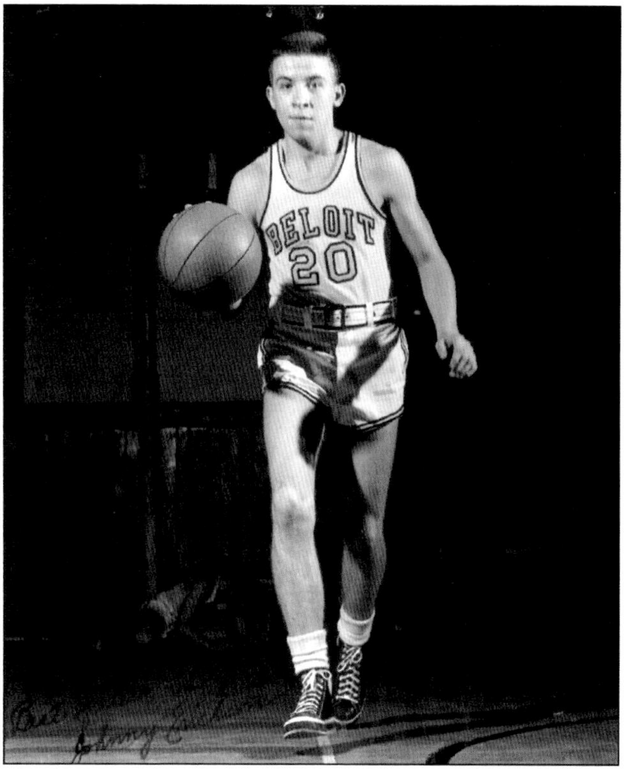

Johnny Erickson was an outstanding player for the Beloit College Buccaneers. After graduating in 1949, he coached for Beloit High School and in 1960 was named head coach for the University of Wisconsin Badgers. His teams finished in the Big Ten's first division three times in nine years. In 1968, he was appointed general manager of the new Milwaukee Bucks. This picture was among those on the wall. (Courtesy of Dr. William Fitzgerald.)

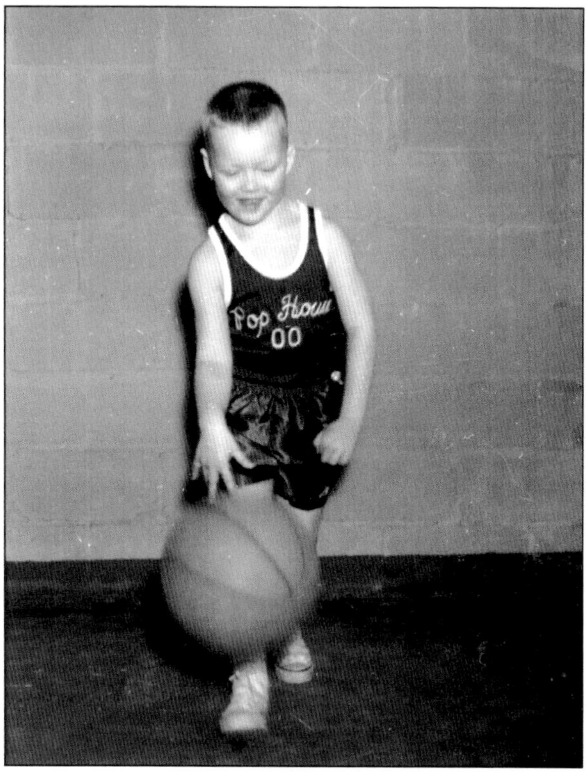

No. 00, Jeff Hanson was an aspiring Pop House basketball player and had the jersey to prove it. This photograph, taken in March 1956, was another of the framed pictures on the Pop House wall in the main dining room. (Courtesy of the Pop House collection.)

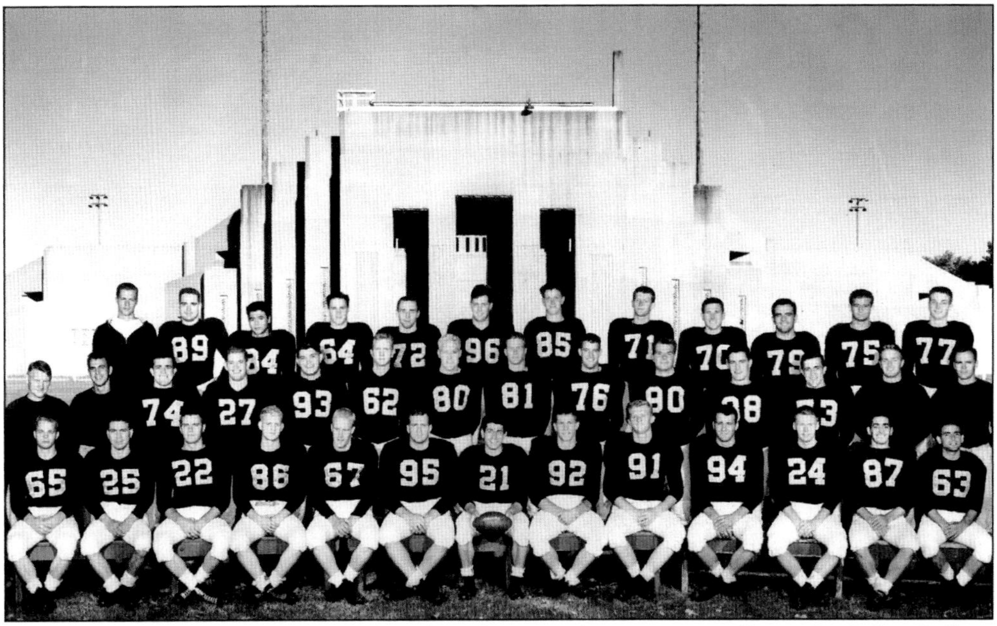

Another of the framed pictures displayed on the main dining room wall was this Beloit College Buccaneers team photograph that appeared in the 1953 college yearbook, *Gold*. This football team went undefeated in 1952 under coach Carl T. "Pill" Nelson, seen in the second row at the far left. (Courtesy of the Beloit College Archives.)

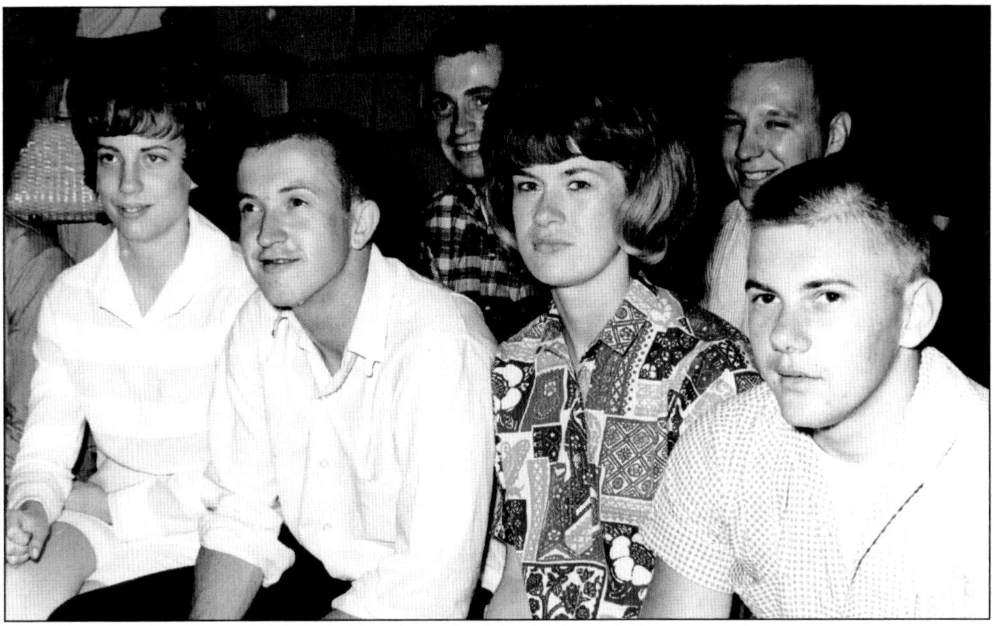

Concerts provided an opportunity to see big-name entertainment, but rules applied and George Stankewitz was strict with their enforcement. The worst thing that could happen to a teenager was to be kicked out of the Pop House. When celebrities performed, everyone was on their best behavior. Waiting for the show are, from left to right, (first row) Jeannie Refue, Stan Showers, Linda Pickett, and Fred Tuttle; (second row) Tom Monahan and Frank Spahos. (Courtesy of the Pop House collection.)

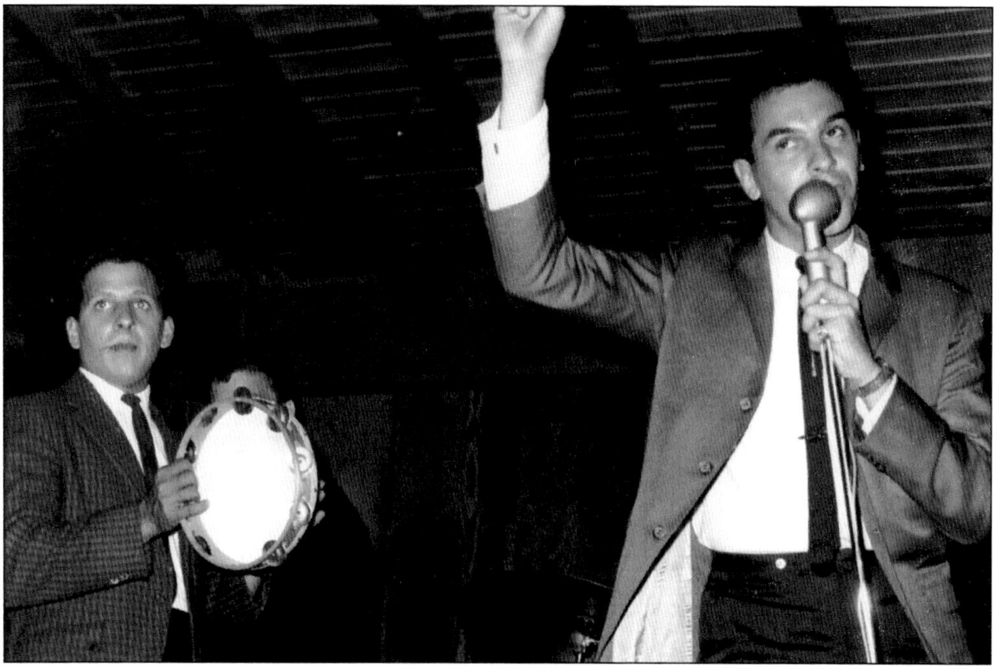

In July 1964, Freddy "Boom Boom" Cannon (right) and Johnny Maestro perform together on the patio stage. Freddy Cannon, known for his electrifying live shows, had a top-10 song, "Palisades Park," in 1962 on the Swan record label. His 1964 recording of "Abigail Beecher" was charting at the time of this Beloit show. Maestro enjoyed great success in 1958 with his doo-wop group, the Crests, and their top-10 song "Sixteen Candles" released on Coed Records. In the early 1960s, he toured as a solo act until eventually forming the group Brooklyn Bridge. They had a Top 40 hit in 1968 with "The Worst That Could Happen." (Courtesy of the Pop House collection.)

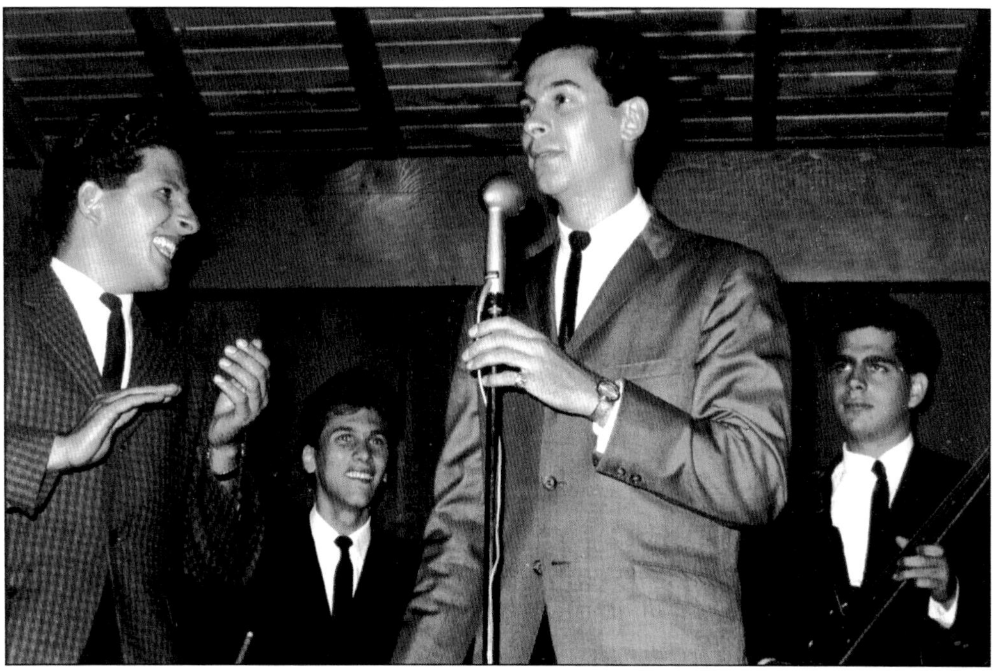

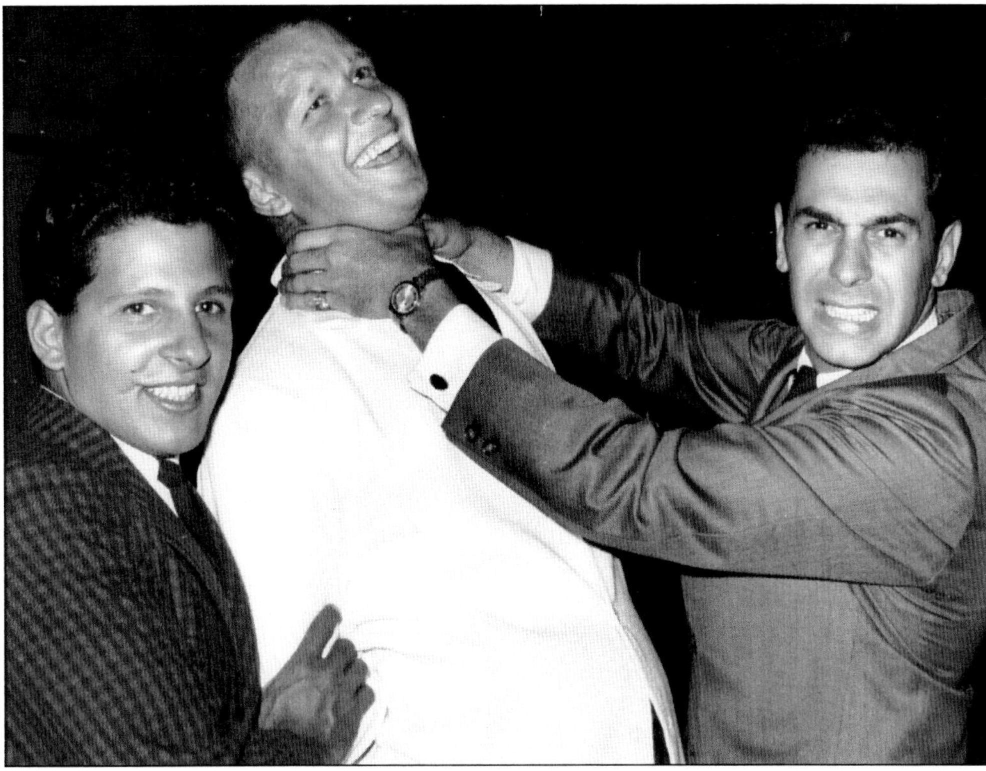

Above, Freddy Cannon and Johnny Maestro are caught joking around with George Stankewitz before the show. It was common for two, three, or more artists to tour together in the early 1960s. Cannon's appearance at the Pop House was part of a contract deal (below) for a package tour brokered by Madison booking agent Ken Adamany that also included small-town shows in Elkhorn and Cleveland, Wisconsin. It was not unusual for contracts involving solo artists to stipulate that the employer furnish local transportation. So Stankewitz would sometimes accompany one of his grillmen to the airport to pick up that evening's headliner. (Courtesy of Ken Adamany.)

THE ATTACHED RIDER(S) ARE HEREBY MADE PART OF THIS CONTRACT.

№ 1503 GAC **GENERAL ARTISTS CORPORATION**

AGVA STANDARD FORM OF ARTISTS ENGAGEMENT CONTRACT

For Promotional and One Night Engagements Not Covered by Club Date or Outdoor Code

NATIONAL HEADQUARTERS
551 FIFTH AVENUE
New York 17, N. Y.
TN 7-5600

American Guild of Variety Artists
(A Branch of the Associated Actors and Artistes of America)
(Affiliated with the AFL-CIO)

AGVA APPROVED
Membership No. ....
Paid to ....
Checked by ....
Date Checked ....
Bond....... MBA....... Welfare.......

AGREEMENT made this 24th day of APRIL, 1964, between KEN ADAMANY hereinafter called the "Operator" and FREDDIE CANNON hereinafter called the "Artist", Membership No. ....

AGVA Branch .... Paid to ....

1. The Operator hereby warrants that he is the operator herein at the present time and for the duration of this contract, and engages the Artist and the Artist hereby accepts said engagement, to present his act under the direction, supervision and control of the Operator, as a VOCALIST consisting of ONE (1) persons, at the WILL ADVISE, ELKORN, BELOIT, CLEVELAND, WISÇONSIN XXXXXXXXXXXXXXXXXXXXXXXXXXXXXXXXXXXXXXXXX for a period of THREE DAYS (3) (XXXXXXXXXXXXXXXXXXXXXXXXXXXXXXXXXXXXXXXXXXXX WILL ADVISE ( ) shows daily, commencing on JULY 1, 1964, xxxxx for which the Operator agrees to pay the Artist, and the Artist agrees to accept, as full payment, the sum of FIFTEEN HUNDRED DOLLARS Dollars ($ 1500.00) xxxxx! payable immediately preceding the first performance on the concluding night of each week's engagement hereunder.

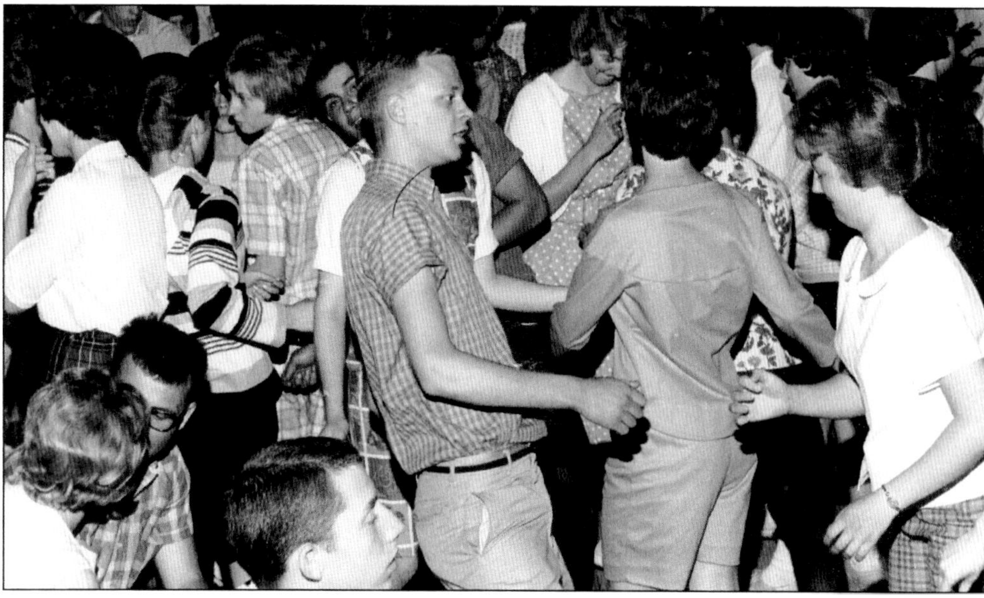

George Stankewitz often would hold record jams on Friday nights after games. He was keenly aware of sports schedules and so was careful not to create conflicts. Most times a grillman or other employee would spin records as customers danced. These dancers are pictured doing the twist out on the patio. The dance was first popularized by Chubby Checker in 1960 with his hit "The Twist." It reached number one in 1960 and then again in 1962. (Courtesy of the Pop House collection.)

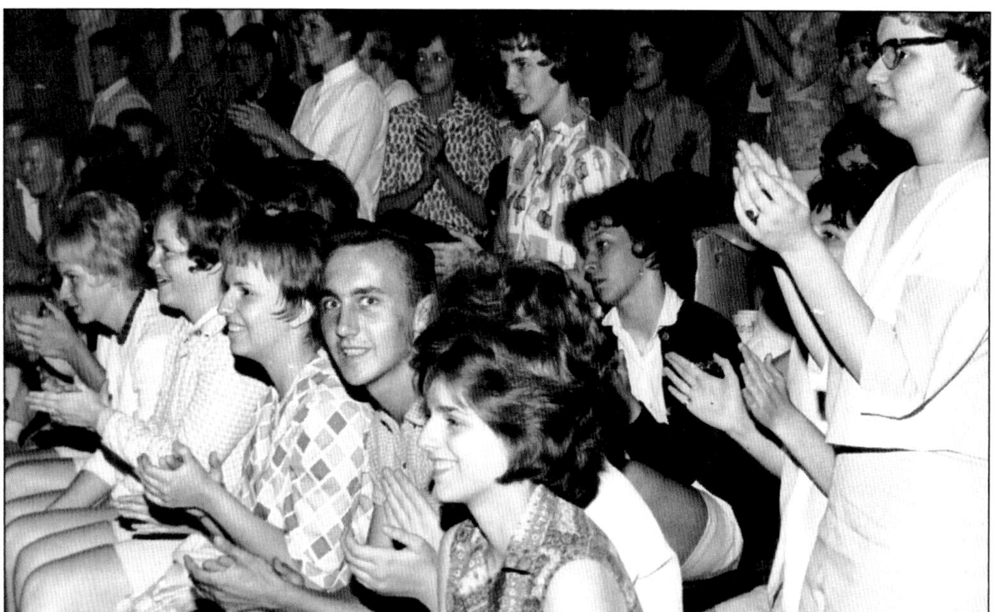

For big-name entertainers, a concertlike environment was created on the patio with bleacher seats or chairs on risers. Crowds often packed in tightly for popular shows. The patio turned out to be a major improvement for Stankewitz that allowed him to hire national acts as they were making their summer tours through the Midwest. Pop House gigs were always good as pickup dates for acts between major concerts. (Courtesy of the Pop House collection.)

To keep the Pop House orderly, Stankewitz established rules based on a constitution and bylaws and governed by a board of directors. Upon reaching 10th grade, students applied for membership. Applications were reviewed by a committee. Once accepted, the student was issued a tan guest card, on the back of which was printed "Guest membership is subject to revocation by the president." (Courtesy of Bob Harrer.)

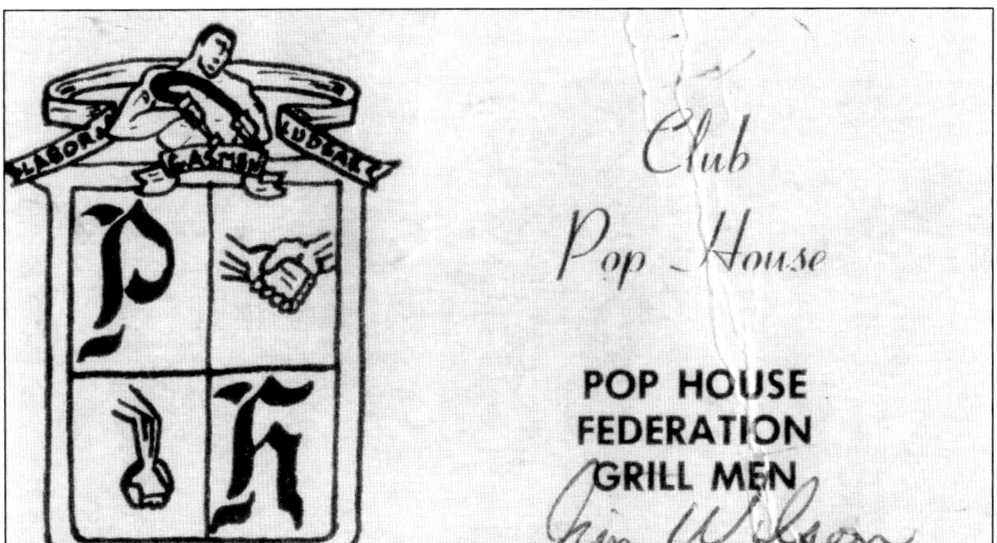

There were special membership cards of different colors printed for the Federation of Grillmen (gold), alumni association (green), and board of directors (red). The logo was modified for the grillmen card. The word *youth* inside the banner was replaced with the word *gasmen*—named for those who operated the gas-fired grill. The modified logo also appeared on the alumni card. (Courtesy of Jim Wilson.)

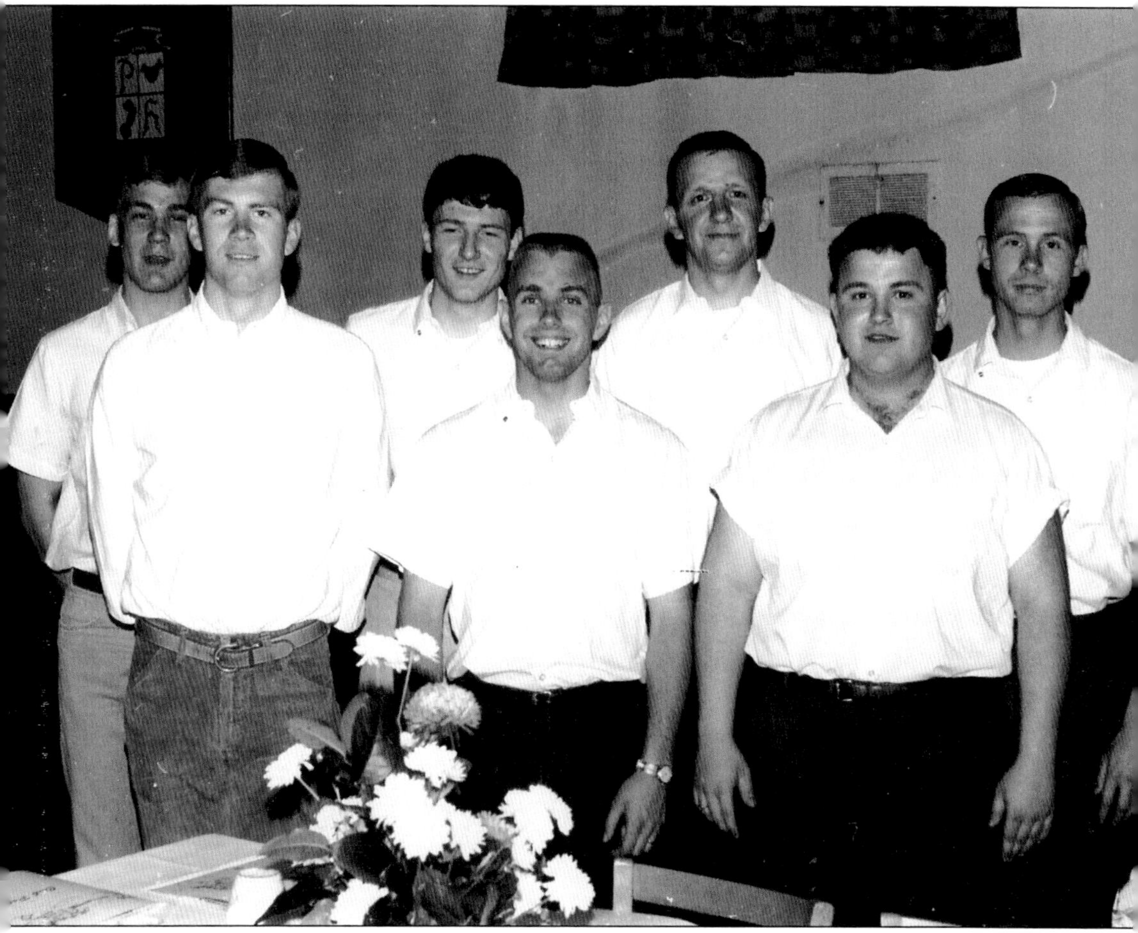

George Stankewitz tried to have seven grillmen on the payroll at any given time. He leaned toward hiring athletes, but that was not a hard-and-fast rule, and no girls were allowed. Grillmen were issued their own unique Federation of Grillmen membership cards. No one had to miss a dance, a prom, a football game, or other school-sponsored activity. Stankewitz would allow time off for school functions and would still have enough guys to cover a shift. He would try to use four from Beloit Memorial High and three from Beloit Catholic High. At times Stankewitz might find himself working with only one other guy, but the grillmen never missed their social functions. All available grillmen were called upon for special events, such as chili festivals. The grillmen in this photograph pose with Stankewitz before a senior girls' breakfast. (Courtesy of the Pop House collection.)

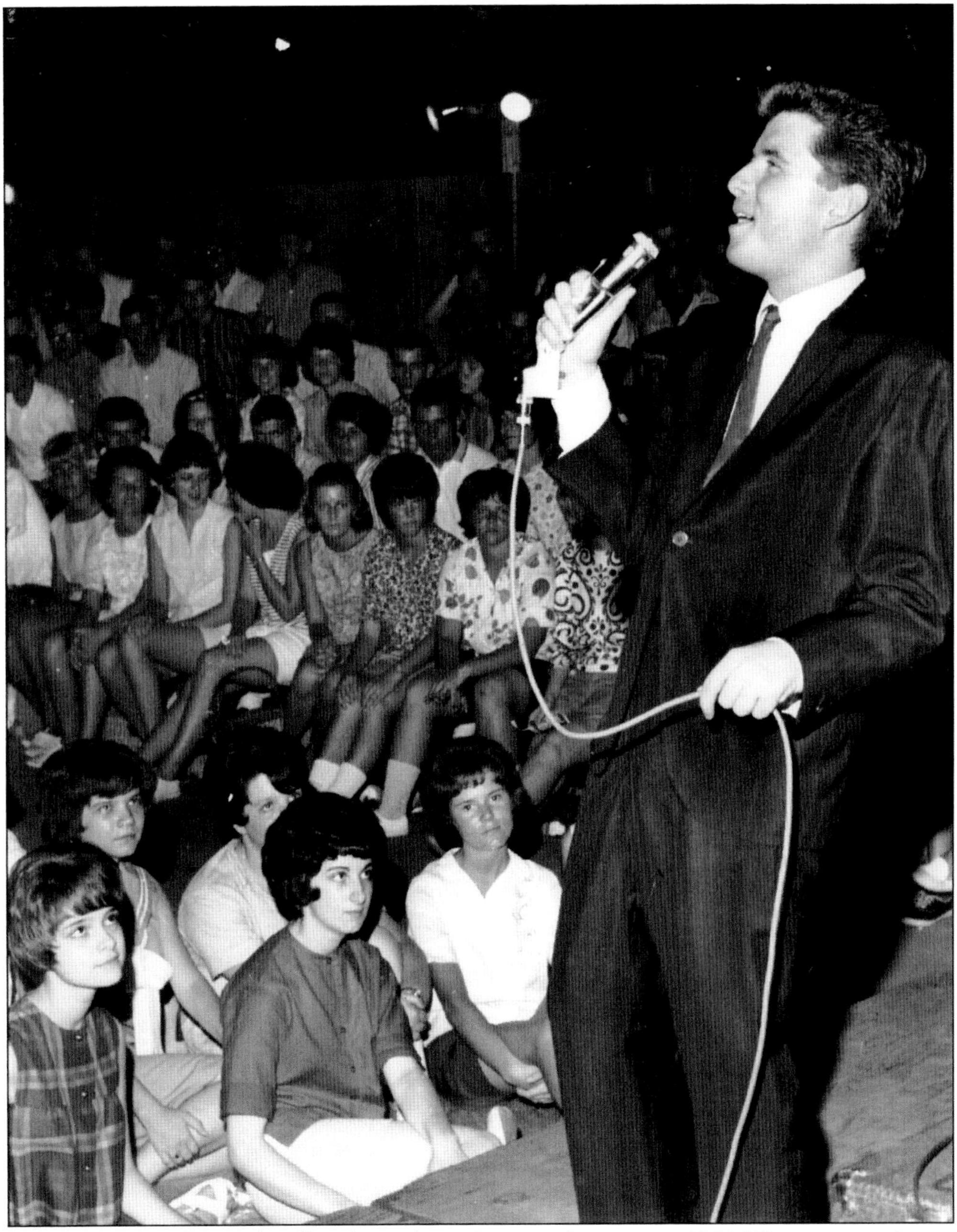

Singer Johnny Tillotson headlined a package show on the patio in 1964. The enrapt audience pictured in this photograph listens to him sing one of his many hit songs. Tillotson had recorded a number of top-10 hits by that time, including "Poetry in Motion" and "Talk Back Trembling Lips." (Courtesy of the Pop House collection.)

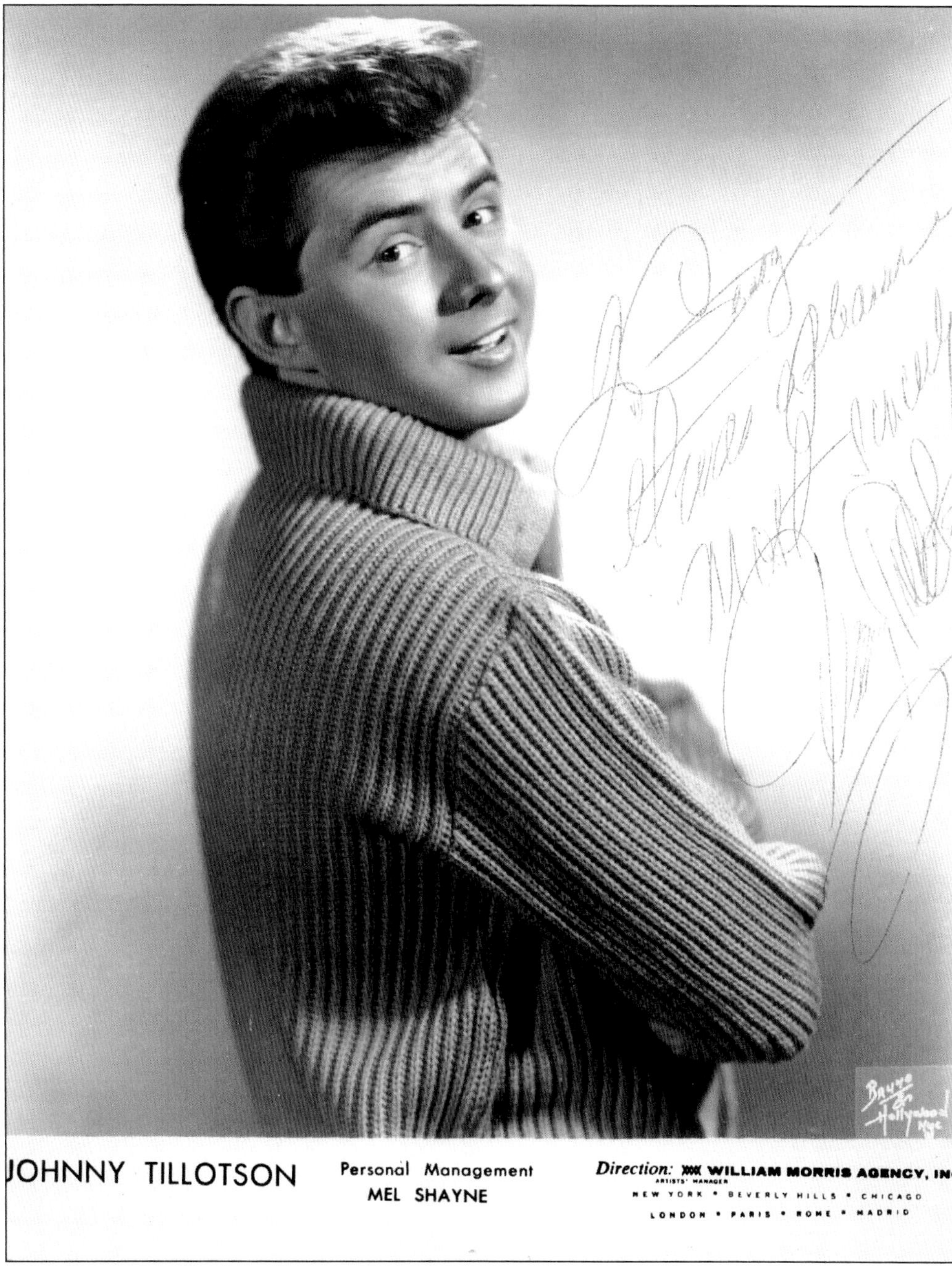

Johnny Tillotson's 1962 song "It Keeps Right on a-Hurtin'" reached top 10 on the country charts, winning him a Grammy nomination and establishing him as one of the first crossover artists. His song "Heartaches by the Number" was nominated for best vocal performance in 1965. Tillotson recorded 26 singles that made it onto the charts and performs at venues around the world. Above his autograph he wrote, "To George — It was a pleasure. Most sincerely." Tillotson was still touring internationally into the 21st century. (Courtesy of the Pop House collection.)

The Tillotson show also included a singer named Bernadette Carroll who toured with him during that summer. She had a national hit with the song "Party Girl" that year. The following year, she sang backup vocals for Lou Christie on "Lightning Strikes." On this photograph, she wrote, "George, Thanks a million! Enjoyed every minute of it. Hope to see you again real soon. Love, Bernadette Carroll." (Courtesy of the Pop House collection.)

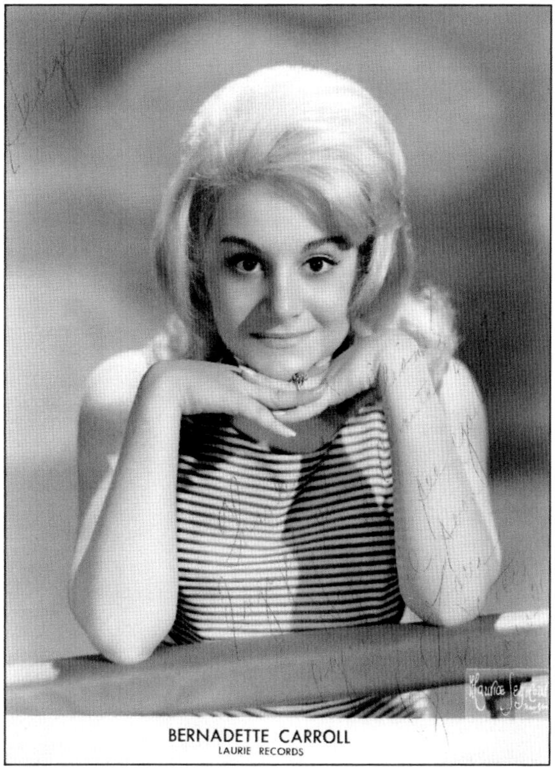

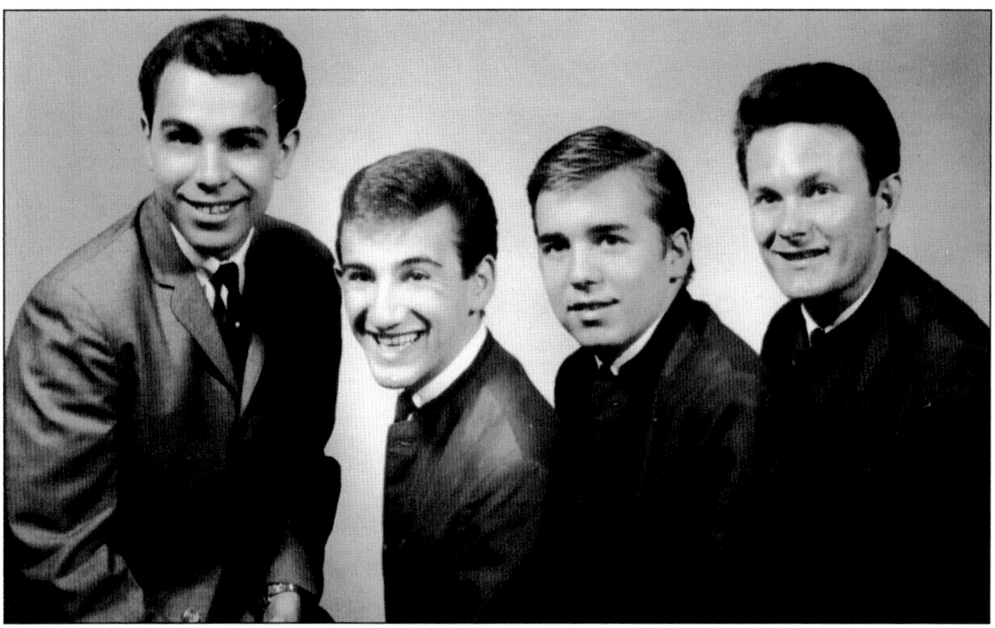

Ronnie Dio and the Prophets, from rural New York, was the backing band for the Tillotson show. Dio eventually began using his middle name, becoming Ronnie James Dio, and pursued a musical career in heavy metal. He played with Deep Purple guitarist Ritchie Blackmore in a band called Rainbow and continued playing heavy metal with his own band named Dio into the 21st century. (Courtesy of the Pop House collection.)

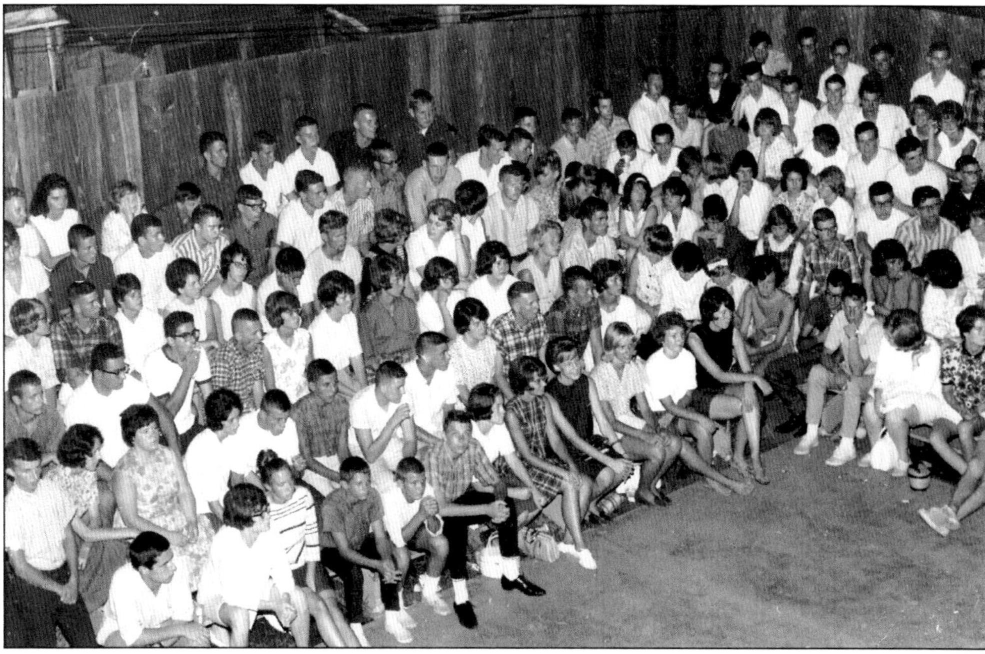

A Dick Clark *Caravan of Stars* show touring nationally during the summer of 1964 featured the Dovells, Dick and Dee Dee, and Paul and Paula. The tour made a stop at Club Pop House in Beloit where the audience is pictured here waiting for the show to open with backing band Danny and the Velaires. (Courtesy of the Pop House collection.)

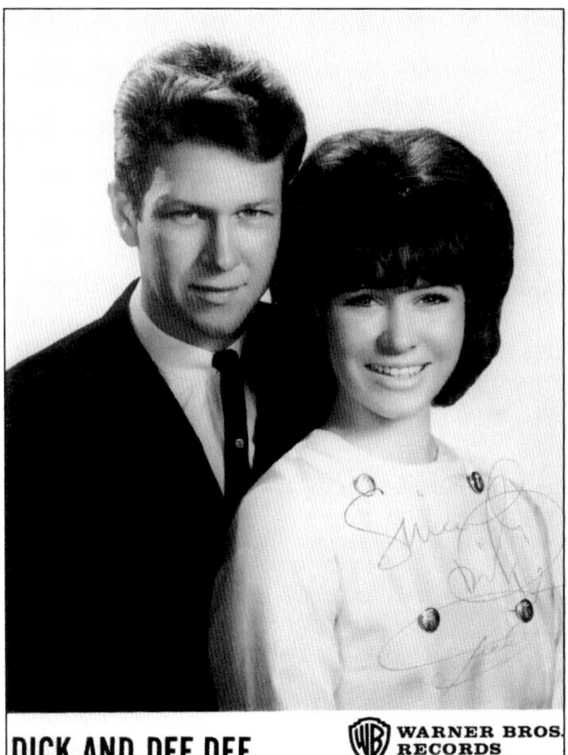

Pop phenomenon Dick and Dee Dee recorded their first song entitled "The Mountain's High" in 1961. The popular duo had eight singles on the *Billboard* charts during the 1960s and made numerous appearances on *American Bandstand* and *Shindig*. Their complete story can be found in Dee Dee's memoir, *Vinyl Highway, Singing as Dick and Dee Dee*, published in 2007. (Courtesy of the Pop House collection.)

By the time the Dovells ("Bristol Stomp") played the Pop House as part of the same tour as Paul and Paula and Dick and Dee Dee, they had pared down from a quintet to a trio led by tenor Jerry Gross. Former member Len Barry ("1-2-3") had left the group for a solo career. The Dovells continued as a trio and recorded as the Magistrates in 1968. Gross and another original member, Mark Gordesky, continue to perform as the Dovells into the 21st century. (Courtesy of the Pop House collection.)

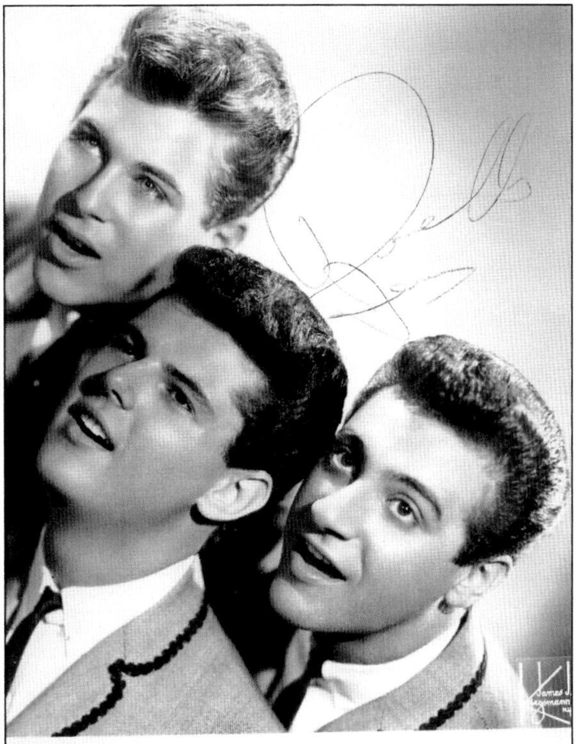

THE DOVELLS

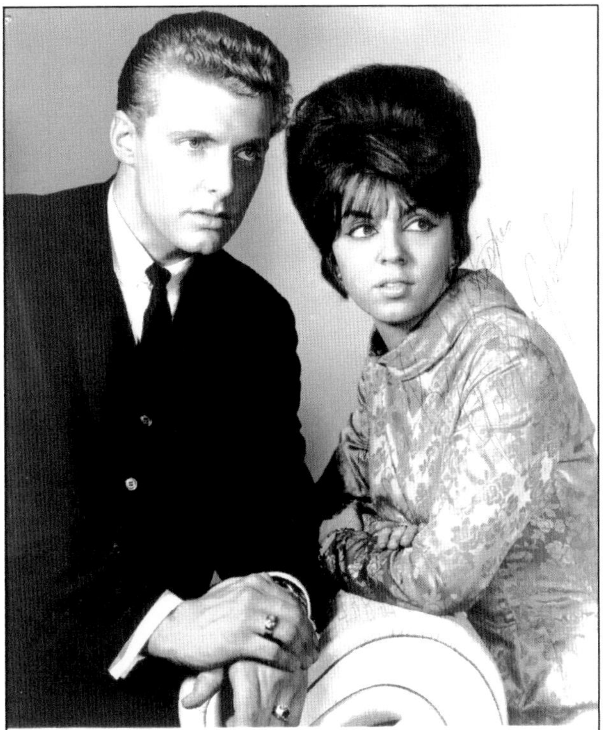

PAUL & PAULA

Ray Hildebrand and Jill Jackson teamed up in 1962 to record a song written by Hildebrand called "Hey Paula." By 1963, it had reached number one on the *Billboard* Hot 100 chart and spent the next 15 weeks as a top seller. Calling themselves Paul and Paula, they headlined the *Caravan of Stars* show on that summer night in 1964. Jackson continued with a solo career, and Hildebrand formed a Christian duo, Land and Hildebrand. They reunited occasionally as Paul and Paula for special events. (Courtesy of the Pop House collection.)

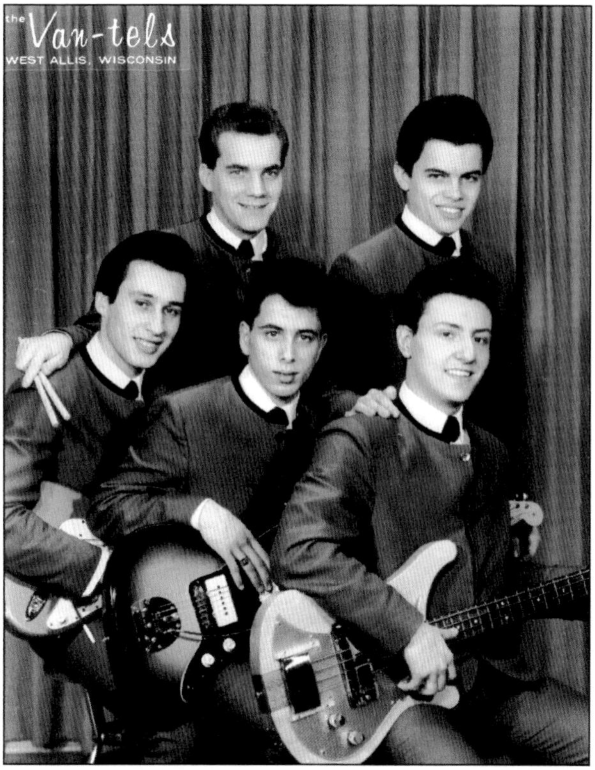

The Van-tels were a Wisconsin band that played the Pop House in August 1964. Their show was described by agent Ken Adamany as "electric" with a "hard-driving rock sound that leans toward the blues." Adamany promoted the Van-tels in the South through the Bill Lowery Agency in Atlanta, with whom he had already established booking rights for the Roemans, a band Lowery represented. (Courtesy of the Pop House collection.)

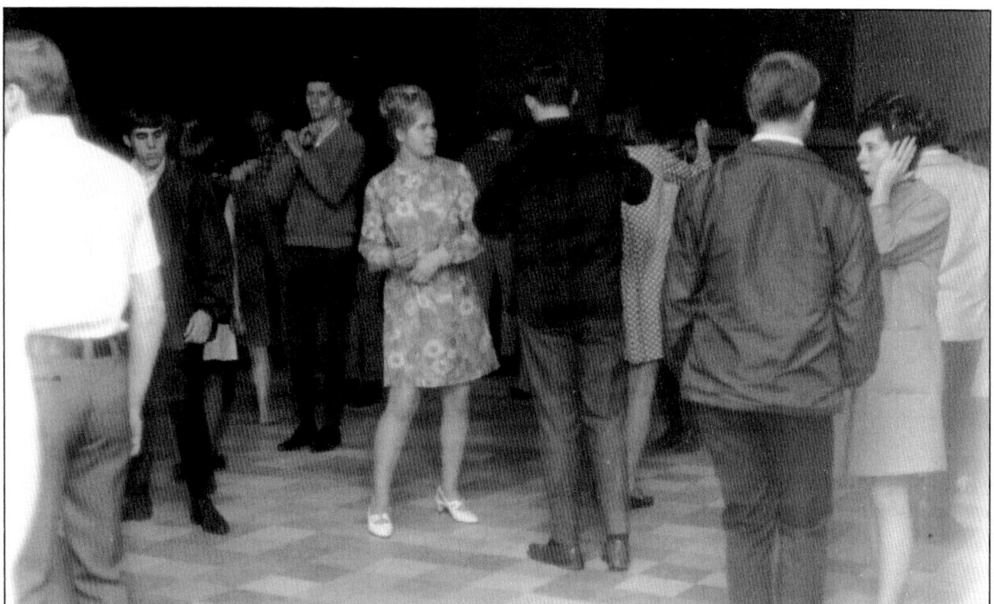

Noise complaints, weather issues, and larger crowds necessitated another expansion of the Pop House that led to construction of the dance hall, or "ballroom" as George Stankewitz preferred to call it. Completed in 1964, it provided an environment protected from the elements with concrete block walls that helped to contain increasing volume levels. (Courtesy of the Pop House collection.)

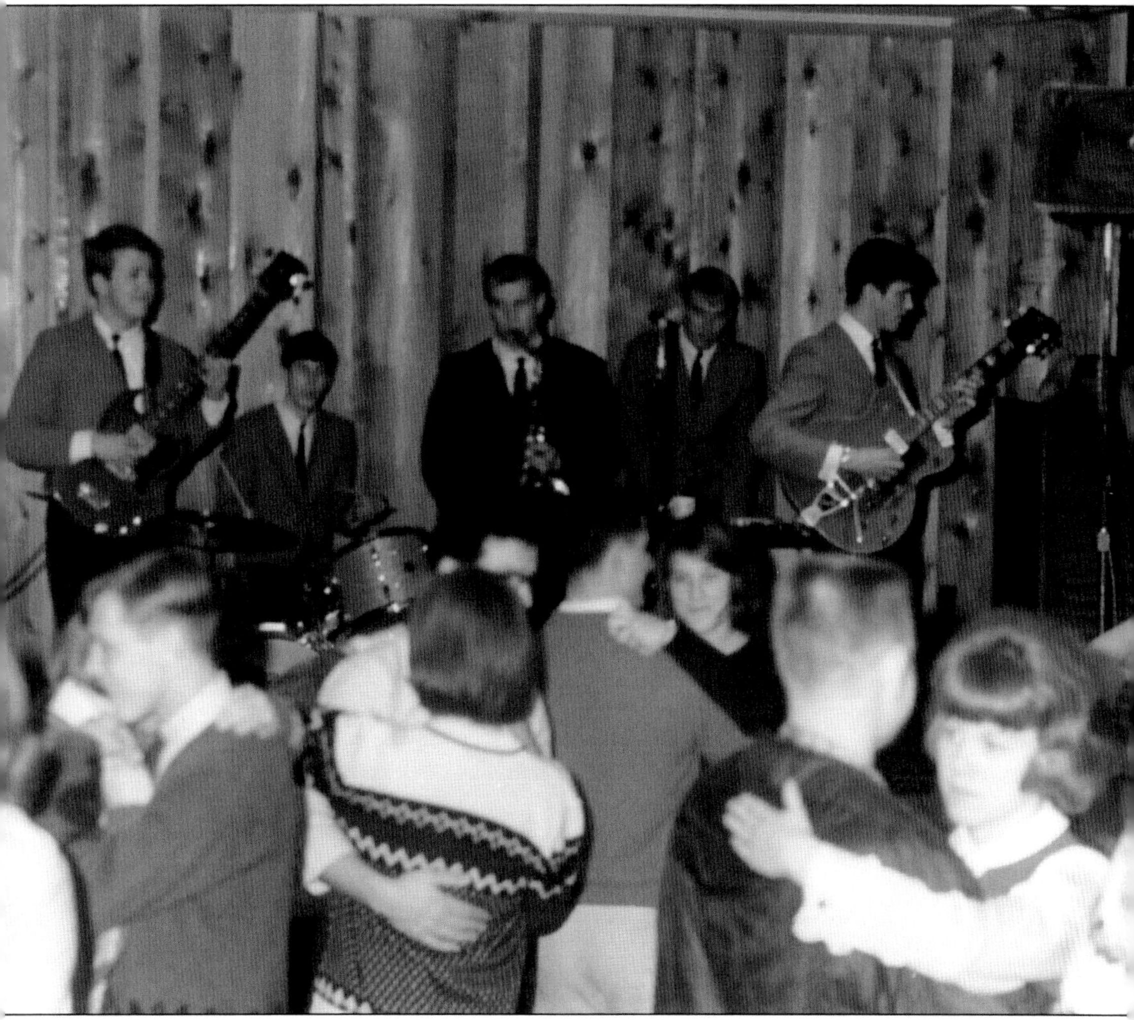

Among the first national acts to play in the new ballroom during the winter of 1964–1965 were the Kingsmen, still riding high on the success of their first big hit "Louie Louie," rock-and-roll anthem to a generation of baby boomers. In this photograph, band members, from left to right, Norm Sundholm, Dick Peterson, Lynn Easton, Barry Curtis, and Mike Mitchell perform on the Pop House stage. Their somber "Death of an Angel" was released in 1964. (Courtesy of the Pop House collection.)

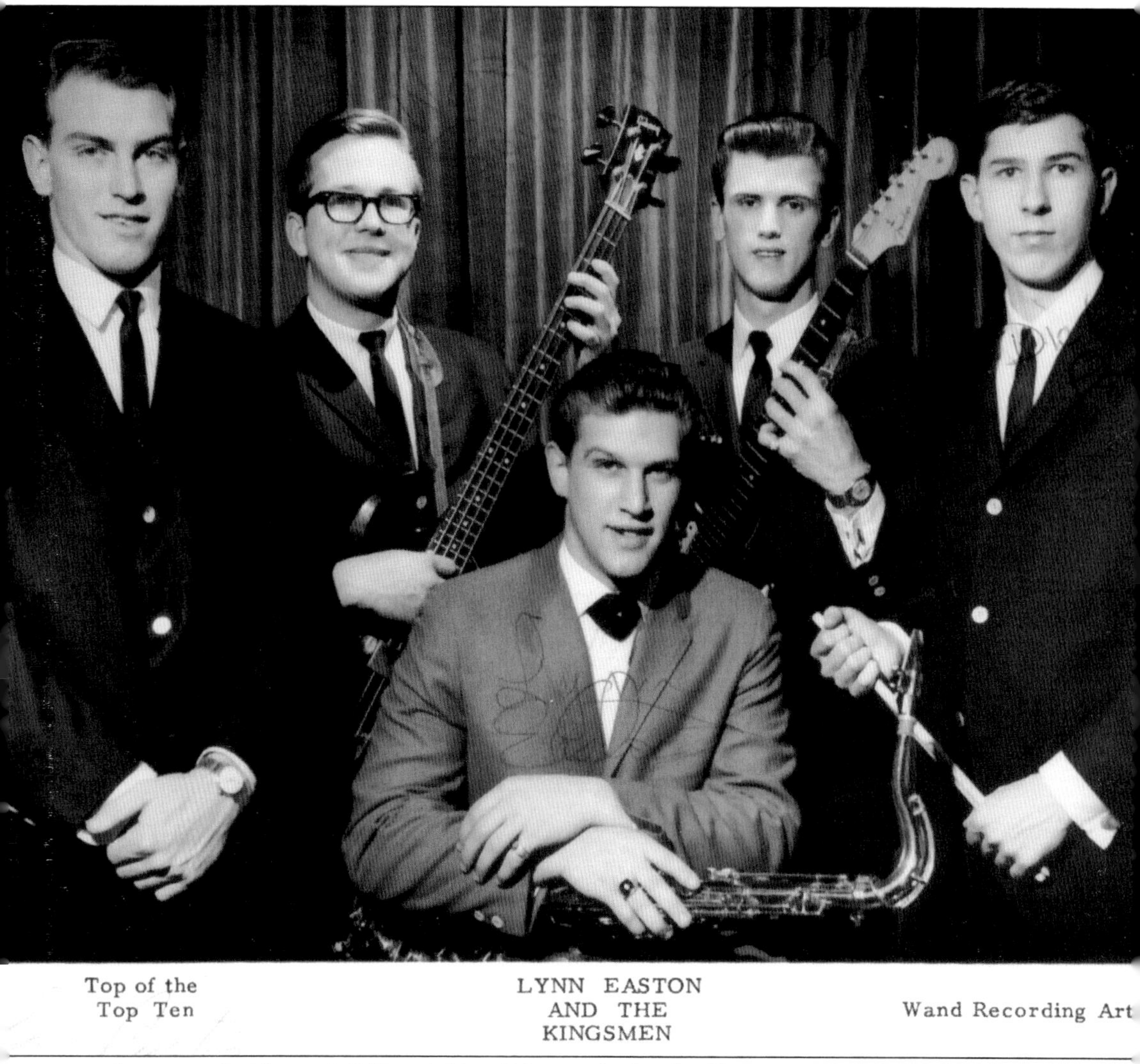

A string of additional *Billboard* Top 100 records for the Kingsmen included "Money," "Little Latin Lupe Lou," and "Jolly Green Giant." Bandleader Lynn Easton wrote on the back of this publicity photograph, "To George of the Pop House, all we can say is what a gas. It's been real." The Kingsmen, featuring original members Dick Peterson and Mike Mitchell, are still performing. (Courtesy of the Pop House collection.)

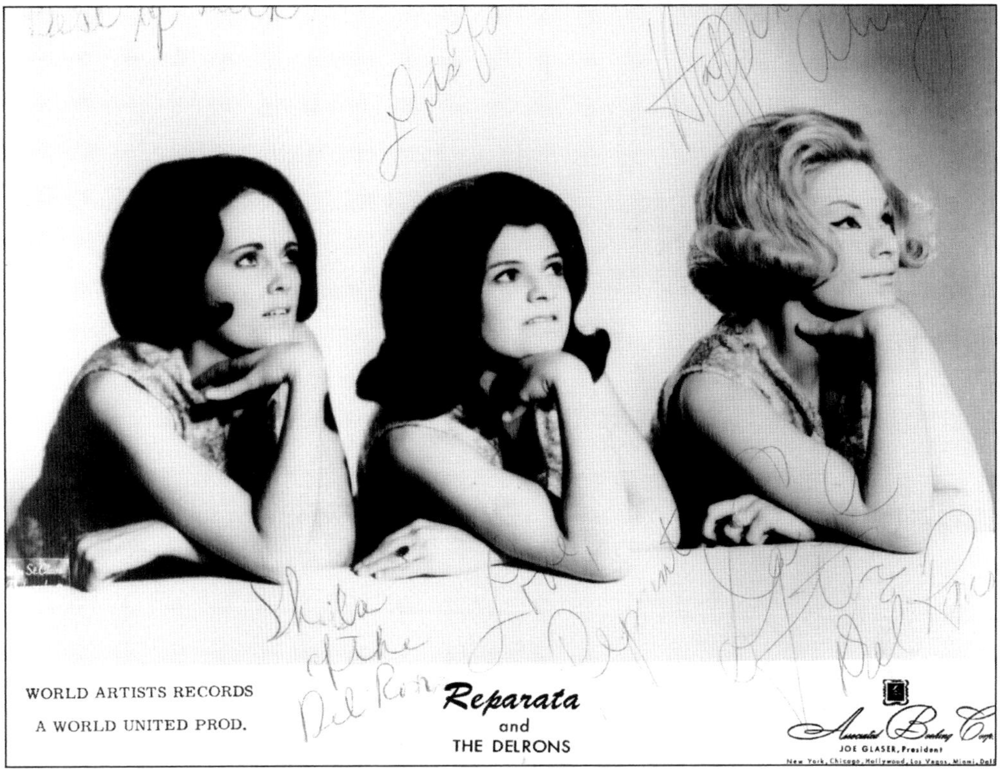

Reparata and the DelRons, a trio of Mary Aiese (Reparata), Carol Drobnicki, and Sheila Reilly, were part of Dick Clark's *Hitsville* show booked in April 1965 by agent Ken Adamany. The tour also featured Lou Christie, the Tradewinds, Round Robin, and Louise Harrison Caldwell (sister of Beatle George Harrison), whose role was to tell Beatles stories in between musical acts. The backing band was Gene Jones and the Impacts. The DelRons' first record, "Your Big Mistake," sold poorly as "da-doo-ron-ron" style was going out of fashion. The Trade Winds included Peter Andreoli and Vincent Poncia, songwriters who had collaborated with Phil Spector on Ronettes and Crystals recordings. The Trade Winds had just released their debut single, "New York Is a Lonely Town." In later years, Poncia produced records for Ringo Starr and Kiss. (Courtesy of the Pop House collection.)

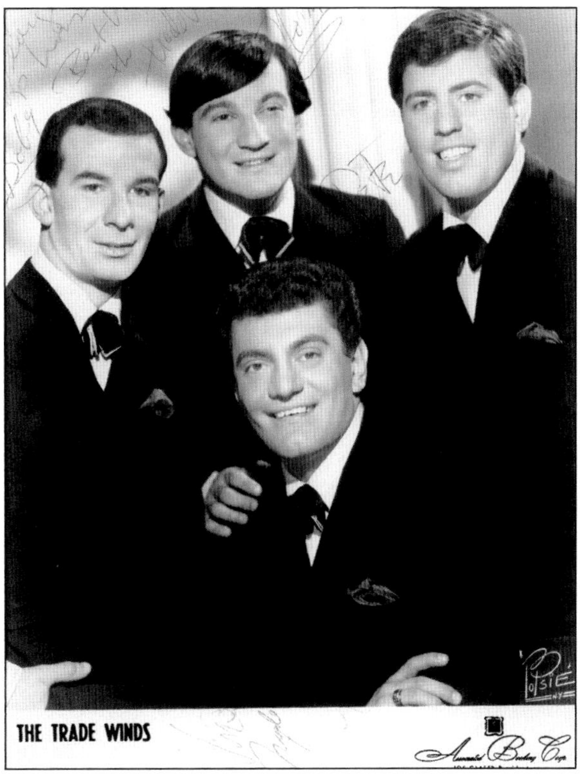

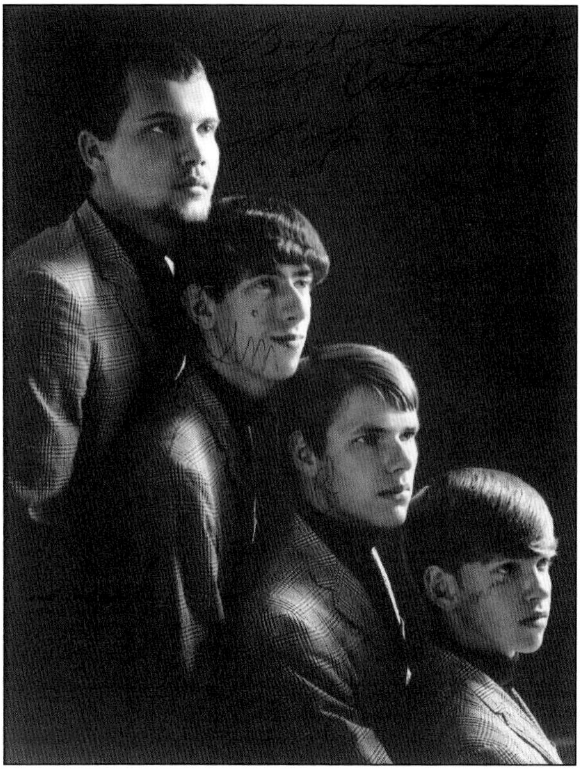

The Castaways (from left to right, Roy Hensley, Jim Donna, Rob Falschow, and Dennis Craswell) emerged from the garage-rock scene of Minneapolis to perform at the Pop House in 1965. Their hit song "Liar, Liar" charted at number 12 that year. The Castaways continue to perform with Donna as the only original member in the lineup. They were inducted into the Minnesota Rock and Country Hall of Fame in 2005. (Courtesy of the Pop House collection.)

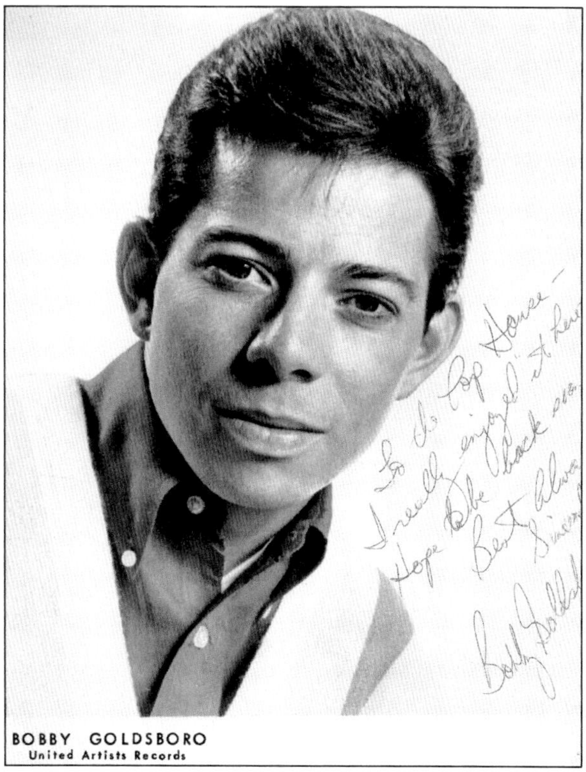

Bobby Goldsboro's 1966 tour through the Midwest brought him to the Pop House for one night in June. At that time, his hits included "See the Funny Little Clown" and "Little Things." The autographed photograph says, "To the Pop House — I really enjoyed it here. Hope to be back soon." The multitalented Goldsboro continues to work as a television producer, composer, painter, and performer. (Courtesy of the Pop House collection.)

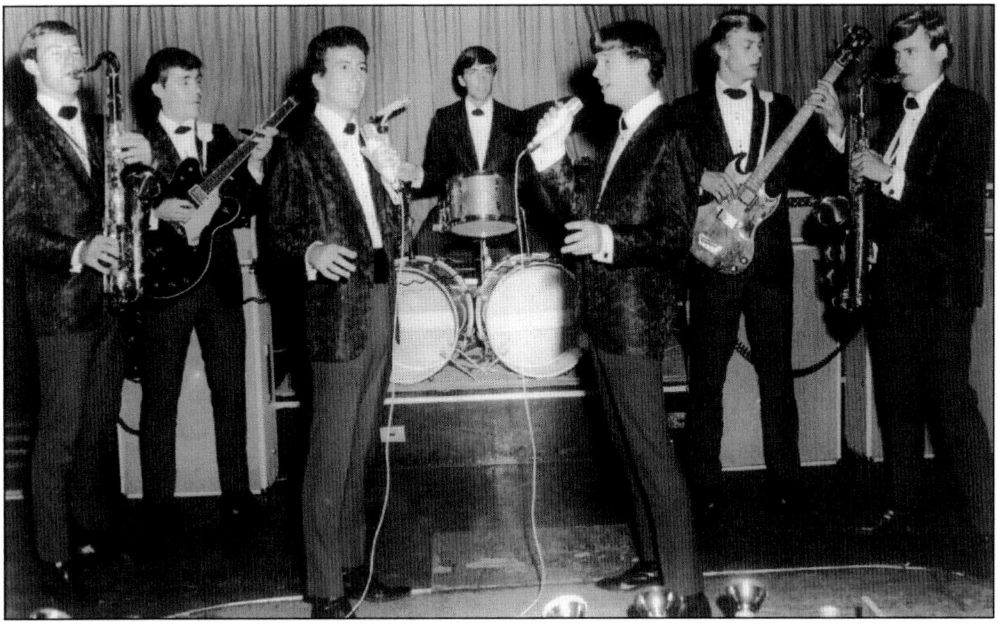

The Fabulous Flippers was one of the most highly acclaimed Midwest show bands of the mid-1960s. Their stage show included synchronized choreography, or steps, combined with band members moving from instrument to instrument and trading lead vocals. The result made the stage look like it was actually moving. The Flippers wore matching suits, and the drummer often would solo with black-lit drumsticks. Band members included Terry Wierman (guitar), Danny Hein (vocals), Dennis Lowen (keyboards), Dennis Fredricks (bass), Doug Crotte (trumpet), Jerry Tammen (drums), and Gary Claxton (saxophone). Their best-known recording was "Harlem Shuffle" on the Quill label. The Fabulous Flippers were inducted into the Iowa Music Hall of Fame in 1998 and into the Nebraska Music Hall of Fame in 1999. (Courtesy of the Pop House collection.)

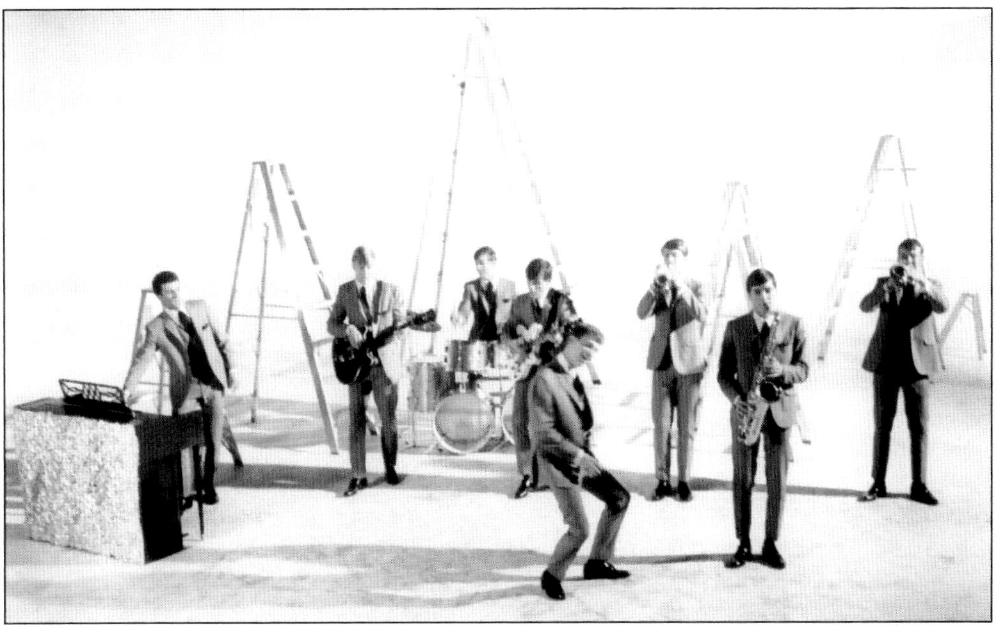

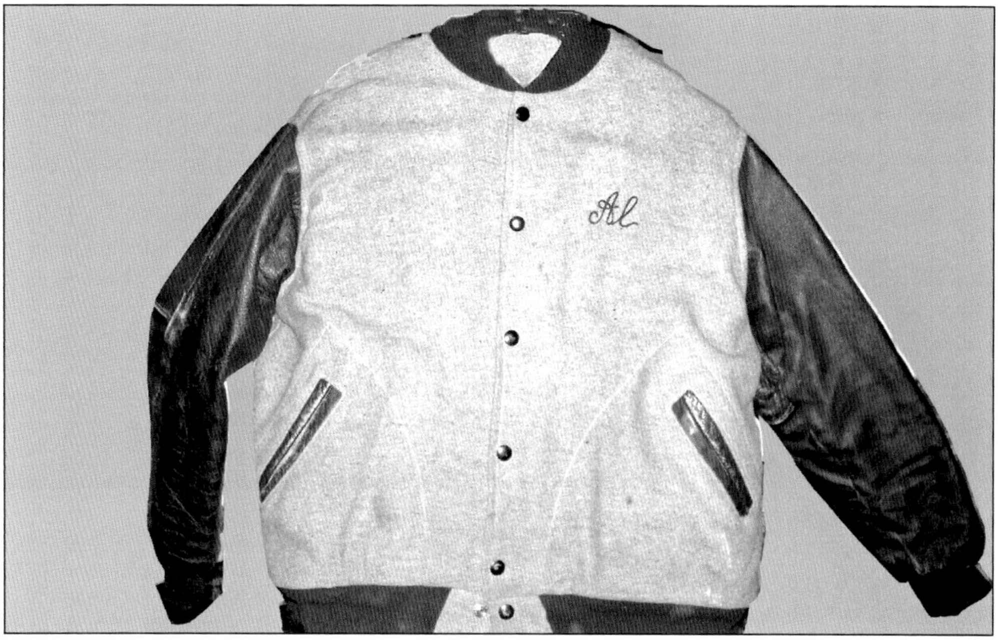

Club Pop House featured a limited line of clothing available from the sport shop run by George Stankewitz's brother Vince Stankewitz. Among the items were baseball jerseys, sweatshirts, and jackets. Many club regulars and alumni wore the Pop House colors just as they would wear their school colors. There were at least two versions of the Pop House jacket. An early version was three-quarter length with the letters *PH* on the left front side. The color was red with black leather sleeves. A later version, pictured here, was gray with black leather sleeves. An embroidered name could be added also. Sweatshirts available included a short-sleeved style shown here. Color choices included red or light blue. The Pop House logo was printed on the front. (Courtesy of Dave Hernandez.)

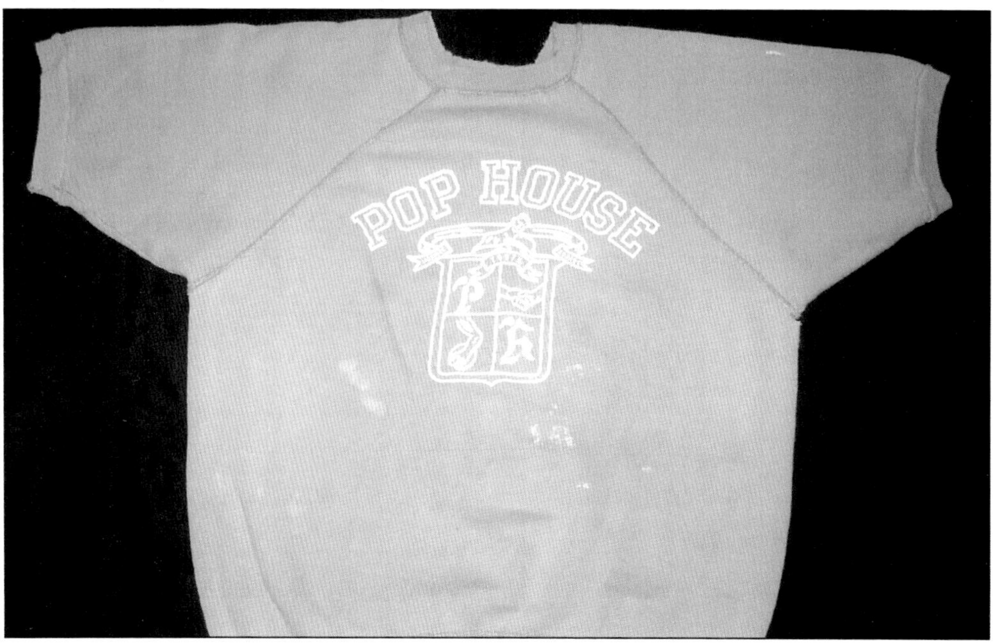

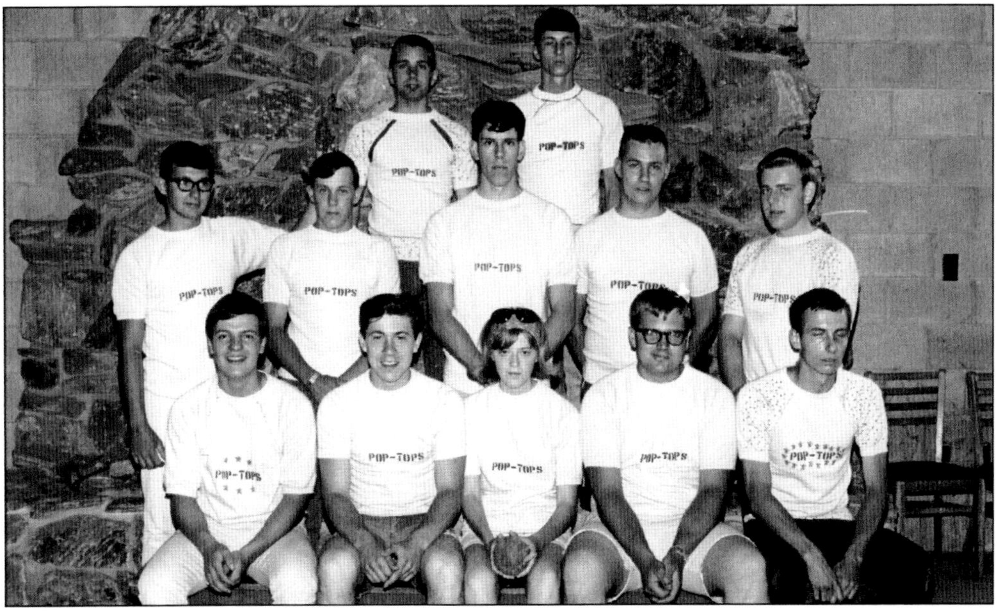

Summer softball leagues continued into the 1960s with intramural competition where several Pop House teams competed against one another. Posing for their team portrait are the 1965 Pop-Tops. The players are, from left to right, (first row) Gary Marshall, Dave Magner, Sherry Strain, Jim Carroll, and Tom O'Donahue; (second row) Greg Samp, Dennis Lasher, Kim Taylor, Tom Jordan, and Dan Burns; (third row) Dennis Elmer and Don Shepherd. (Courtesy of the Pop House collection.)

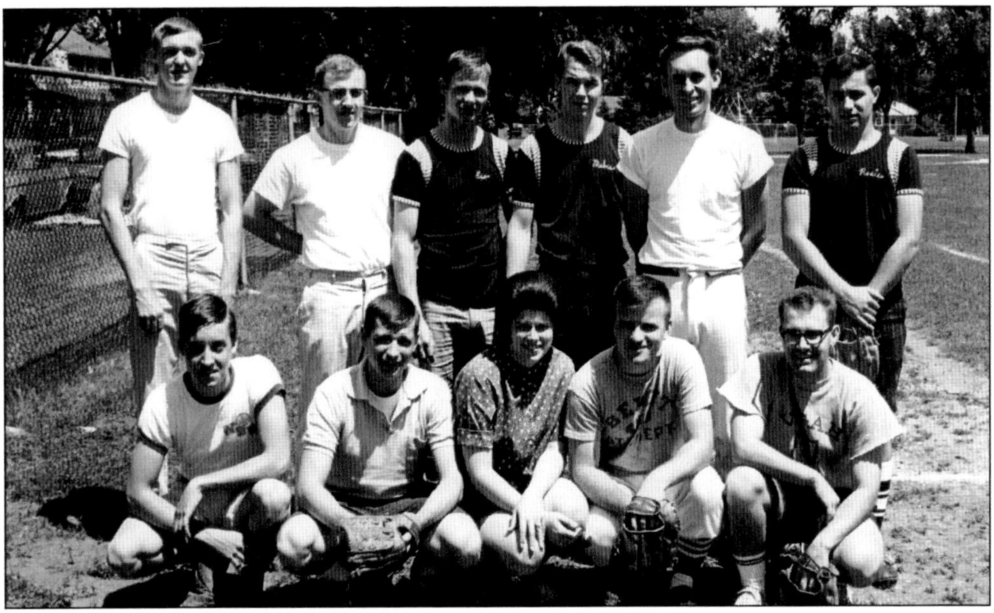

Pictured here is another of the many softball teams that played in intramural games during the summer. The Humpers competed in 1966 and include, from left to right, (first row) Roger Goodwin, Jim Long, Donna Luebke, Mike Hutchinson, and Dave Lynch; (second row) Dave Peacock, Bill Dietsch, Jim Sand, Don Schoville, Kent Hamblin, and John DeNoto. Several of the players reunite annually to reminisce about old times. (Courtesy of Mike Hutchinson.)

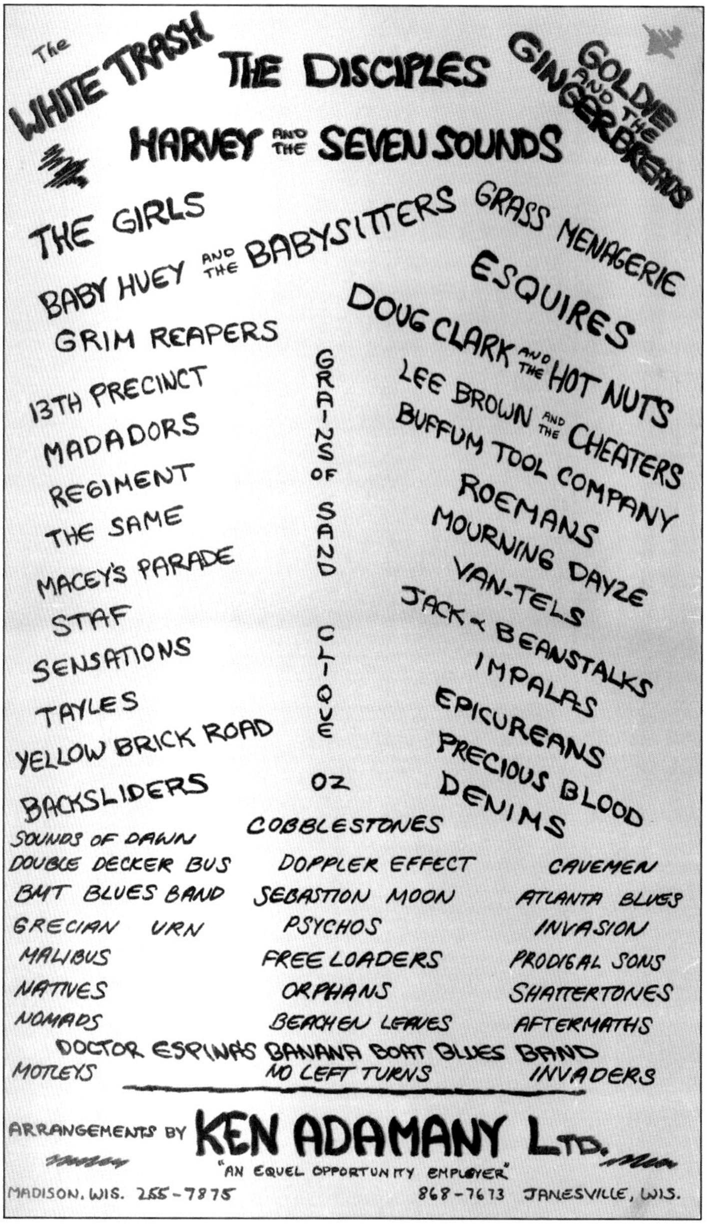

With the decade well underway, the Pop House had become a major entertainment venue for Beloit teenagers. For most dances, the club featured regional bands or the jukebox. Garage bands were omnipresent, but aspirations to play on the Pop House stage were met only infrequently because professionalism and showmanship were the accepted standards. For the audience, dancing had overtaken sitting and watching. George Stankewitz established successful business relationships with a handful of booking agents around the Midwest but perhaps none as noteworthy as that with Ken Adamany Music Enterprises. Based in Madison but with an office close by in Janesville, Adamany represented more than 100 Stateline area bands and had business connections with others who represented national acts. Pictured here is a list of bands represented by Adamany in 1967, including the Disciples, the Roemans, and the Van-tels. These and many more not listed were about to take the Pop House by storm. (Courtesy of Dave Hernandez.)

The Roemans backed Tommy Roe on his recordings of "Sheila," "I Think I Love You," "Diane from Manchester Square," and "Susie Darlin." Original band members were Lanny Langford (vocals), Bertie Higgins (drums), Ronnie Swartzkopf (guitar), Bob Glover (guitar), and Joe Pappalardo (bass). Upon splitting with Roe in 1964, the Roemans recorded and toured on their own. They appeared at the Pop House in June and July 1965, having been booked all over the Stateline area by Ken Adamany. For that tour, Berry Oakley replaced bassist Joe Pappalardo. Oakley joined the Allman Brothers Band in 1969. Drummer Bertie Higgins pursued a successful solo career in the early 1980s with such hits as "Key Largo" and "Just Another Day in Paradise." (Courtesy of Ken Adamany.)

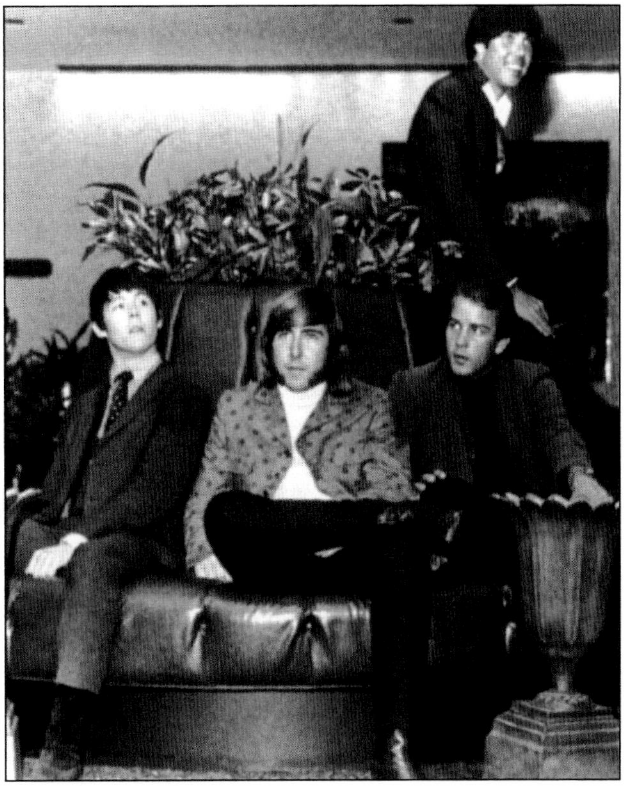

Contract Blank

AMERICAN FEDERATION OF MUSICIANS OF THE UNITED STATES AND CANADA

(HEREIN CALLED "FEDERATION")

KEN ADAMANY Music Enterprises

A. F. of M. License No. 6561

MADISON and JANESVILLE, WISCONSIN

LOCAL NUMBER #729 THE ROEMANS

THIS CONTRACT for the personal services of musicians, made this 25th day of June, 1965, between the undersigned employer (hereinafter called the "employer") and Five (5) (including the Leader) musicians (hereinafter called "employees").

WITNESSETH, That the employer hires the employees as musicians severally on the terms and conditions below. The leader represents that the employees already designated have agreed to be bound by said terms and conditions. Each employee yet to be chosen shall be so bound by said terms and conditions upon agreeing to accept his employment. Each employee may enforce this agreement. The employees severally agree to render collectively to the employer services as musicians in the orchestra under the leadership of Lanny Langford as follows:

Name and Address of Place of Engagement The Pop House/ Beloit, Wisconsin

Date(s) of Employment Friday, ~~July 9th~~, 1965 July 8

Hours of Employment 8:00-12:00

Type of Engagement (specify whether dance, stage show, banquet, etc.) Dance

The employer is hereby given an option to extend this agreement for a period of — weeks beyond the original term thereof. Said option can be made effective only by written notice from the employer to the employees, not later than — days prior to the expiration of said original term, that he claims and exercises said option, and a copy of said notice shall be filed with the local in whose jurisdiction the engagement is to be played.

WAGE AGREED UPON $ ~~$300.00~~ ~~EXACTLY THREE HUNDRED DOLLARS~~ 225 TWO HUNDRED TWENTY FIVE (Terms and Amount)

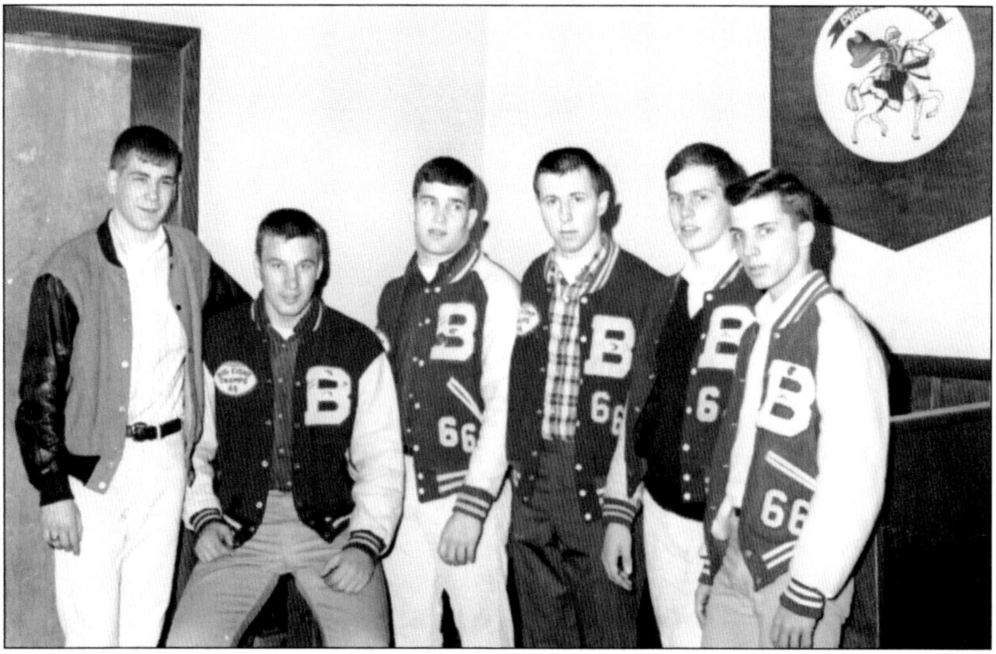

The Beloit Memorial High Purple Knights were the Big Eight Conference baseball champions in 1965. Pictured here posing with Pete Martin (left) in his Pop House jacket are, from left to right, team members Tom Johnson, Bill Getzke, Harold Stanford, Gary Olin, and unidentified. It was the first state championship in baseball for the Purple Knights. (Courtesy of the Pop House collection.)

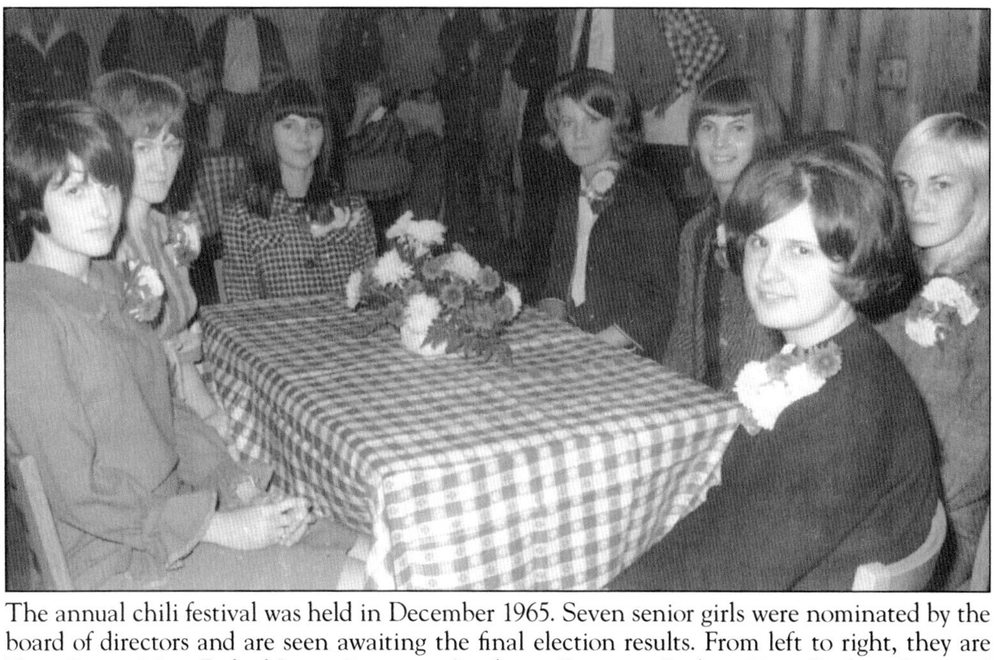

The annual chili festival was held in December 1965. Seven senior girls were nominated by the board of directors and are seen awaiting the final election results. From left to right, they are Terry Piazza, Mary Egdorf, Jenny Pargman, Stephanie Bierman, Barbara King, Barbara Bier, and Virginia Belvedere. Jenny Pargman won the balloting and reigned as chili queen for the coming year. (Courtesy of the Pop House collection.)

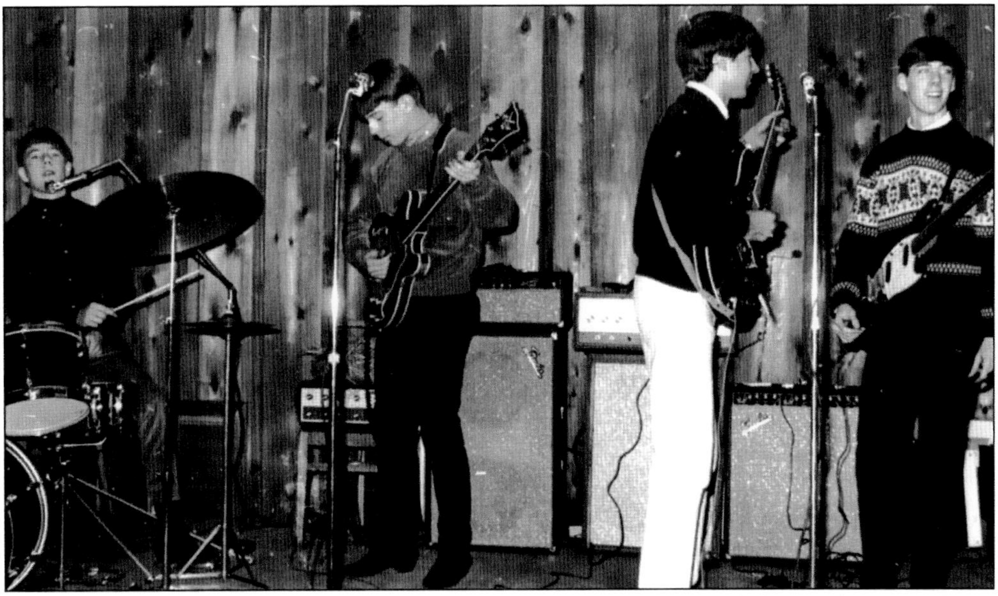

Warming up for the 1965 chili festival dance are the Esquires, from left to right, twins Dave and Dana Buck, Brad Palmer, and Tom Harrison. They played cover versions from the current WLS Silver Dollar Survey, often better than the original artists, and occasionally added visual bits to their show. For a rendition of Nancy Sinatra's "These Boots Are Made for Walking," a pair of boots sat on one side of the stage. Toward the song's end, at the line "Are you ready boots? Start walkin'," a stagehand pulled wires attached to the boots to make them "walk" across the stage. The Esquires recorded a single in 1967, "Am I to Blame," on the Feature label owned by Ken Adamany. Below, the Esquires pose for a publicity photograph on the grounds of the Lincoln-Tallman Home in Janesville. (Above, courtesy of the Pop House collection; below, courtesy of Dana Buck.)

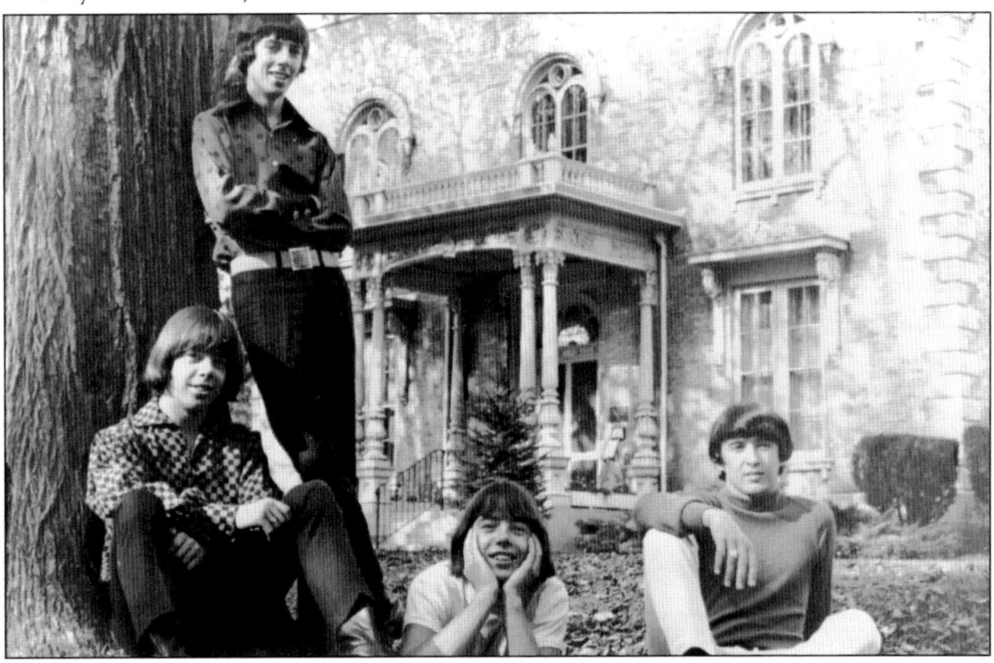

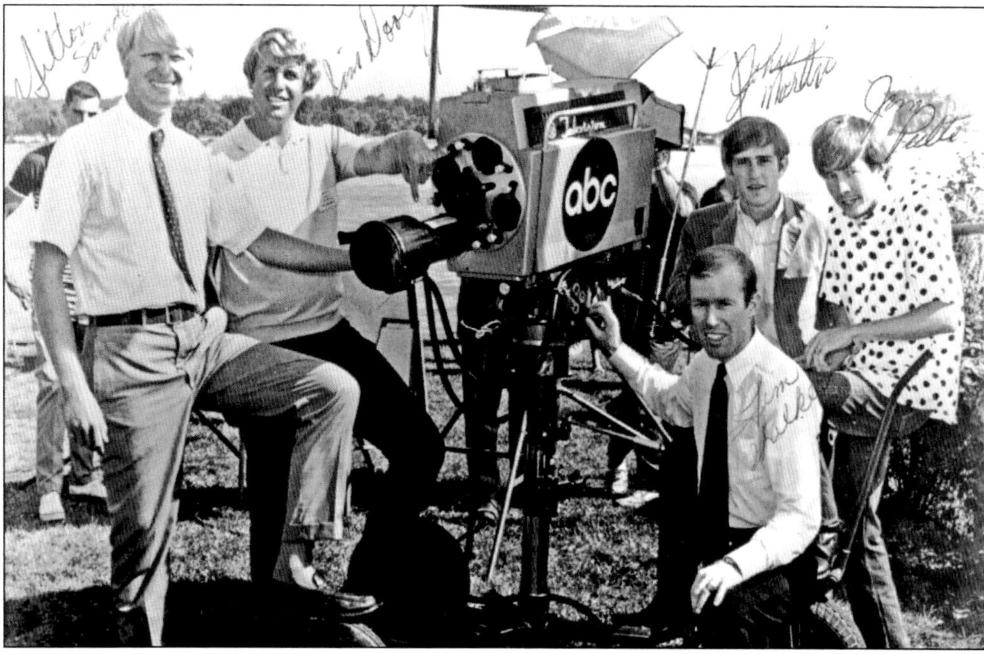

John "Moon" Martin, composer of the song "Bad Case of Lovin' You (Doctor, Doctor)," a hit for Robert Palmer in 1979, played the Pop House in December 1966 with his band from Oklahoma called the Disciples. In 1969, the band moved to California, changed its name to Southwind, and recorded its first of three country-rock albums. The publicity photograph here shows band members Milton Sanders, Jim Dooley, Martin, Jim Pulte, and Jim Walker. Pulte also had success as a songwriter and recorded with a band called the Tractors. The Disciples were one of Ken Adamany's most popular bands, playing to packed houses wherever they went. (Above, courtesy of the Pop House collection; below, courtesy of Ken Adamany.)

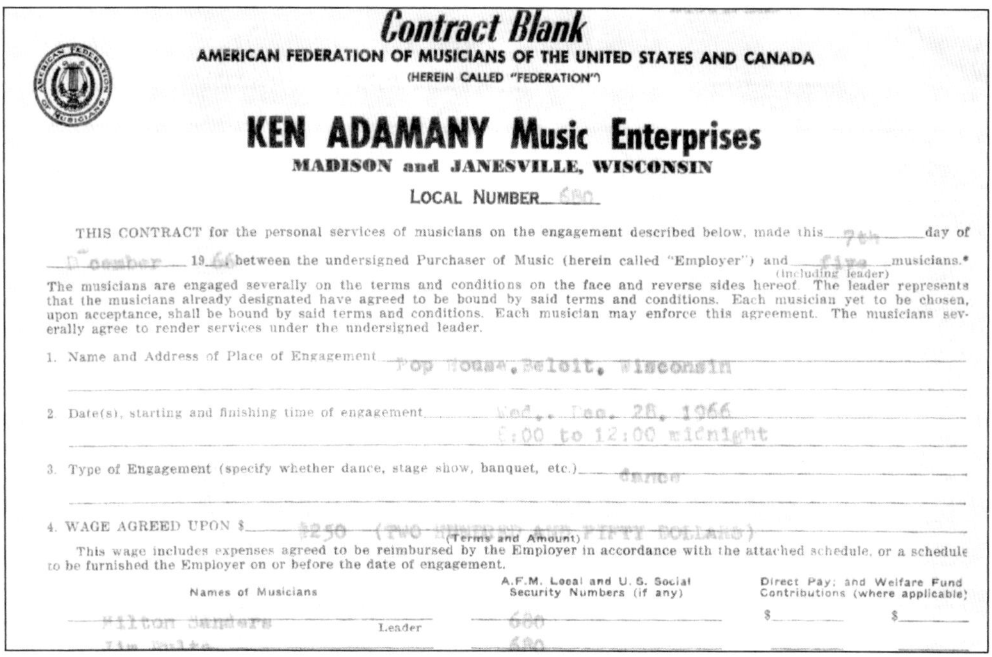

Contract Blank

AMERICAN FEDERATION OF MUSICIANS OF THE UNITED STATES AND CANADA
(HEREIN CALLED "FEDERATION")

KEN ADAMANY Music Enterprises

MADISON and JANESVILLE, WISCONSIN

LOCAL NUMBER 680

THIS CONTRACT for the personal services of musicians on the engagement described below, made this 7th day of December 19 66 between the undersigned Purchaser of Music (herein called "Employer") and five (including leader) musicians.*
The musicians are engaged severally on the terms and conditions on the face and reverse sides hereof. The leader represents that the musicians already designated have agreed to be bound by said terms and conditions. Each musician yet to be chosen, upon acceptance, shall be bound by said terms and conditions. Each musician may enforce this agreement. The musicians severally agree to render services under the undersigned leader.

1. Name and Address of Place of Engagement Pop House, Beloit, Wisconsin

2. Date(s), starting and finishing time of engagement Wed., Dec. 28, 1966 8:00 to 12:00 midnight

3. Type of Engagement (specify whether dance, stage show, banquet, etc.) dance

4. WAGE AGREED UPON $ $250 (TWO HUNDRED AND FIFTY DOLLARS) (Terms and Amount)
This wage includes expenses agreed to be reimbursed by the Employer in accordance with the attached schedule, or a schedule to be furnished the Employer on or before the date of engagement.

Names of Musicians		A.F.M. Local and U. S. Social Security Numbers (if any)	Direct Pay; and Welfare Fund Contributions (where applicable)	
Milton Sanders	Leader	680	$	$
Jim Pulte		680		

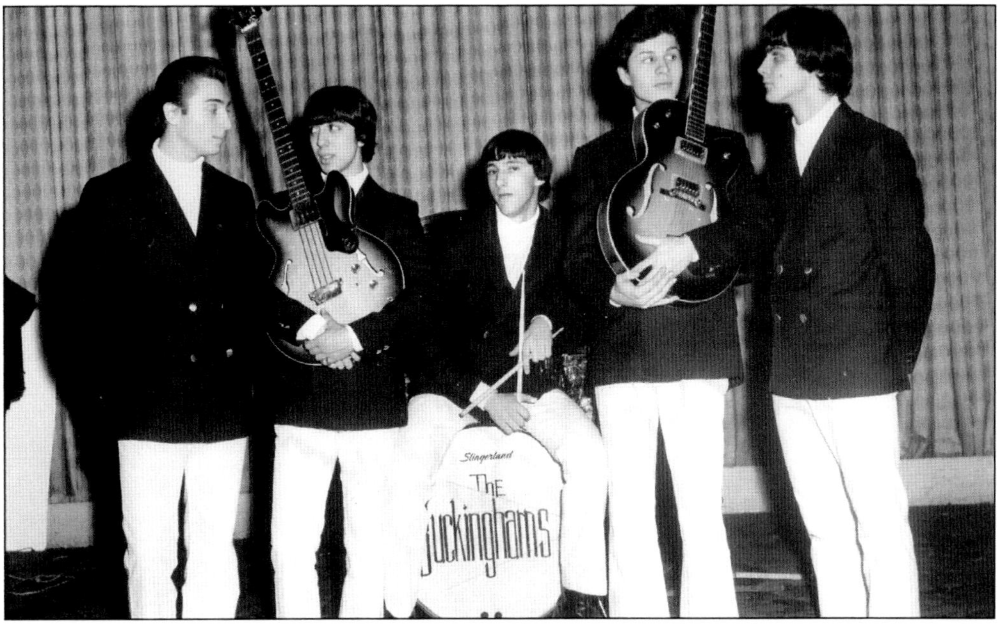

The Chicago-based Buckinghams (from left to right, Marty Grebbs, Nick Fortuna, John Poulas, Carl Giammarese, and Dennis Tufano) performed at the Pop House in 1966 on the way to national success with their first hit, "Kind of a Drag." The following year, they had five songs on the charts, three in the top 10. They also appeared on the Smothers Brothers and Ed Sullivan television programs. (Courtesy of the Pop House collection.)

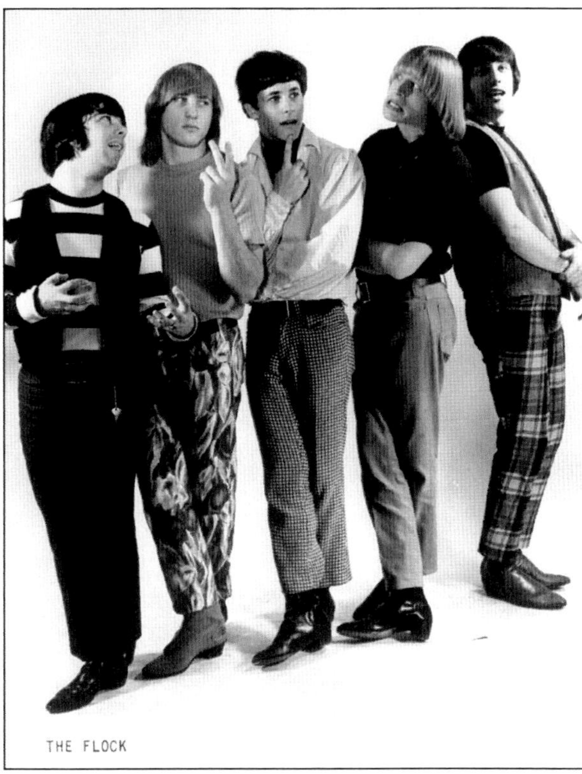

THE FLOCK

The Flock (from left to right, Fred Glickstein, Rick Canoff, Ron Karpman, Ricky Mann, and Jerry Smith) were from Chicago and had a local hit, "Take Me Back." When violinist Jerry Goodman joined the band in 1968, they developed a jazz-rock sound. Their 1966 appearance featured wall-shaking volume, and the closing line "We're going to do one more song and then we're going to get the Flock out of here." (Courtesy of the Pop House collection.)

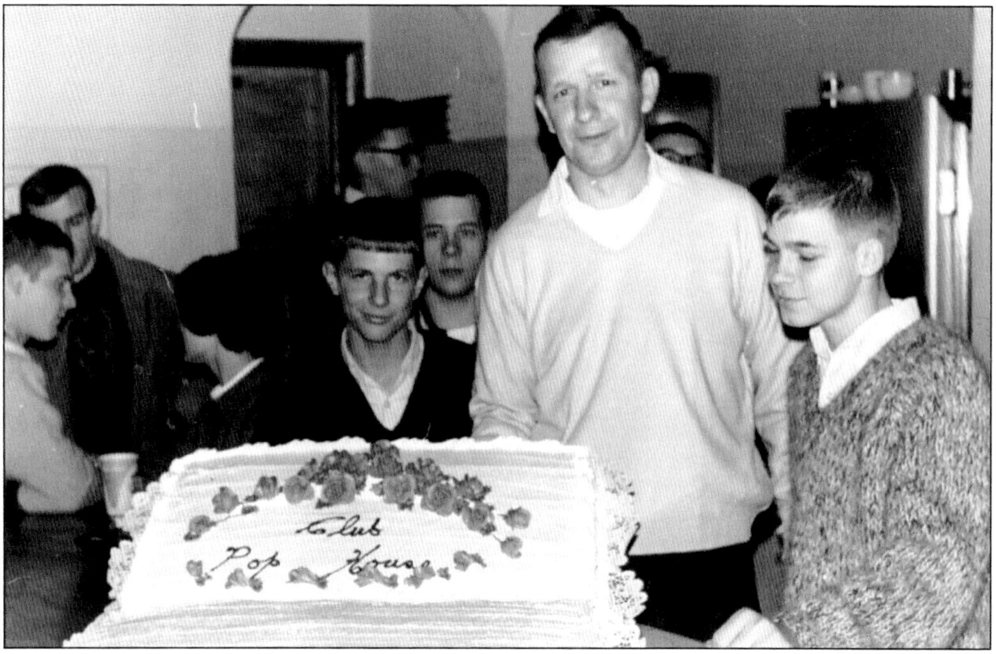

The year 1966 marked the 25th anniversary of the Club Pop House, and George Stankewitz celebrated the occasion with a cake that he shared with his customers. Flanking Stankewitz in this photograph are grillmen Bruce Rudolph (left) and Chris Martin, both seniors from the Beloit Memorial High School class of 1967. (Courtesy of the Pop House collection.)

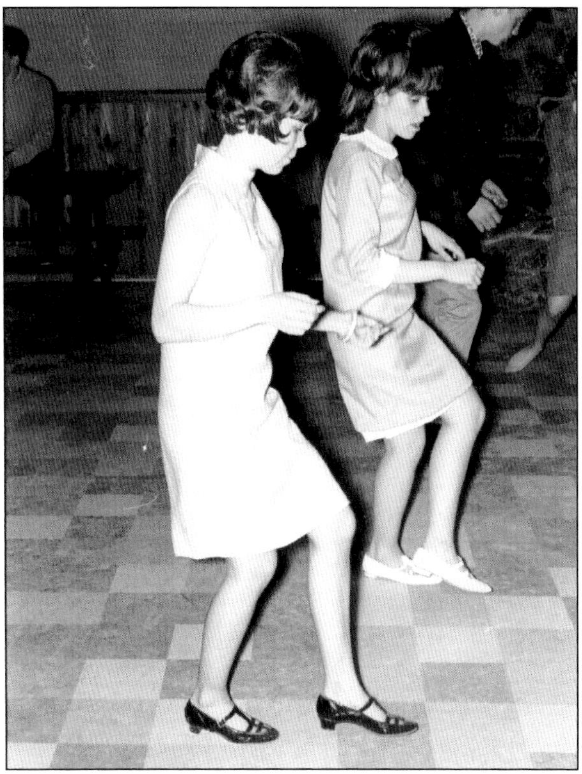

Of course, the celebration included music and dancing. Deb Haefner (left) and Kris Krafjack are pictured here doing the stroll. A precursor to the line dancing of today, the stroll is thought to have originated on *American Bandstand* in the mid-1950s and was popularized further by a song called "The Stroll" by the Diamonds. (Courtesy of the Pop House collection.)

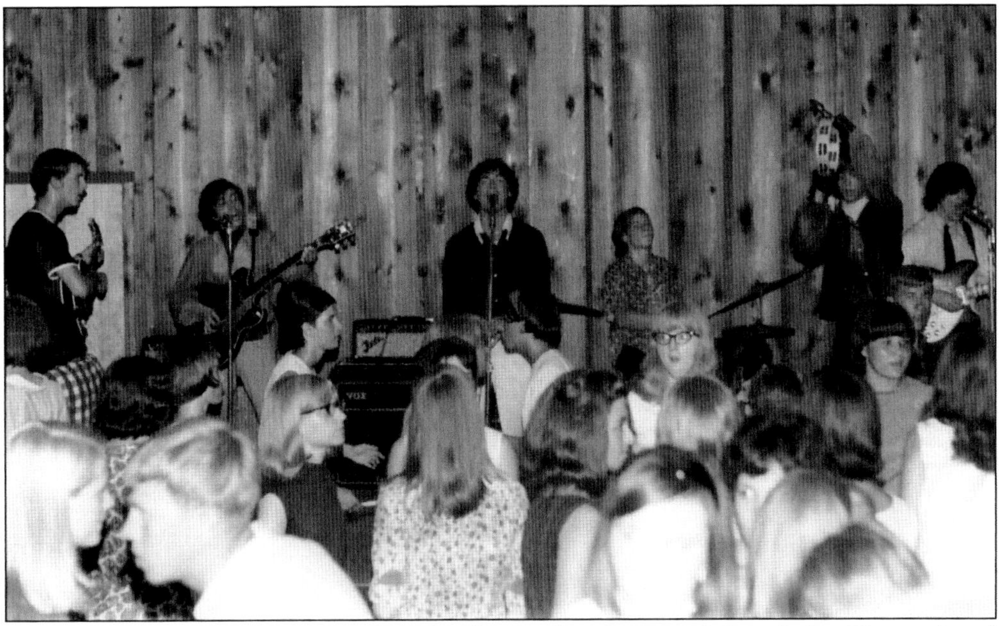

Shortly after the 1966 release of their first hit single, "Sugar and Spice," the Chicago-based Cryan' Shames (from left to right, Gerry "Stonehenge" Stone, David "Grape" Purple, Tom "Toad" Doody, Dennis Conroy, Jim "J. C. Hooke" Pilster, and Jim Fairs) play for a packed house in the Pop House ballroom. A successful recording career produced a string of hits such as "I Wanna Meet You" and "It Could Be We're in Love." (Courtesy of the Pop House collection.)

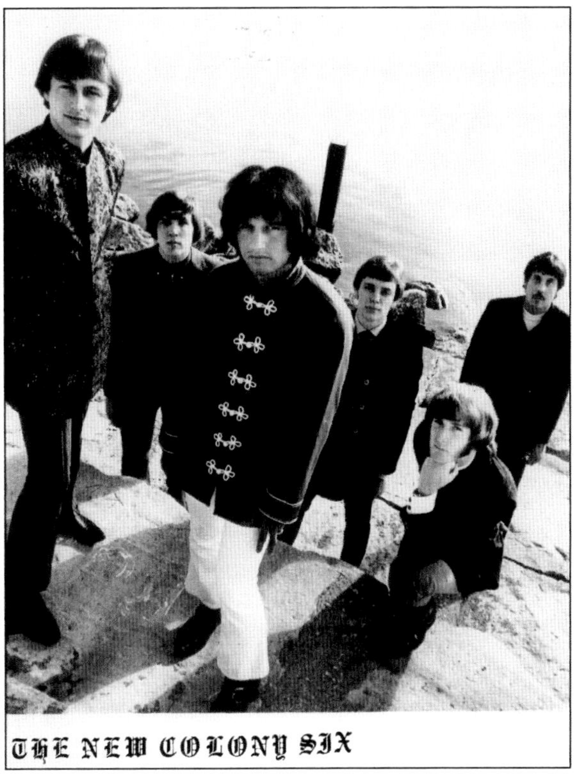

The New Colony Six, another Chicago band, had two national hits, "I Will Always Think about You" and "Things I'd Like to Say." Their shows in 1966 and 1967 at the Pop House combined rave-up rock and psychedelic forays along with their better-known ballads. Band members included Ray Graffia, Gerry Van Kollenburg, Les Kummell, Chic James, Pat McBride, and Ronnie Rice. (Courtesy of the Pop House collection.)

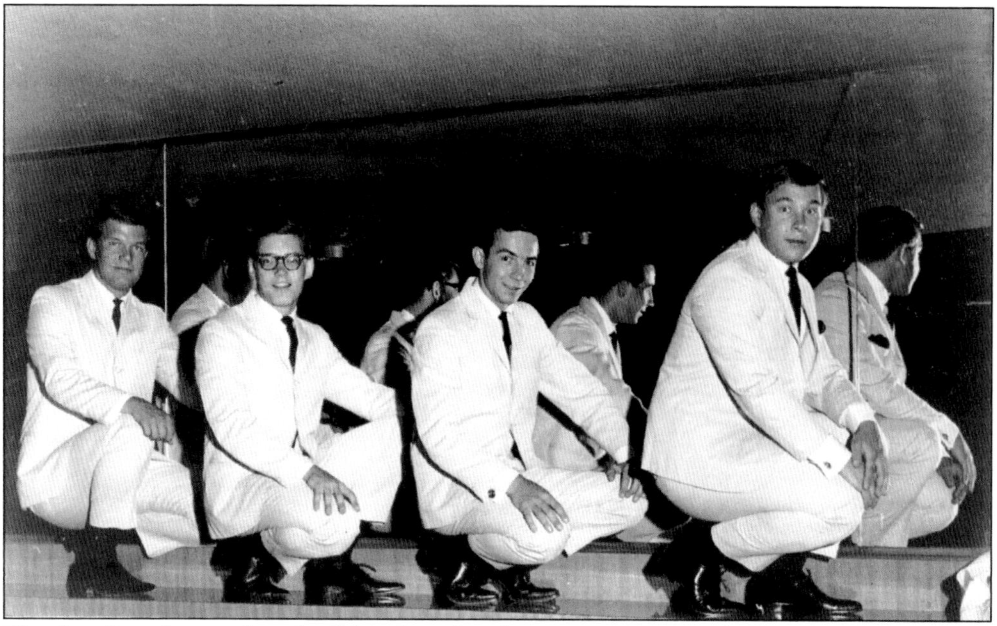

The first Canadian rock-and-roll band to play the Pop House was Chad Allan and the Guess Who, having just released the song "Shakin' All Over." For their Pop House appearance, the band lineup included Randy Bachman, Chad Allan, Jim Kale, and Garry Peterson. Subsequently, Burton Cummings joined the band and Chad Allan left. (Courtesy of the Pop House collection.)

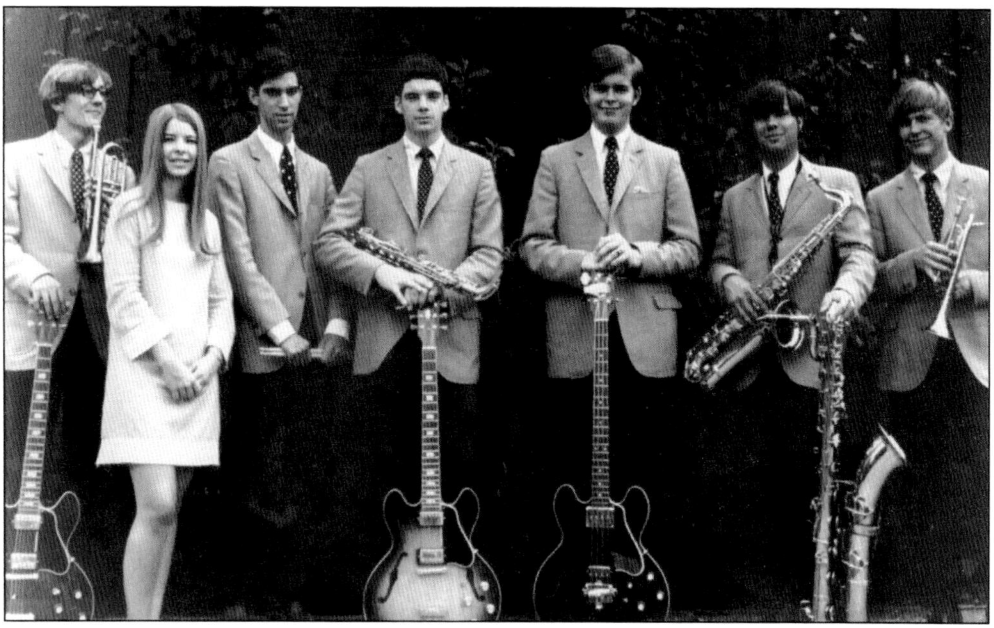

Minneapolis-based Marcia and the Lynchmen offered a variety of musical styles ranging from hard rock to rhythm and blues. Vocalist Marcia Harris was backed up by a band whose members were multi-instrumentalists. Primarily a cover band, they did record one original song, "Won't Turn Back," that received airplay in the Twin Cities. Their show at the Pop House followed the record's release in 1967. (Courtesy of the Pop House collection.)

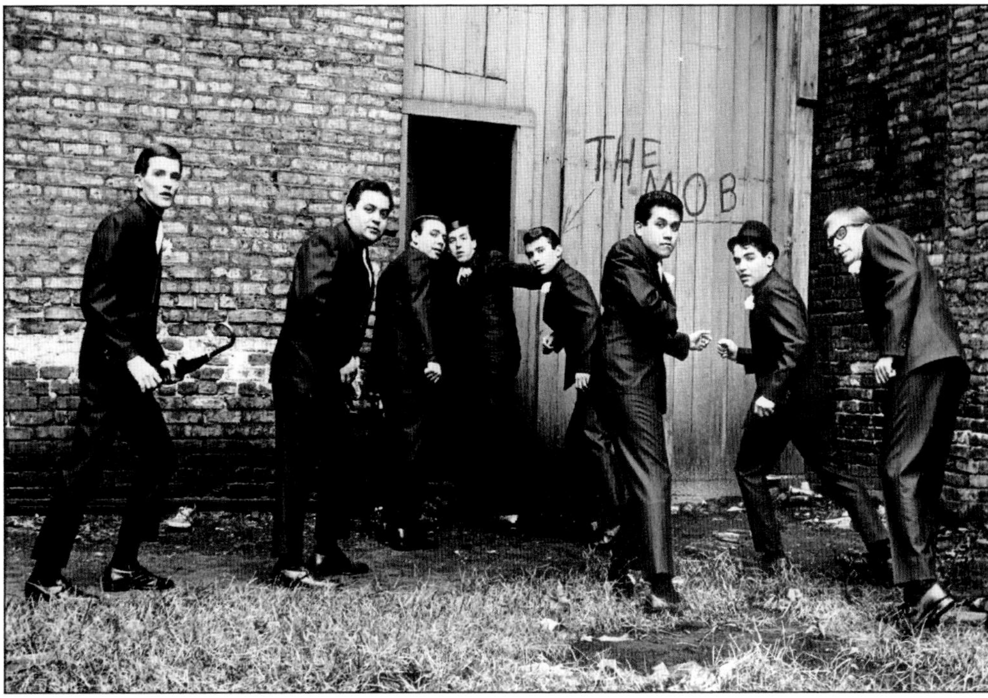

Pictured from left to right, Gary Beisbier, "Big Al" Herrera, Mike Sistak, Jimmy "Soul" Holvay, Tony Nedza, "Little Artie" Herrera, Bobby "the Cheeze" Ruffino, and Jimmy Ford comprised an exciting Chicago-based show band, the Mob. Their Pop House appearances in 1966 and 1967 generated packed houses. Audiences were blown away by the powerful horn arrangements, vocals, and showmanship. The Mob recorded a number of original songs, including "Open the Door," "I Dig Everything about You," and "Give It to Me," all penned by Holvay and Beisbier. But the songwriting duo saw their biggest success composing million-selling records for the Buckinghams, including "Kind of a Drag," "Don't You Care," "Hey Baby," and "Susan." (Courtesy of the Pop House collection.)

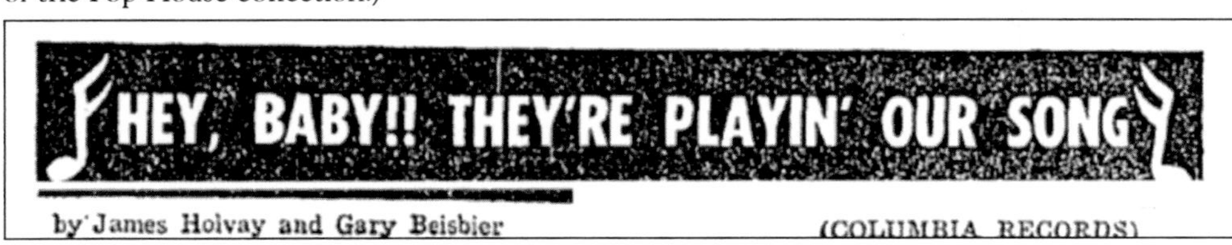
HEY, BABY!! THEY'RE PLAYIN' OUR SONG

by James Holvay and Gary Beisbier (COLUMBIA RECORDS)

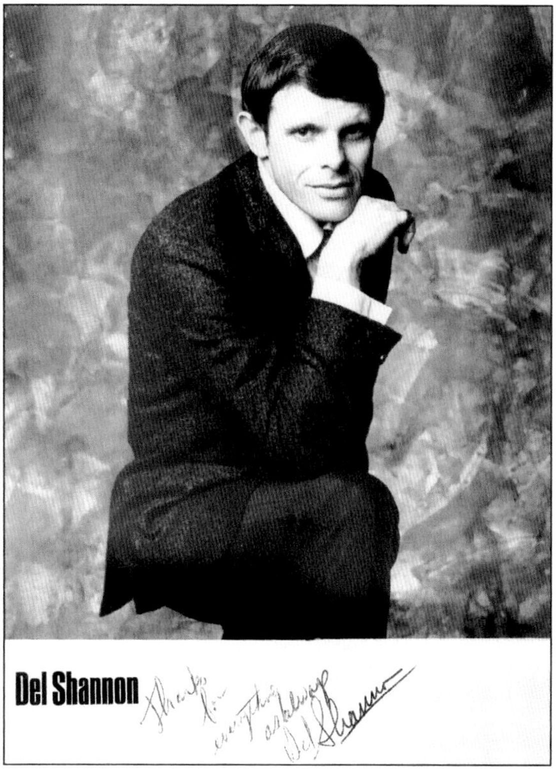

Del Shannon performed in the summer of 1966 while touring the Midwest. He showcased his hit songs "Runaway," "Hats Off to Larry," and "Little Town Flirt," among others. On the day of the Pop House show, Shannon arrived riding in a red Cadillac Coupe de Ville accompanied by his driver named Jimmy. On this publicity photograph he wrote, "Thanks for everything as always." (Courtesy of the Pop House collection.)

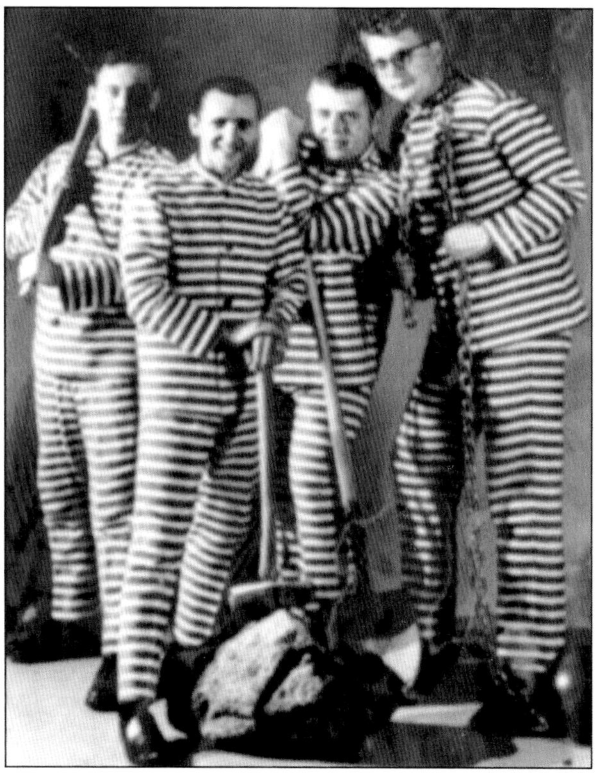

A Wisconsin band, the Shane Gang (from left to right, Jon St. John, Shane Todd, Jerry Raimer, and Darrell Meister), was Shannon's backing band for his summer tour. St. John recalls that guitarist Jerry Raimer needed some dental work done. During the afternoon sound check, Raimer's wife yelled, "Get some teeth, Jerry!" It became an inside joke with Shannon and the band for the rest of the evening. (Courtesy of Jon St. John)

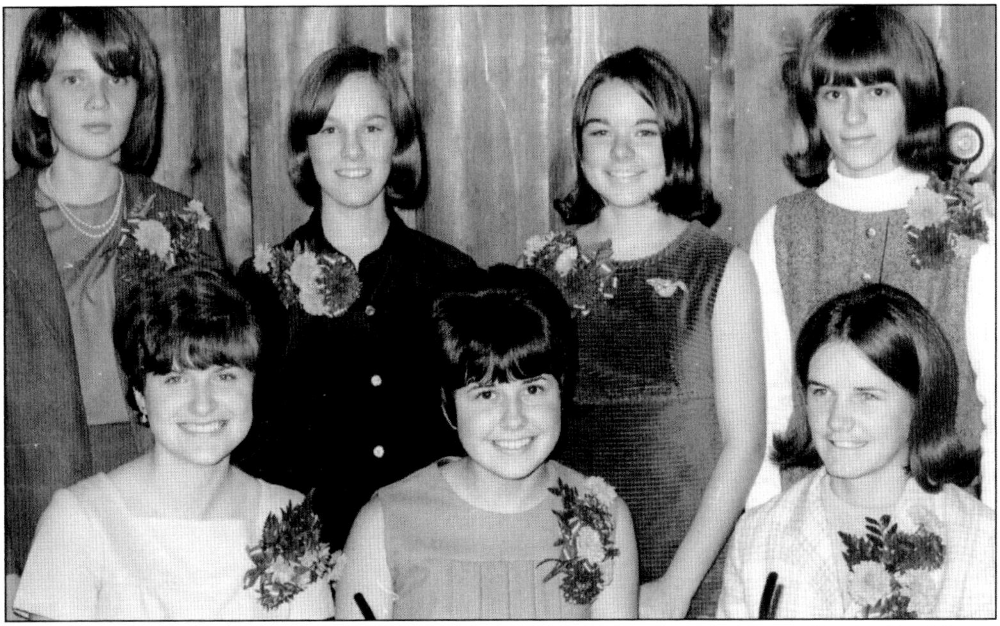

The annual chili festival introduced the customary slate of senior girls selected by the Pop House Board of Directors. All the young ladies received a corsage and were seated at a table reserved for them. The 1966 candidates are pictured here. From left to right are (first row) Holly Broderick, Nancy Belvedere, and Pam Daugherty; (second row) Karyn Vandennoven, Sue Hansen, Dee Dee Rundquist, and Sally McCleary. (Courtesy of Nancy Champion.)

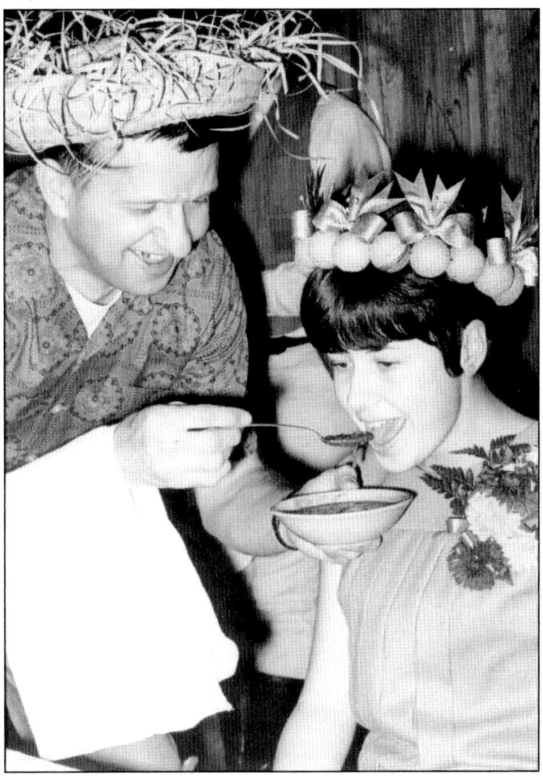

As was the custom, George Stankewitz served the first bowl of the season's fresh batch of chili to the newly elected chili queen. Once the queen was served, the official chili season was deemed underway. The queen might be called upon to reign over any special events throughout the coming months. Here chili queen Nancy Belvedere gets the first spoonful of chili from Stankewitz. (Courtesy of Nancy Champion.)

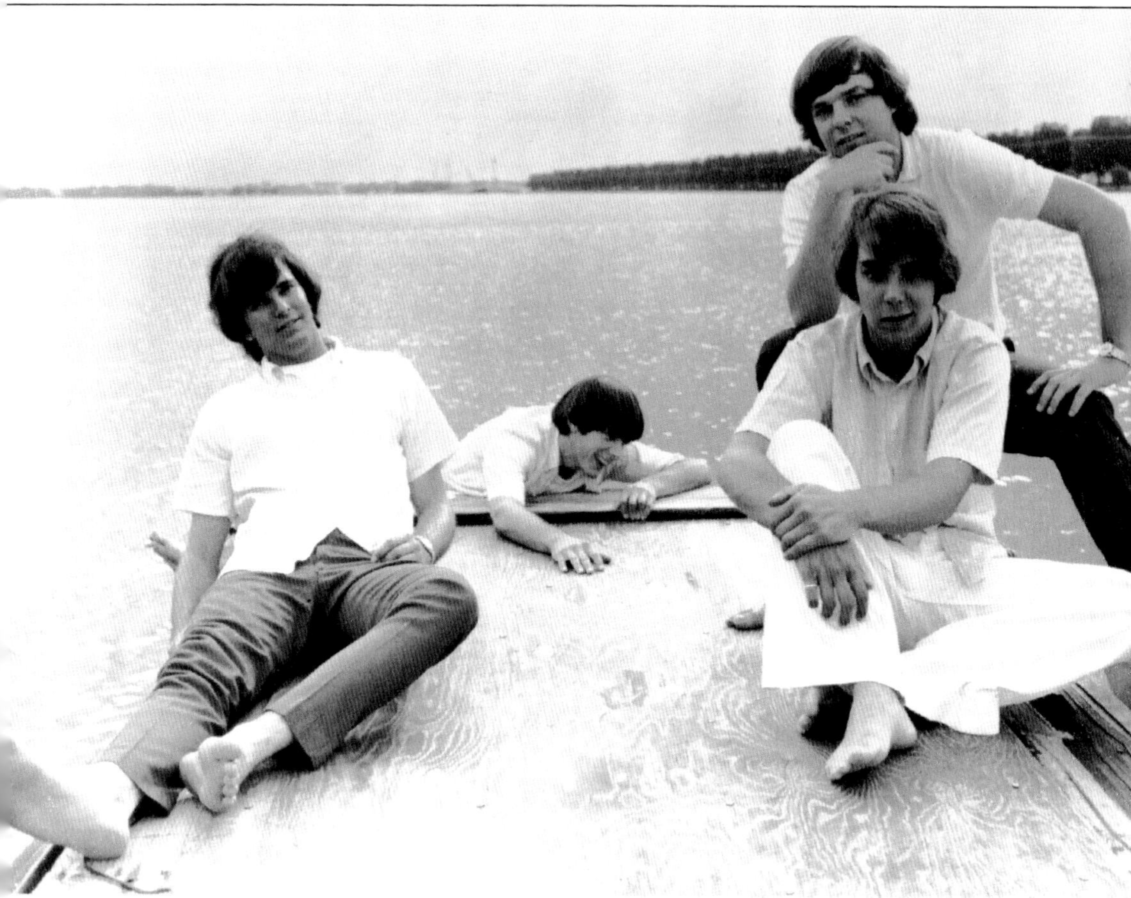

THE **Beau Gentry**

INDIALANTIC, FLORIDA

KEN ADAMANY LTD.
Janesville & Madison, Wis.
Detroit, Michigan Aspen, Colorado

The Beau Gentry originally formed in 1965 in Indialantic, Florida, with, from left to right, Russell DaShiell (guitar), John Cox (drums), Lance Massey (guitar), and Doug Killmer (bass), behind Massey. They specialized in playing Beatles songs and sounding "just like the record, featuring dual guitars and three-part harmonies," according to DaShiell. During the summer of 1966, agent Ken Adamany booked them for a Wisconsin tour. One of their first gigs was at the Club Pop House, and the place was packed. Cox was replaced by drummer Rick Jaeger. The Beau Gentry continued to enjoy appreciative audiences in the Stateline area. Realizing they had found a solid market for their music, the band decided to stay in the area, moving to Janesville full time. DaShiell and Killmer, along with Beloit drummer Bill Meeker, later achieved studio and touring success with Norman Greenbaum ("Spirit in the Sky"). Jaeger recorded and toured with Dave Mason ("Headkeeper"). Russell DaShiell still writes and records original music in California and is developing an animated feature film sound track called *Foreverland Forest*. Lance Massey remained in Wisconsin, writing and performing country-rock music. (Courtesy of Ken Adamany and Russell DaShiell.)

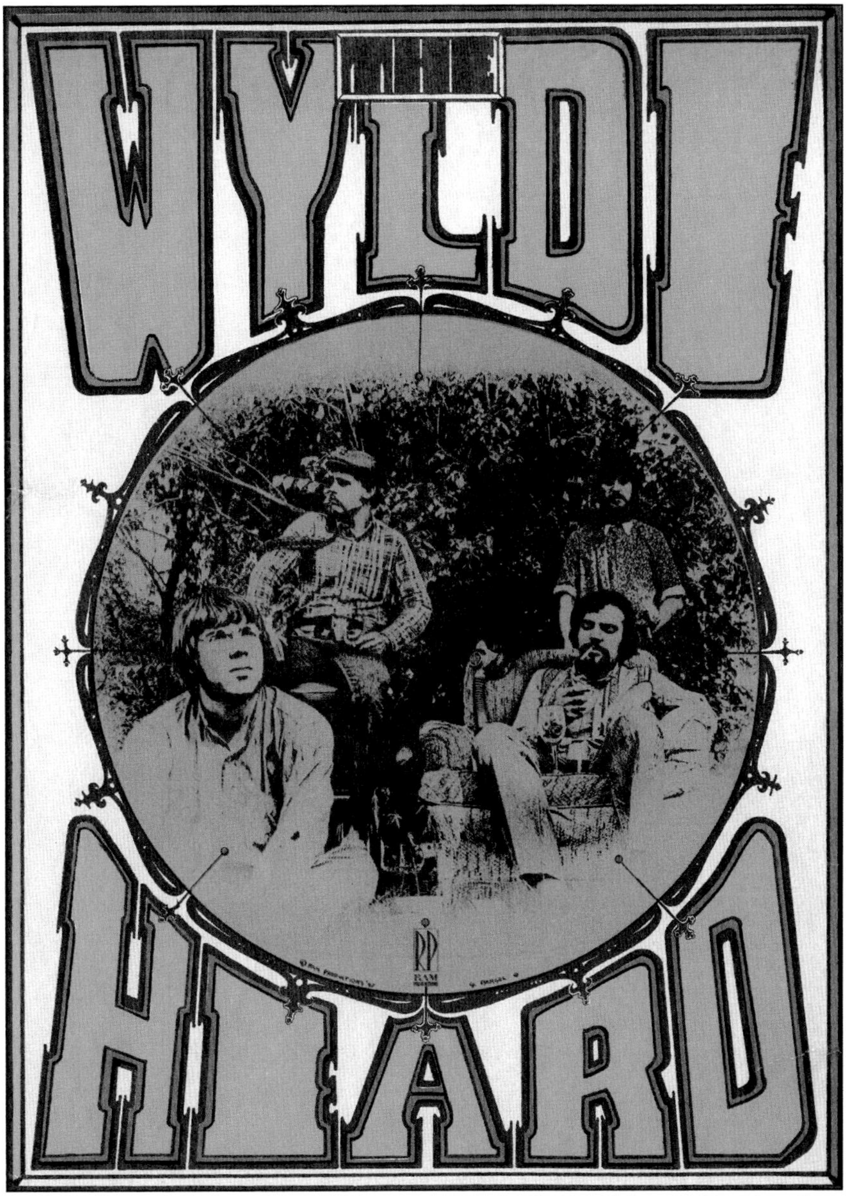

The Heard was a band from Peoria whose music was influenced by the Beatles, Stones, and Byrds, among others. During the late 1960s, band members Jim Croegaert (keyboards), Paul "Bird" Burson (guitar), Bill Sutton (bass), and Ron "Drummer" Bednar (drums) headquartered in Janesville where they were booked at the Pop House and throughout the Midwest by Ken Adamany. Croegaert wrote two songs, "Take It on Home" and "Stop It Girl," they recorded on the Feature label. In 1967, it was released nationally on the Phillips label, and the company added "Wylde" in front of the band's name to make them the Wylde Heard. Upon the breakup of the Wylde Heard, Croegaert and Sutton joined Russell DaShiell (guitar) and Rick Jaeger (drums) of the Beau Gentry to form a short-lived band called Masque. Croegaert eventually joined a group of musicians who, like himself, wanted to perform original music. The band became known as Hope, a contemporary Christian rock group based in La Crosse. Today Croegaert is still writing inspirational music in Evanston, Illinois. (Courtesy of Jim and Janalee Croegaert.)

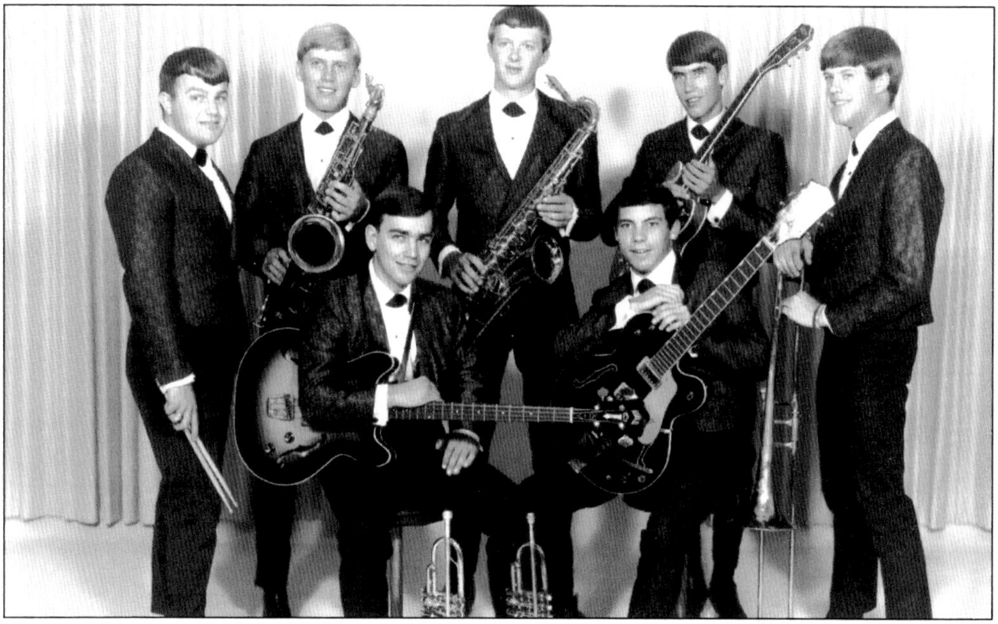

The Marvelous Marauders were a show band from Minnesota patterned after another "blue-eyed soul" group, the Fabulous Flippers. Drummer Jerry Cadwell remembers the night in 1967 they played, saying, "The place was jammed to the ceiling and it was hot for a March night." Other band members included Roger Branson, Dick Larson, Steve Livingston, Barry Ufkin, Randy Geise, and Dick Scherier. (Courtesy of the Pop House collection.)

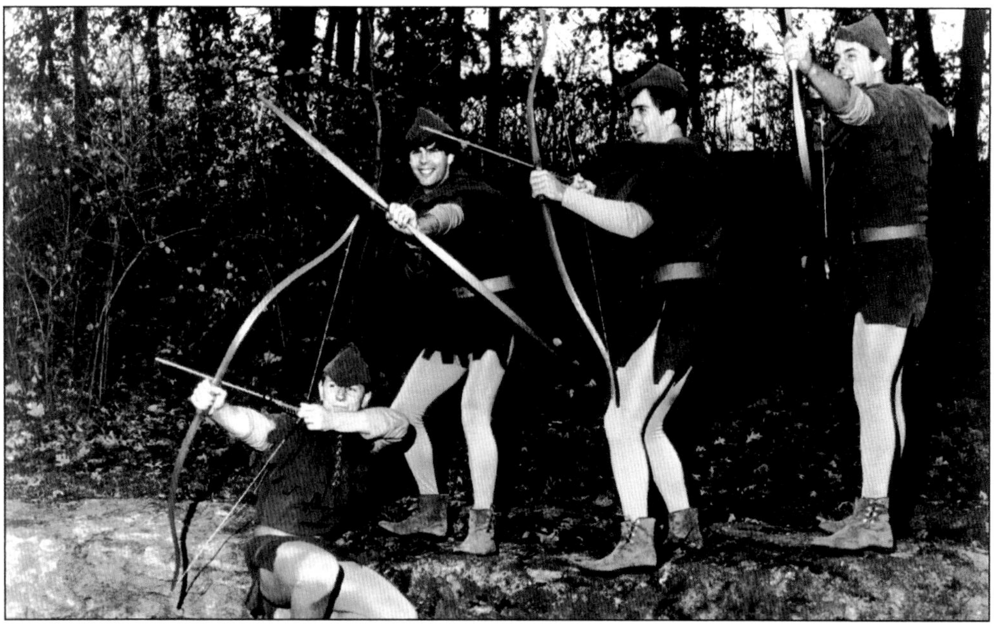

Dressed in green tights with matching Robin Hood jackets and caps, Robin and the Three Hoods was an unforgettable Madison band comprised of Dave Reed, Jim Schwartz, Bob Bernhagen, and Bruce Benson. They rocked the Pop House in 1966 with their stage antics and their spirited cover version of the song "I Wanna Do It" that had originally been recorded by Bobby Comstock in 1963. (Courtesy of Ken Adamany.)

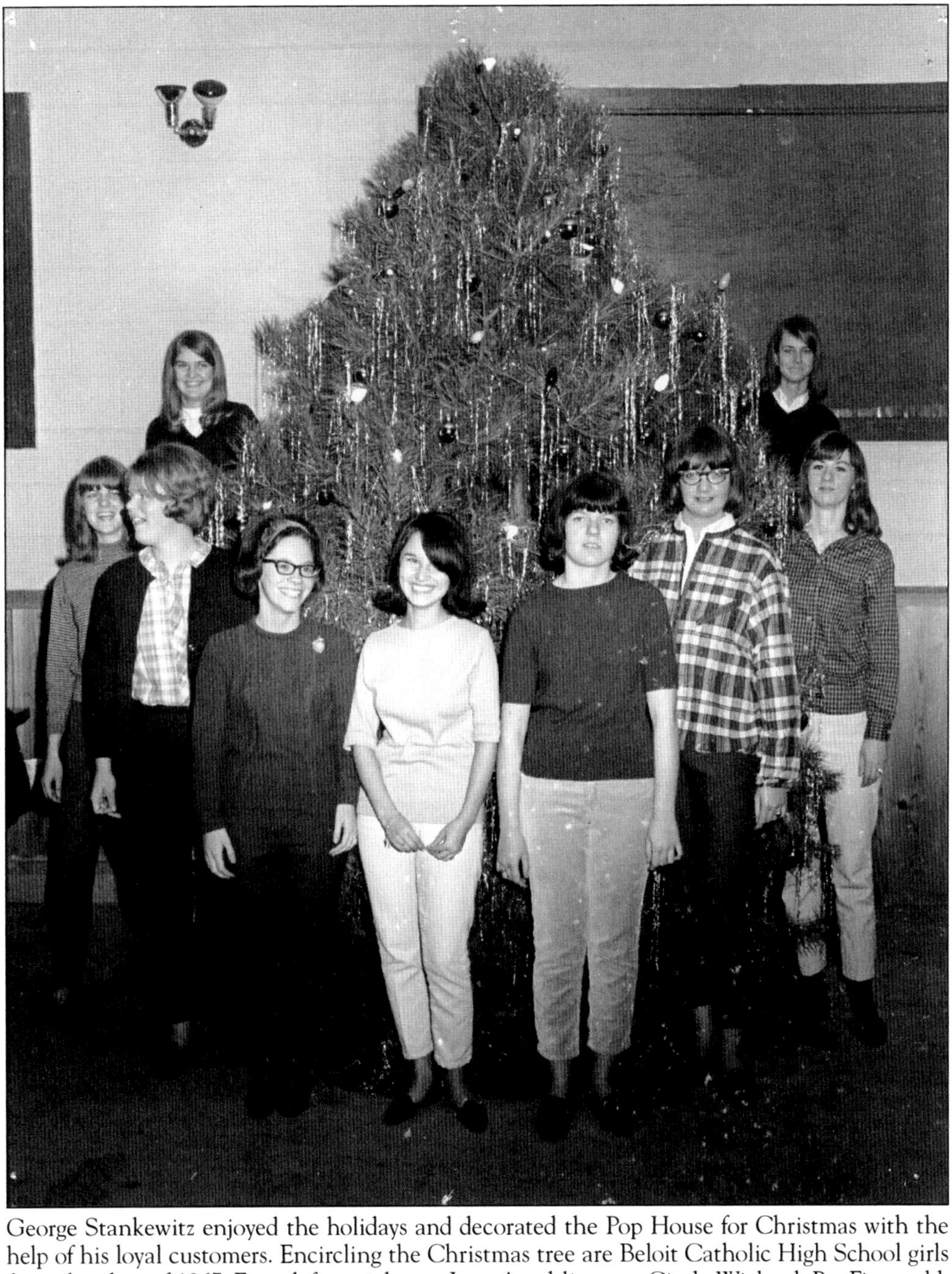

George Stankewitz enjoyed the holidays and decorated the Pop House for Christmas with the help of his loyal customers. Encircling the Christmas tree are Beloit Catholic High School girls from the class of 1967. From left to right are Jane Aeschlimann, Cindy Wieland, Pat Fitzgerald, Linda Senes, Gloria Sierra, Patty Yanulis, Sue Fogle, Michele Chekouras, and Ann George. (Courtesy of the Pop House collection.)

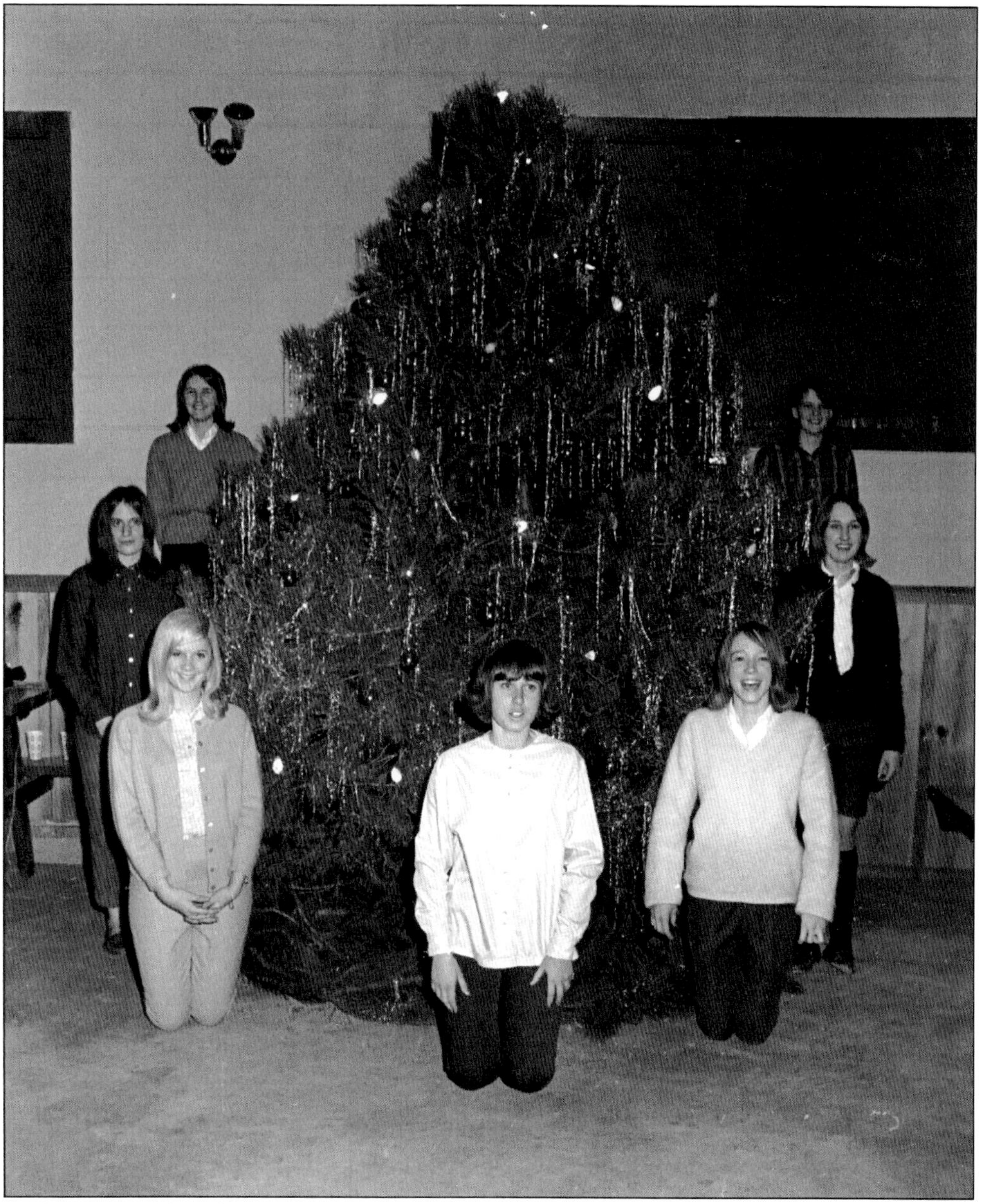

In the spirit of fair play and equal time, Beloit Memorial High School girls from the class of 1967 were gathered around the tree for the same pose. In this photograph are, from left to right around the tree, Pam Daugherty, Linda Harris, Myrna Leibfried, Bobbi Tadder, Kathy Justus, Joann Healless, and Karyn Vandennoven. (Courtesy of the Pop House collection.)

Three

CHANGING TIMES

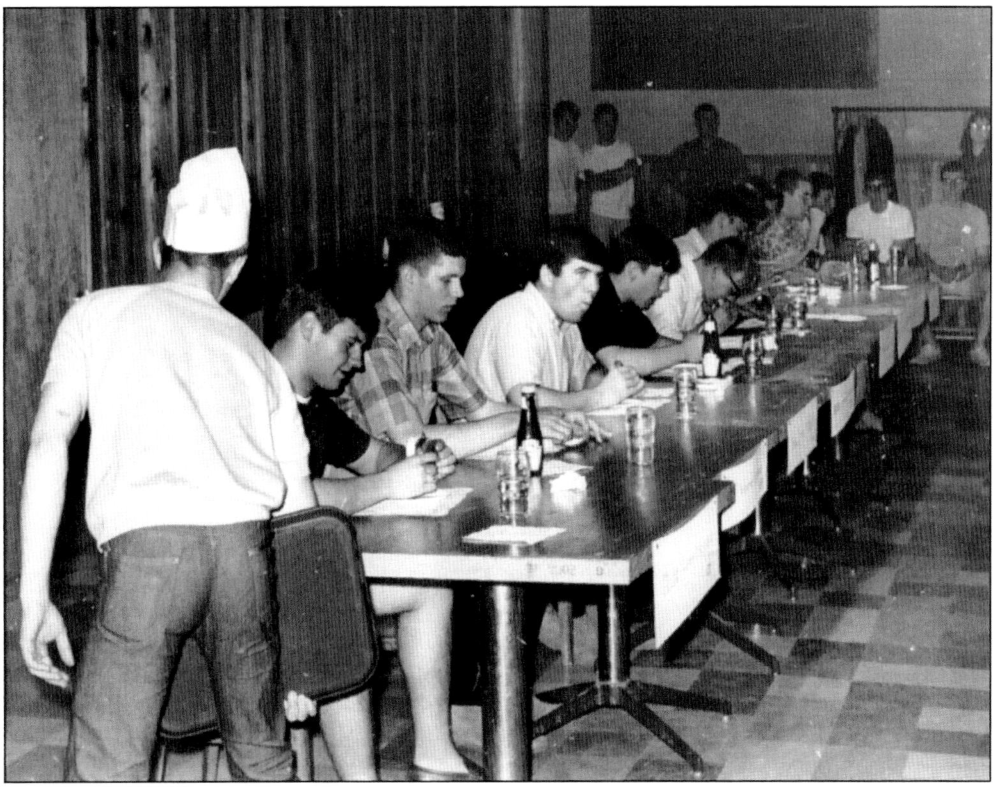

The turbulence of the late 1960s created both rising discontent and general apathy among students. George Stankewitz succeeded in maintaining an environment where events of the day could be put on hold for a while. Club Pop House was the place to forget about time for a while. A new diversion was created in the spring of 1967—a hamburger-eating contest. Bill Kruse, seated third from the left, won the first competition by downing 13 burgers. (Courtesy of the Pop House collection.)

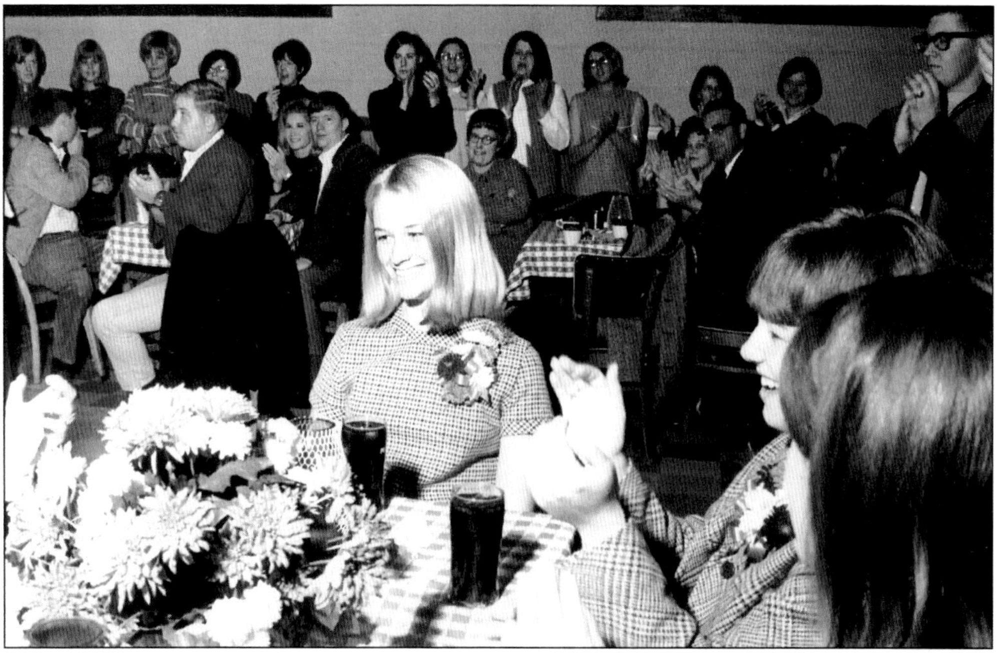

As the 1960s were drawing to a close, so was one of the annual events that had been so popular since it first started in 1949. In the fall of 1967, the final chili festival was celebrated. Linda Dale was the last in a long line of chili queens. She is pictured here receiving a round of applause upon the announcement of her victorious election. (Courtesy of the Pop House collection.)

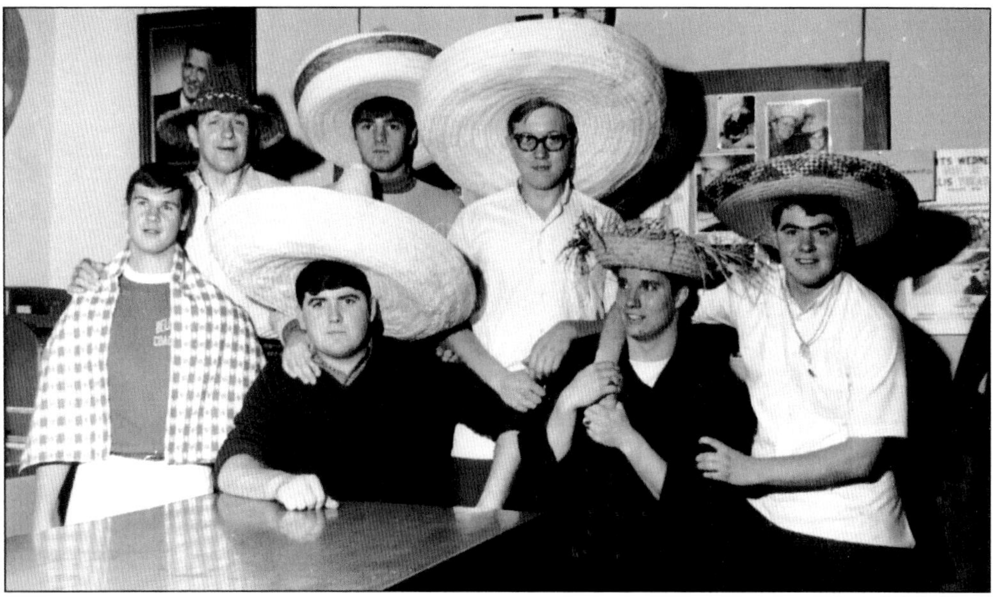

It was the last time George Stankewitz and the grillmen would wear sombreros for a chili festival. The secret ingredient previously known only as "M.O." could now be revealed—magic onions. Stankewitz used generous amounts of dehydrated onions in the chili. Posing before the 1967 festivities are, from left to right, (first row) Glenn Poburka, Bill Kruse, Tom Roehl, and Clark Moriarty; (second row) Stankewitz, Mike Piccione, and Bob Staack. (Courtesy of the Pop House collection.)

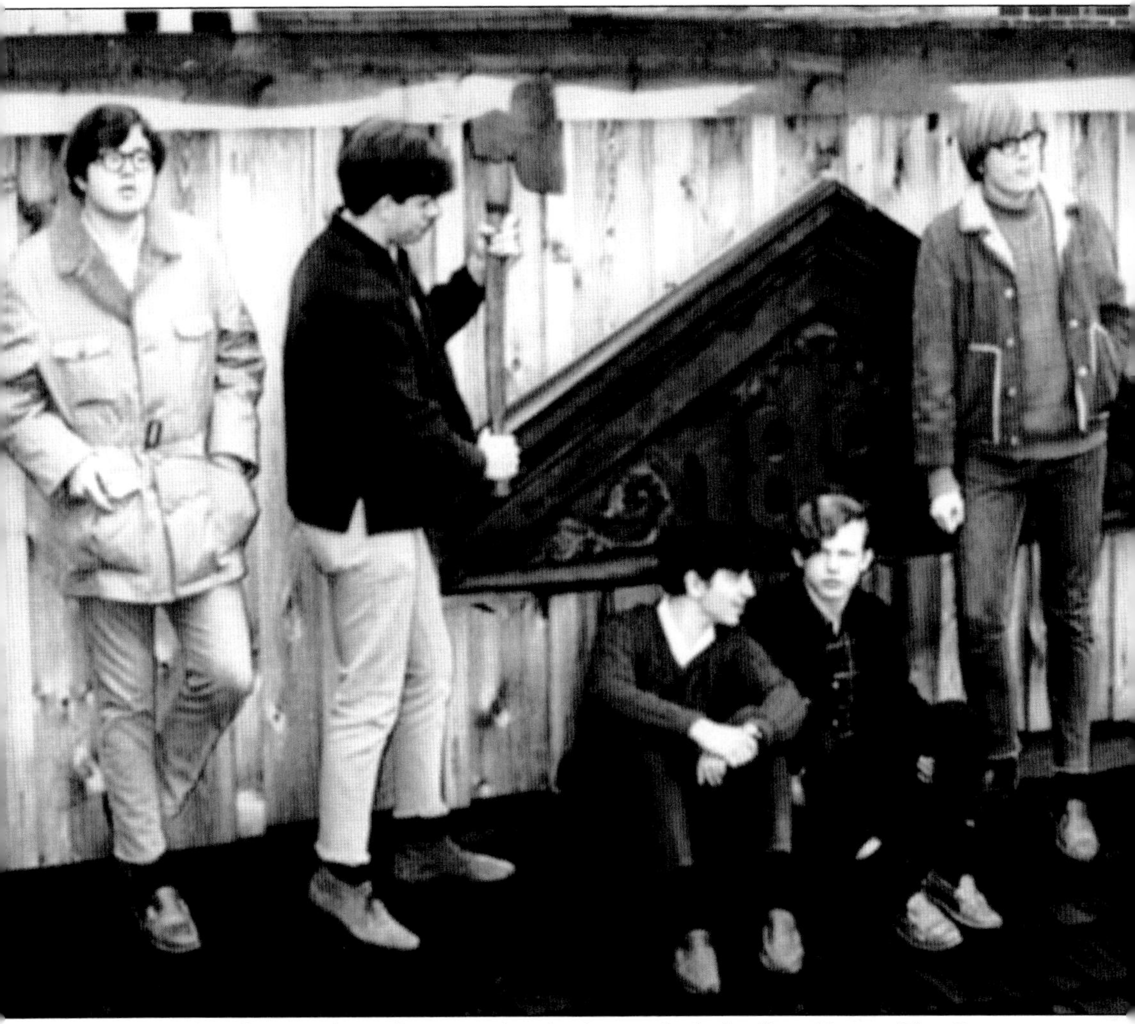

Rockford produced a number of top-tier bands that rocked the Pop House. The Paegans performed there often between 1966 and 1968. The band recorded a cover version of the Beatles' very popular "Good Day Sunshine" on the Rampro label, which received airplay on local radio stations. More impressive is the fact that they were each only 15 years old at the time. A favorite among audiences all over the Stateline area, the band consisted of, from left to right, Brad Carlson, Rick Schneider, Jerry Parlapiano, Steve Carlson, and John Furland. They booked primarily under Ken Adamany, who also represented a Rockford band called the Grim Reapers with whom the Paegans shared an intense rivalry. Eventually Paegans drummer Carlson changed his name to Bun E. Carlos and joined up with members of the Grim Reapers when they formed Cheap Trick. John Furland continued a successful career in music that eventually landed him in Nashville where he still works in the business today. (Courtesy of John Furland.)

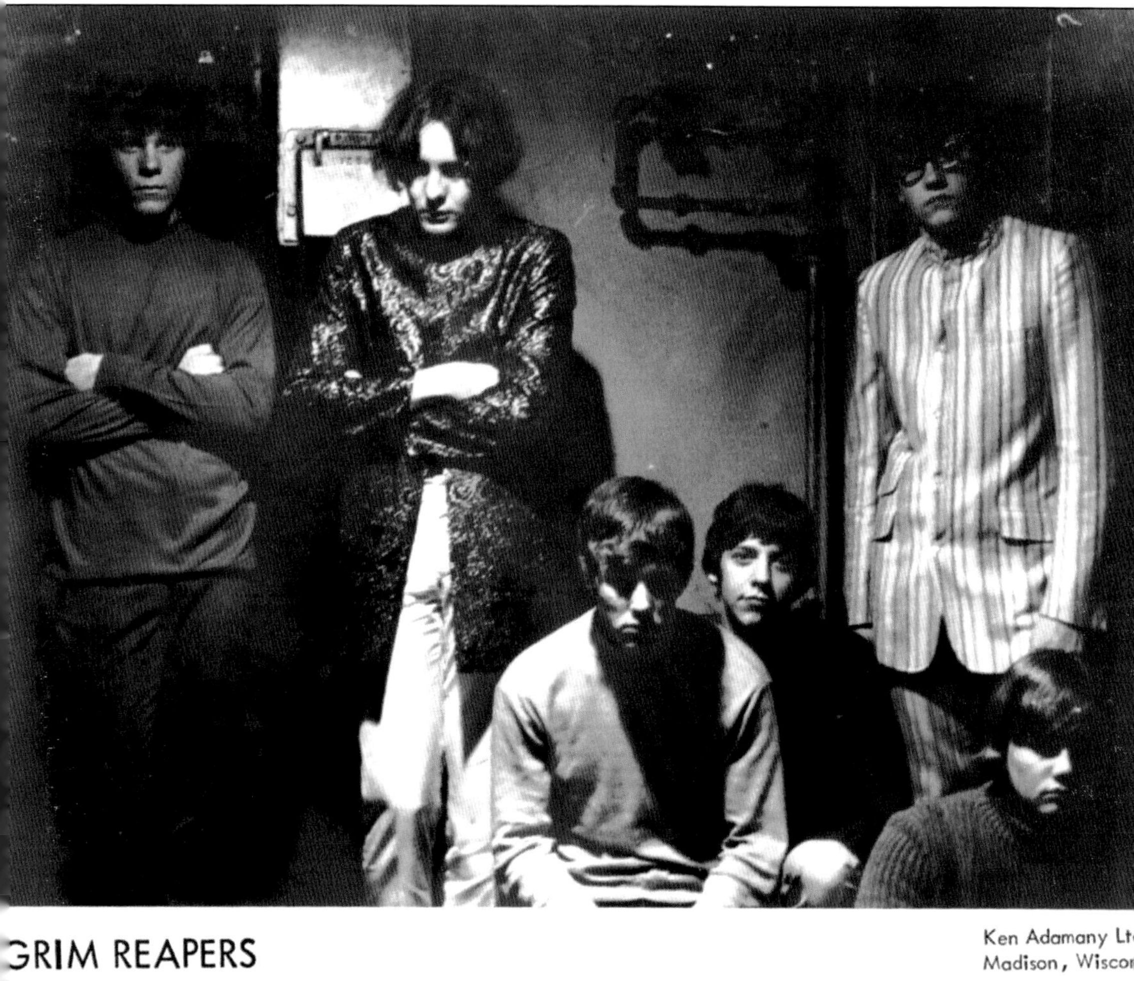

Another of Ken Adamany's bands from Rockford was the Grim Reapers, who also played the Pop House often between 1966 and 1968. Comprised of Rick Nielsen, Bill Walsh, Gary Schuder, Jim Zubiena, Joe Sundberg, and Ross Anderson, the group played hard-driving rock-and-roll cover versions and some original numbers. Their energy and stage presence reminded many people of the Rolling Stones. The Grim Reapers were to have been the opening act for an Otis Redding engagement in Madison before he perished in a plane crash on his way there on December 10, 1967. Shortly thereafter, the band changed its name to Fuse and released an unsuccessful album in 1969. Further personnel changes, including the addition of Brad Carlson (Bun E. Carlos) from the Paegans, eventually resulted in the band changing its name to Cheap Trick. Cheap Trick has enjoyed great recording and touring success that continues to the present day. (Courtesy of Ken Adamany.)

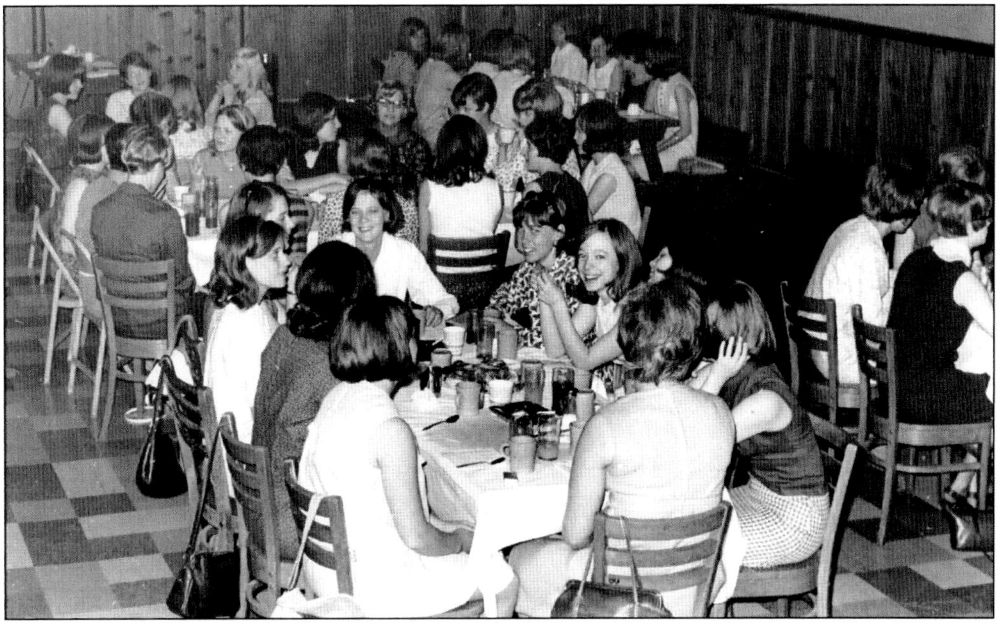

The senior girls' breakfast continued to increase in popularity throughout the 1960s, as evidenced by the number of girls seen here. The added floor space of the ballroom provided a comfortable environment for spreading out the tables to accommodate up to 100 or more participants. This photograph provides only a partial view of the ballroom facing the northeast corner. (Courtesy of the Pop House collection.)

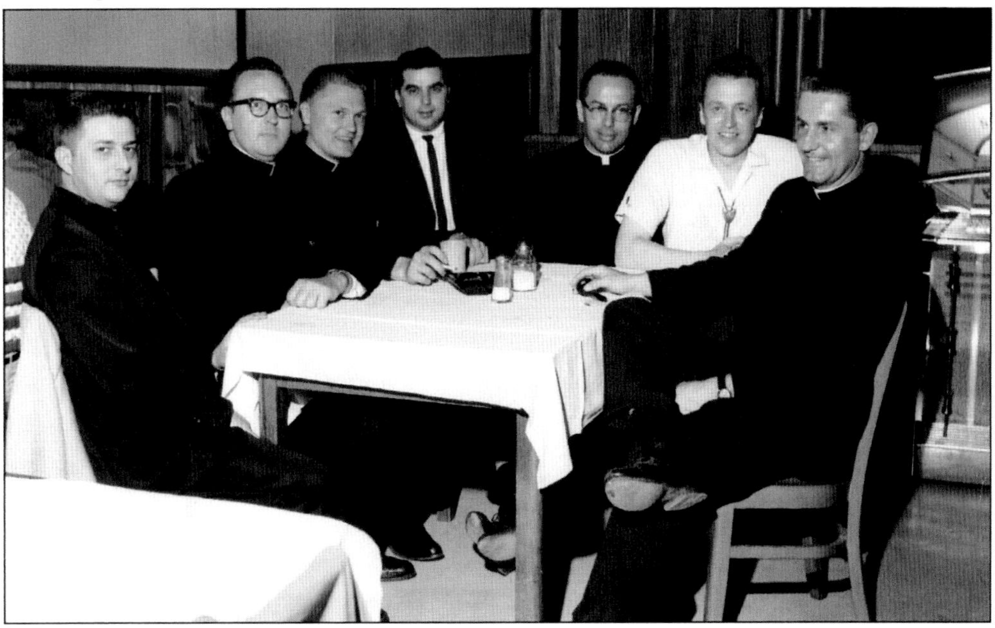

A member of St. Jude's Parish, George Stankewitz was well known in the Catholic community. He also maintained good relations with the high schools. Here both cleric and lay teachers from Beloit Catholic High were invited to observe the Pop House operations. Pictured from left to right are unidentified, Rev. Bernard Pierick, Rev. Roger Nilles, Jack Farina, Rev. Peter Fagan, Richard Godin, and Rev. Raymond Lenahan. (Courtesy of the Pop House collection.)

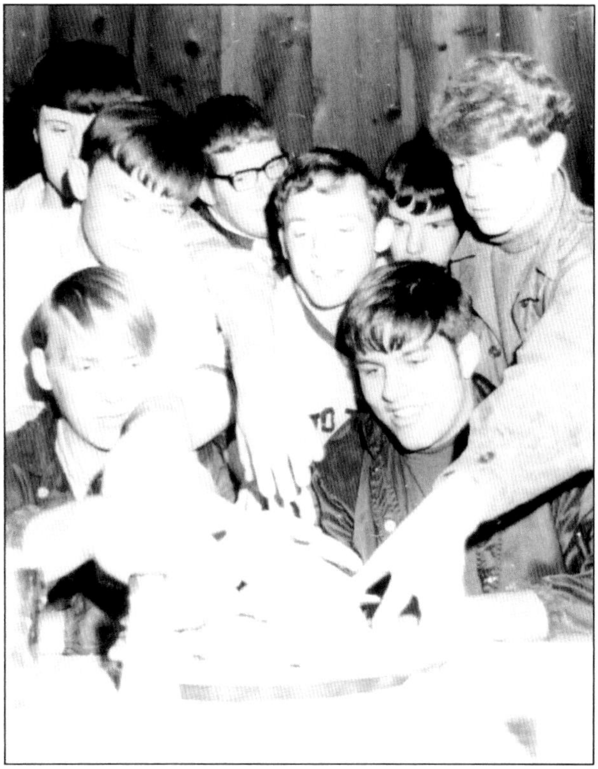

The spring hamburger-eating competition became an annual event for a couple of years. In the spring of 1969, contestants gathered for this group portrait. Hands reaching for the plate of burgers belong to the following bodies: (first row) Dwight Hall and Floyd "Chico" Wells; (second row) Casey Singles, Kevin Schmale, and Tim Miller; (third row) Charlie Loucks, Jim Corcoran, and Dan Taylor. (Courtesy of the Pop House collection.)

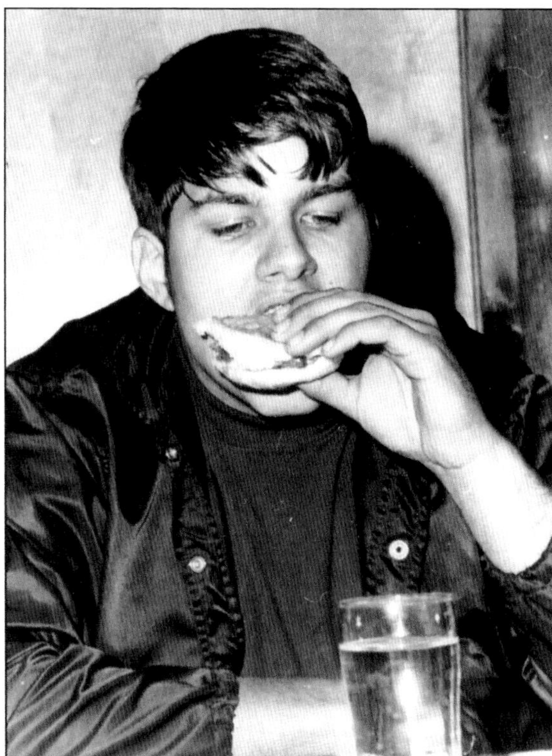

The winner of the spring 1969 hamburger-eating contest was Floyd "Chico" Wells, who is seen here consuming one of the 11 burgers that earned him the championship. (Courtesy of the Pop House collection.)

Mike Masterson is pictured here on grill duty at the Pop House. The last documented hamburger-eating contest on record was held in May 1970. The competition that year included both a girls' division and a boys' division. George Stankewitz selected the contestants with input from his trusted grillmen. The burgers were prepared, and the contest was underway. (Courtesy of the Pop House collection.)

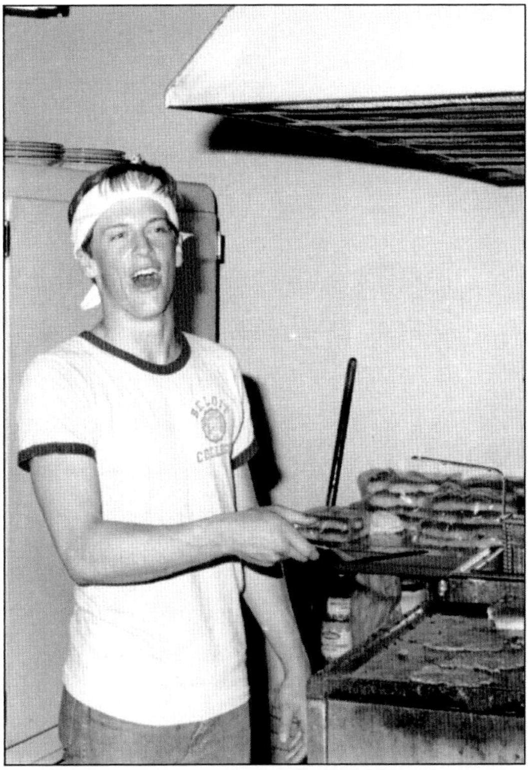

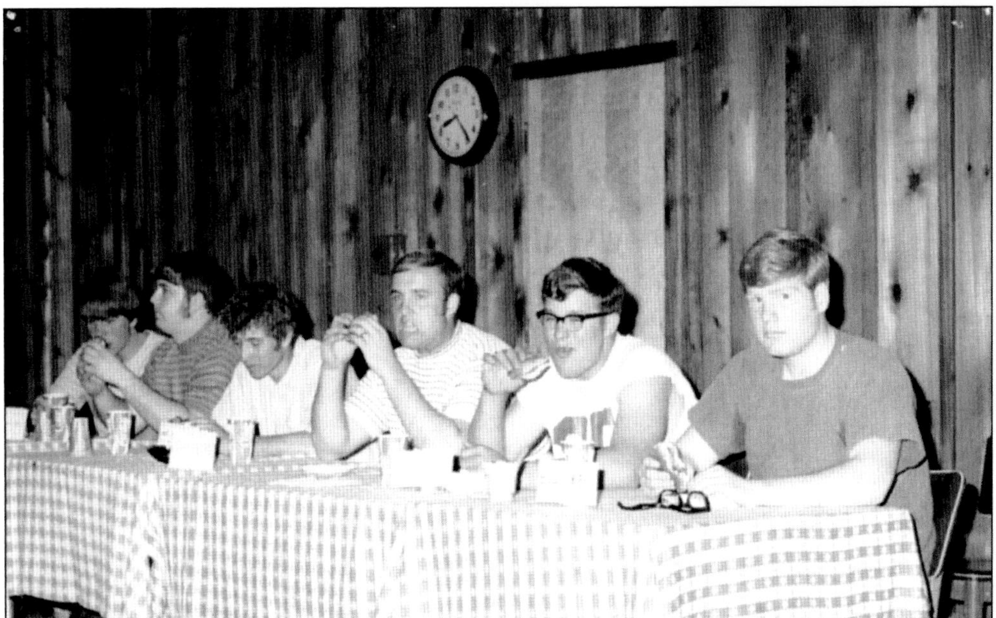

Typically there were between 6 and 12 contestants. The rules of the competition were kept simple. One hamburger had to be consumed every five minutes. Contestants were allowed to drink only water. The first one to "out-consume" the other contestants was ruled the winner and earned bragging rights for the year. (Courtesy of the Pop House collection.)

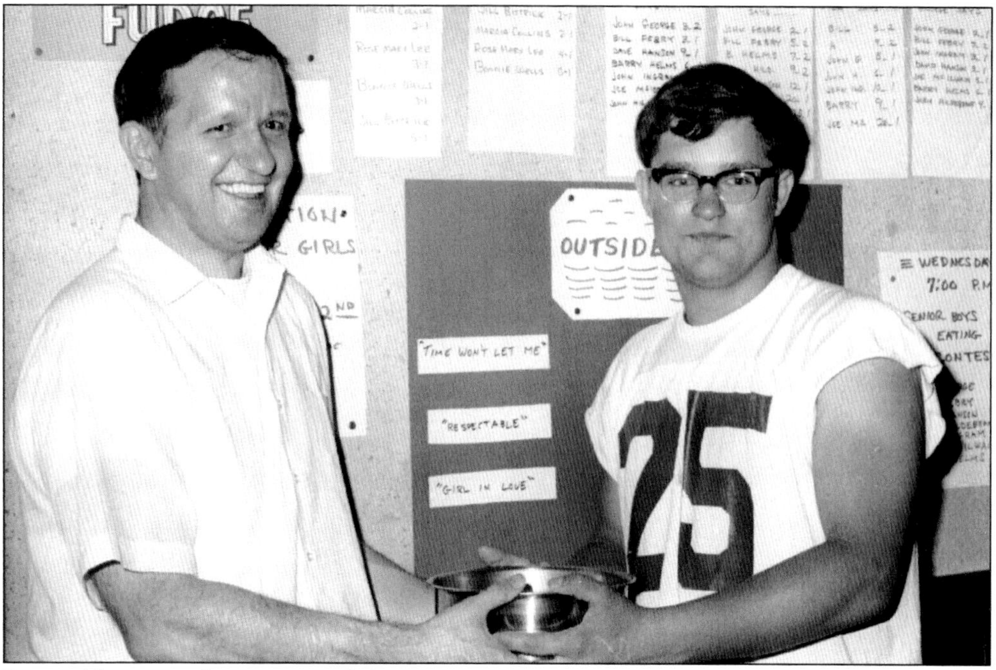

Pictured here are the winners of the 1970 competition. Unfortunately, no records exist that report the final number of burgers eaten. In the photograph above, John Hildebrandt receives a trophy for consuming the most hamburgers. Below, runner-up Rosemary Lee, winner of the first senior girls' hamburger-eating contest receives her trophy—an empty burger bun. Note the Outsiders publicity photograph on the board. The Outsiders had a hit song, "Time Won't Let Me," in 1966. Another sign on the bulletin board promotes the upcoming senior girls' breakfast on Friday, May 22. (Courtesy of the Pop House collection.)

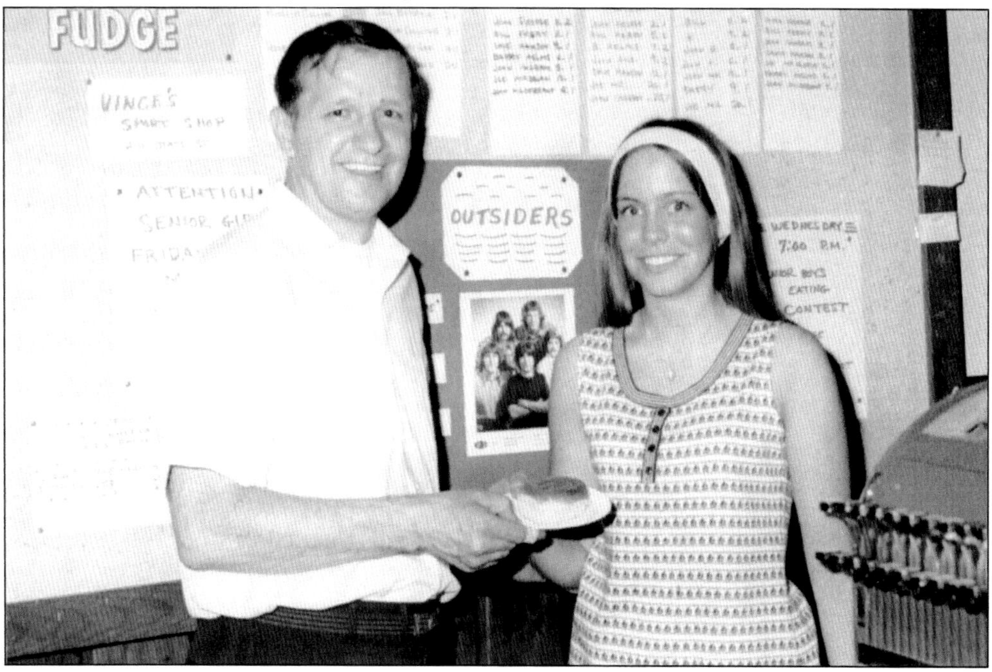

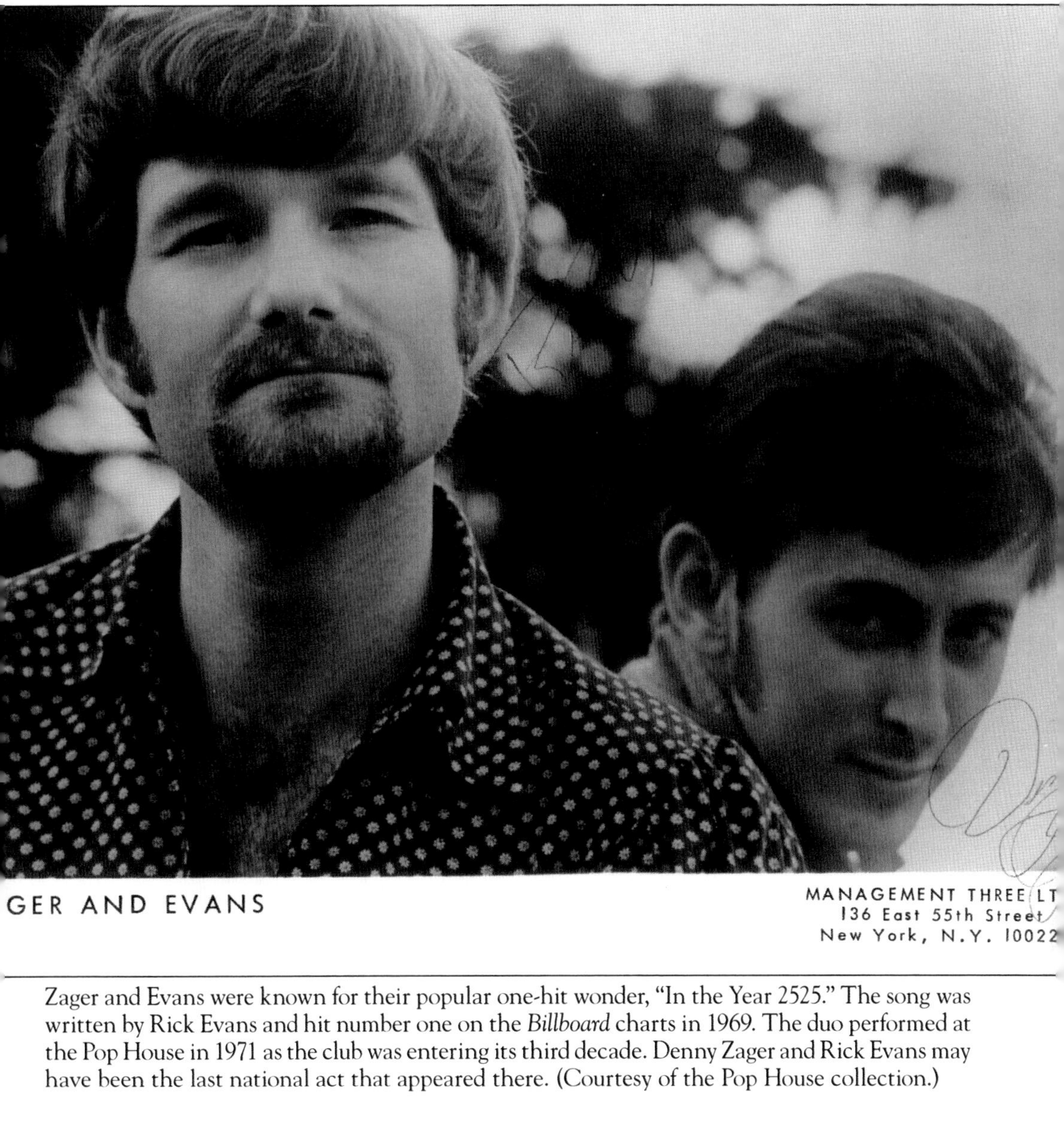

Zager and Evans were known for their popular one-hit wonder, "In the Year 2525." The song was written by Rick Evans and hit number one on the *Billboard* charts in 1969. The duo performed at the Pop House in 1971 as the club was entering its third decade. Denny Zager and Rick Evans may have been the last national act that appeared there. (Courtesy of the Pop House collection.)

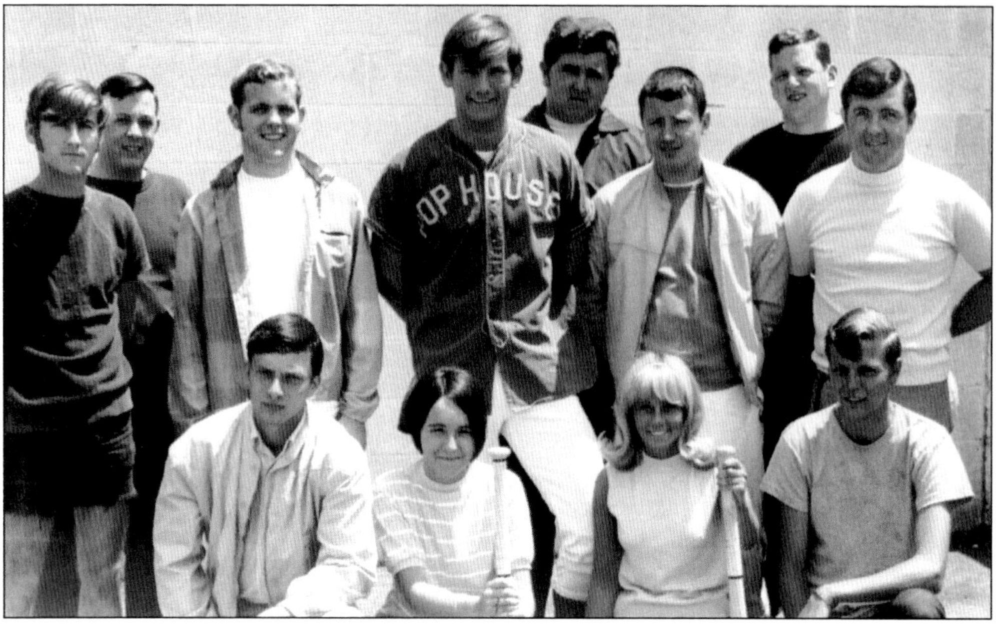

An uncommon sight in the 1970s was someone wearing an original Pop House baseball jersey from the past leagues of the 1940s and 1950s. Here team captain David Luebke is pictured wearing one of the few remaining jerseys that were available. Standing behind Luebke is Larry "Bear" Scott, a Beloit Catholic High School Hall of Fame honoree who participated in numerous softball leagues, basketball, and Turkey Bowl games. (Courtesy of the Pop House collection.)

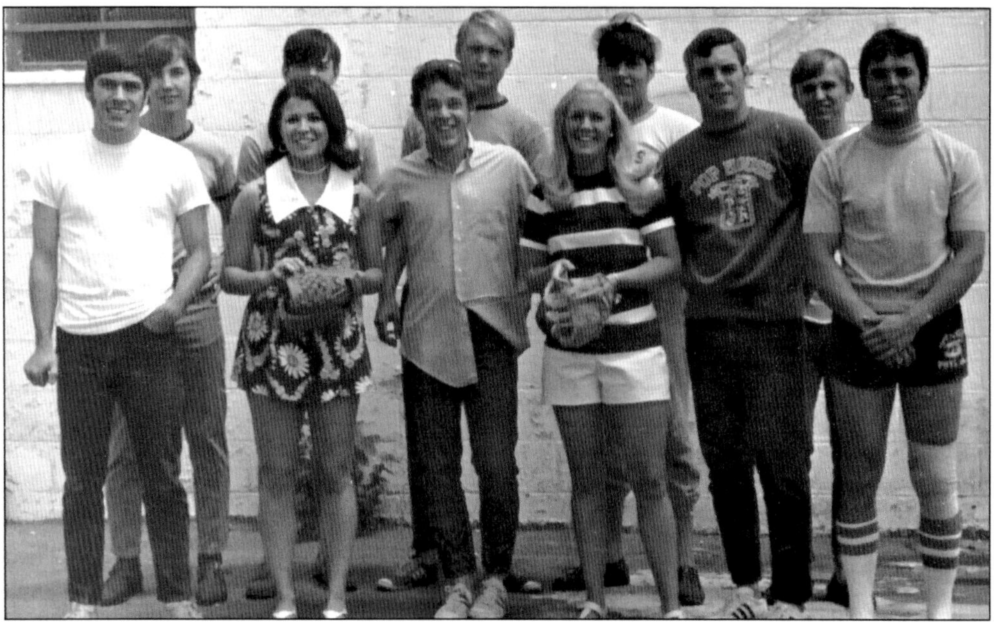

Another example of Pop House apparel can be seen in this team photograph. Team members are, from left to right, (first row) Torry Hill, Marilyn Hall, Kevin Schmale, Martha Tangye, Steve Van Oss (wearing the Pop House sweatshirt), and Fred Jackson; (second row) Dan Kirkpatrick, an unidentified player, Dwight Hall, Floyd "Chico" Wells, and Jerry Reseburg. (Courtesy of Ida and Richard Lenz.)

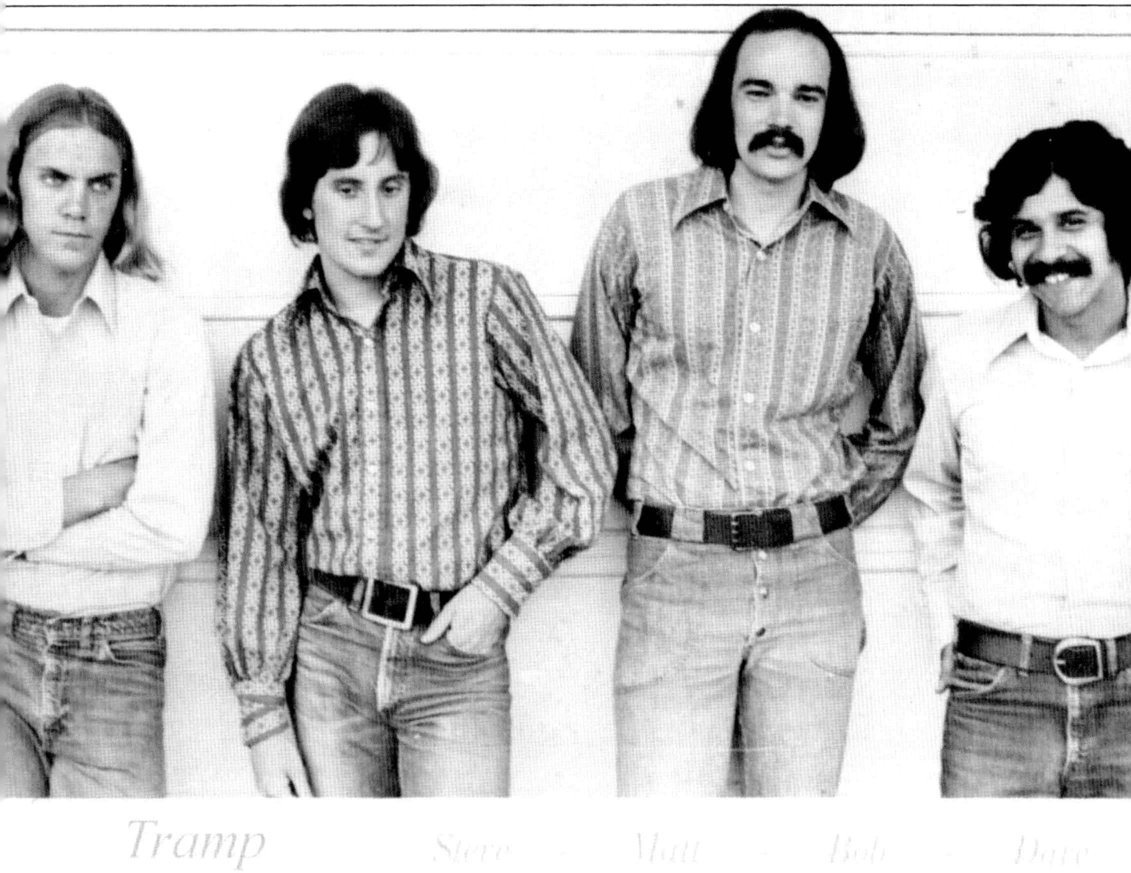

The Beloit band Tramp performed at the Pop House in 1973. Pictured from left to right are Steve Marks (drums), Matt Goodwin (guitar), Bob Slawson (bass), and Dave Hernandez (organ). Not pictured here but joining Tramp for their Pop House show was Roger Noss (saxophone.) Hernandez, an accomplished keyboardist, had previously been in the Chevelles, the Village Gate, the Hernandez Brothers Band, and the Denims. Denims drummer Jeff Grob played with the band Looking Glass, which recorded "Brandy (You're a Fine Girl)." Among other gigs, Tramp also opened a show for the Mob at the Waverly Ballroom that year. Hernandez continues to perform in the area with his brother Jim. (Courtesy of Dave Hernandez.)

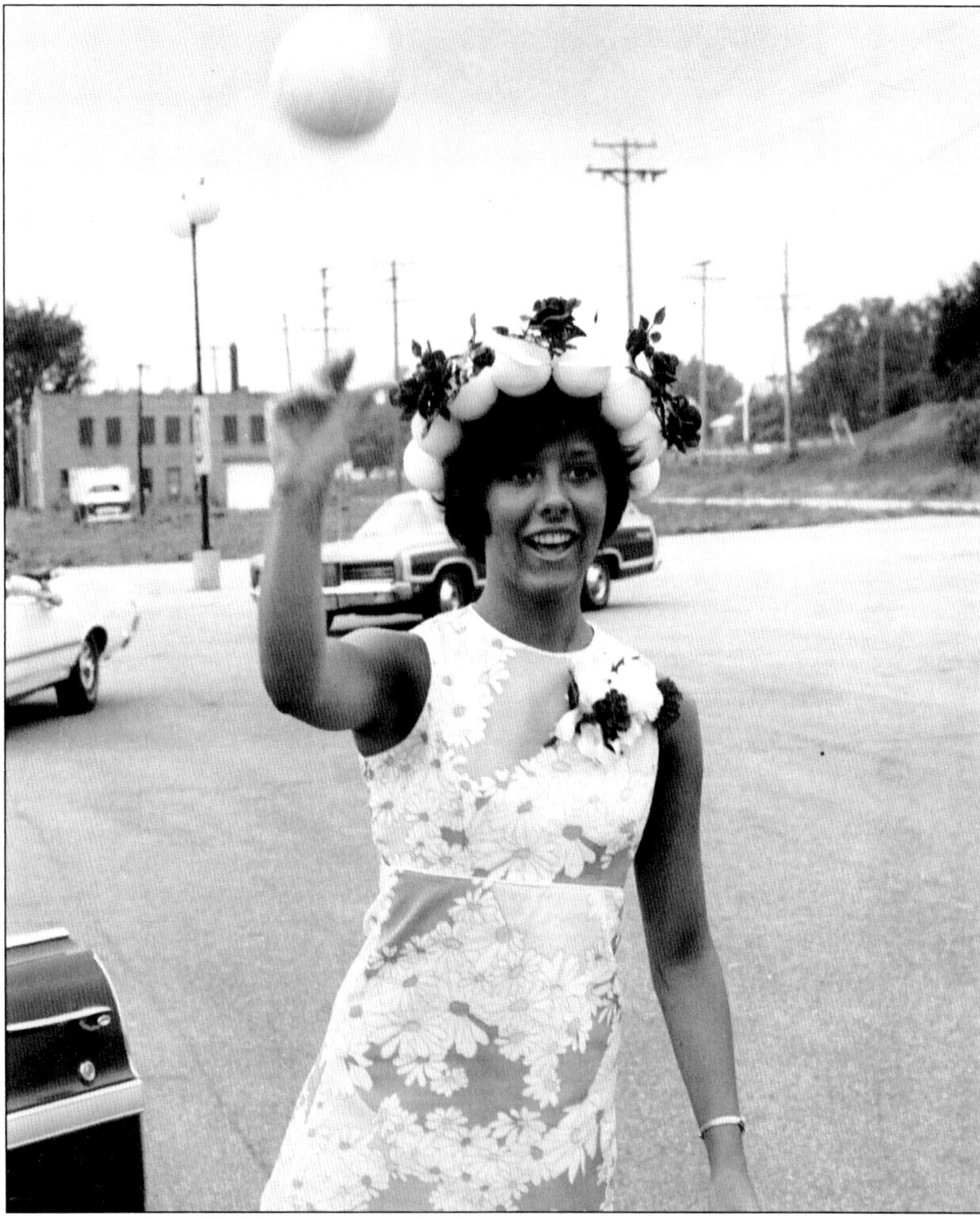

Parade queen Linda Walsh throws out the first ball to kick off the opening game of the 1971 Club Pop House Slow-Pitch League. The official opening of the softball season commenced on a Sunday afternoon with the annual parade from the Pop House to Hinkley Field at the corner of Liberty Avenue and Moore Street. George Stankewitz served as league commissioner. The coronation of the 1971 parade queen was held following the parade in a brief pregame ceremony. Queen Linda Walsh was elected from a field of five candidates. The runners-up served as members of the parade court. They were Jill Hanson, Maridee Schmale, Roberta Tyler, and Judy Warner. Pop House softball leagues were a popular activity in the 1960s and 1970s. Participation was open to both current members and alumni, many of whom maintained their ties to the Pop House for years after high school graduation. Games were scheduled on Sundays so there would be few conflicts with summer work schedules. (Courtesy of the Pop House collection.)

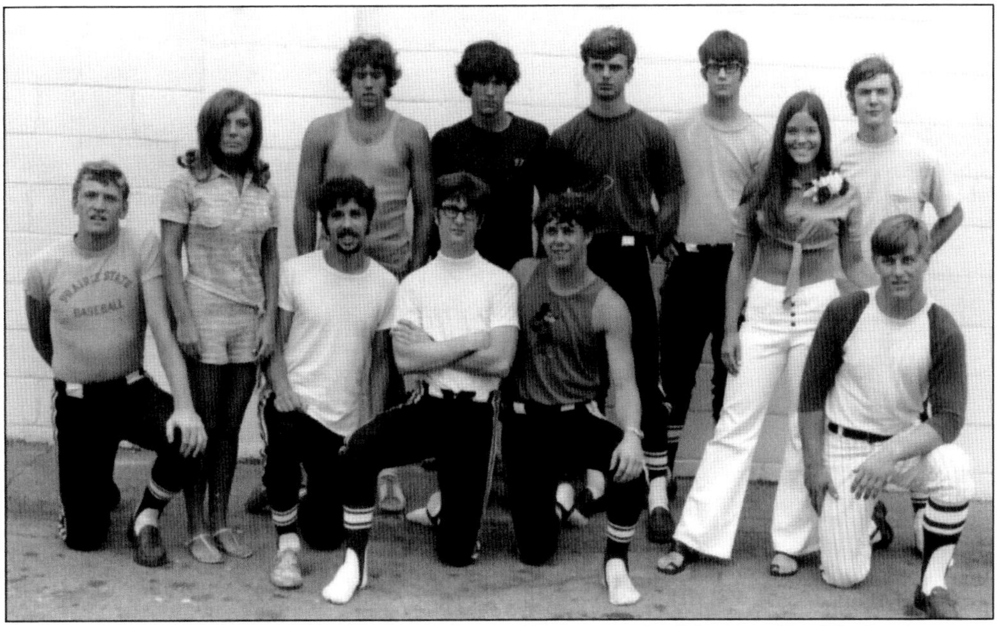

Eight teams made up the league in 1971: the Grillmen, coached by Tom Roehl; the Castouts, headed by Bob Eicher; the Rookies, led by Dave Hanson; the WAFS, coached by Bob Staack; the Dunlaps, headed by Harry Stanford; the Beavers, coached by D. J. Masterson; the Neophytes, headed by Dan Rorabeck; and the Tarz, led by Gary Polglaze. Two of the 1971 teams are pictured here. The photograph above shows the Beavers. Coach D. J. Masterson is wearing the tank top, kneeling in the front row. Parade court member Maridee Schmale is wearing white bell-bottoms and has a corsage. Below are the Rookies. Coach Dave Hanson is in the back row, second from the right. Standing in front is Jill Hanson of the parade court. (Courtesy of Ida and Richard Lenz.)

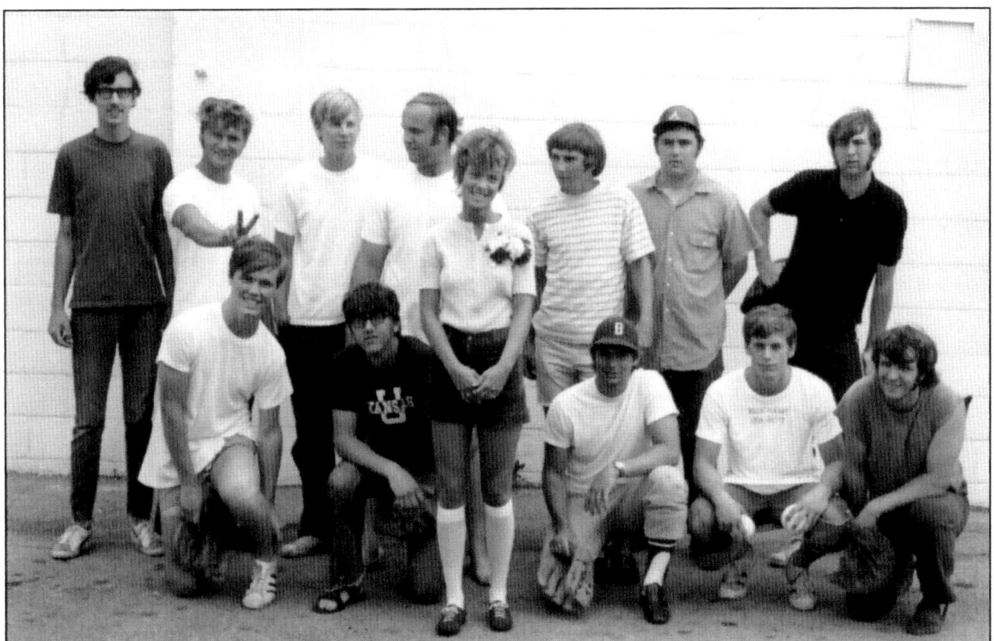

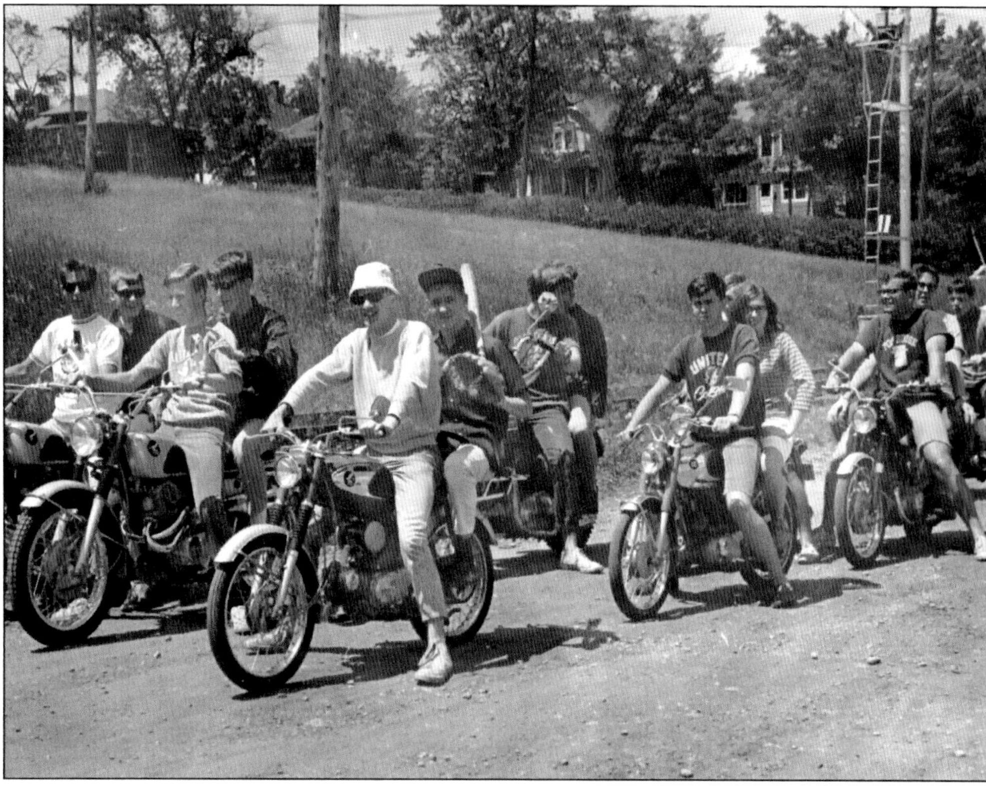

From the early days of the Pop House, George Stankewitz enjoyed organizing ceremonies and parades. His customers, many of whom remained Pop House alumni for years, never had a problem obliging him. If there was any kind of gimmick or some unusual twist that could be used to embellish an event, then all the better. Two parade embellishments are illustrated in these photographs. Above, a procession of Honda motorcycles carrying team members is ready for the parade to the playing field. Below, coach Harry Stanford of the Dunlaps carries a coffin in his Buick Skylark convertible, with a sign on the car that reads, "We'll knock 'em dead." (Courtesy of the Pop House collection.)

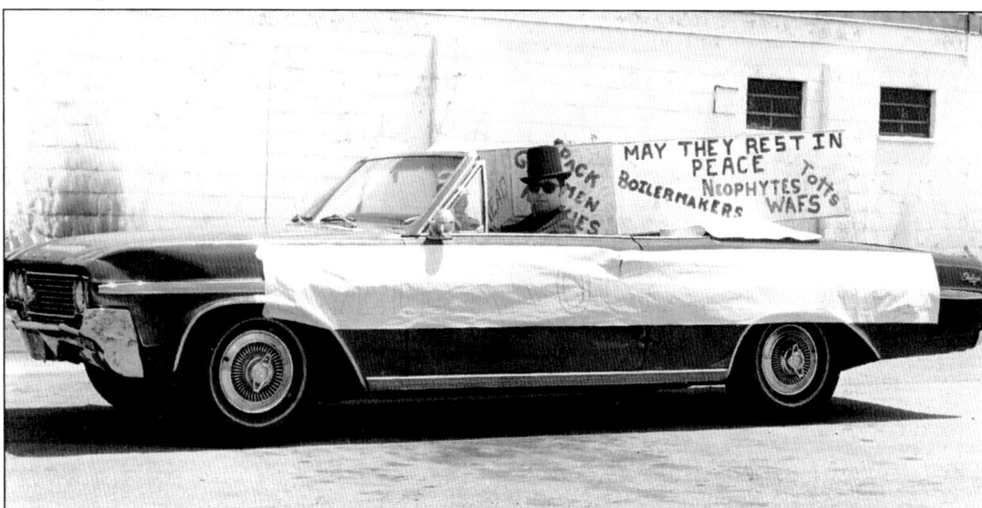

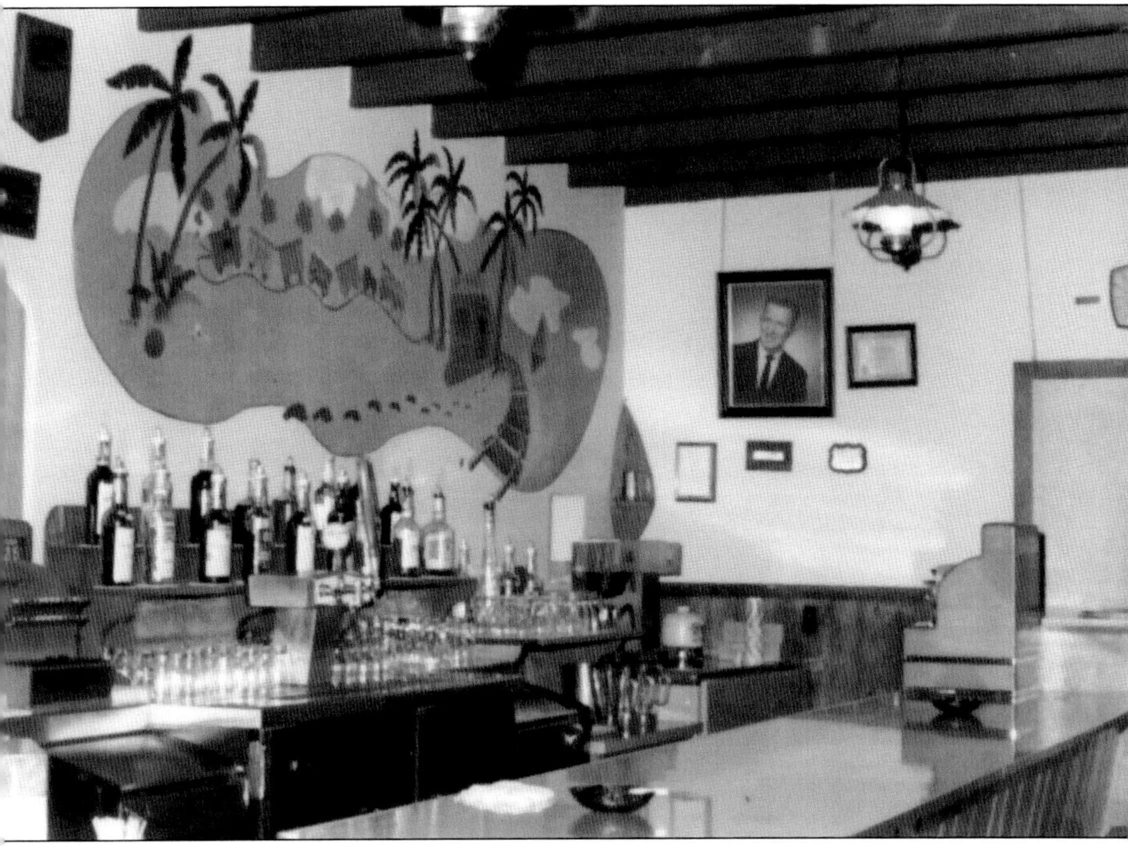

Business at the Pop House continued unabated until March 1972, when Wisconsin lowered its drinking age to 18. Seeing an immediate decline in customers who were now heading for the taverns, George Stankewitz reluctantly brought liquor into the Pop House in November of that year. It was not his favorite business decision. The change was not noticeable by standing outside the building. But once inside, the new beer taps and rows of liquor bottles dominated what had once been a simple lunch counter. There were attempts to allow the under-18 crowd in for entertainment on special nights when Stankewitz would put away the liquor bottles and empty the beer taps. In the long run, though, it created more complications with workloads and business operations. Of the new law Stankewitz said, "[It] didn't do the kids any favor. It made me feel as if something had been taken away from them." The Pop House mural still adorned the wall, moved there from the original building during the 1958 construction. (Courtesy of Dr. William Fitzgerald.)

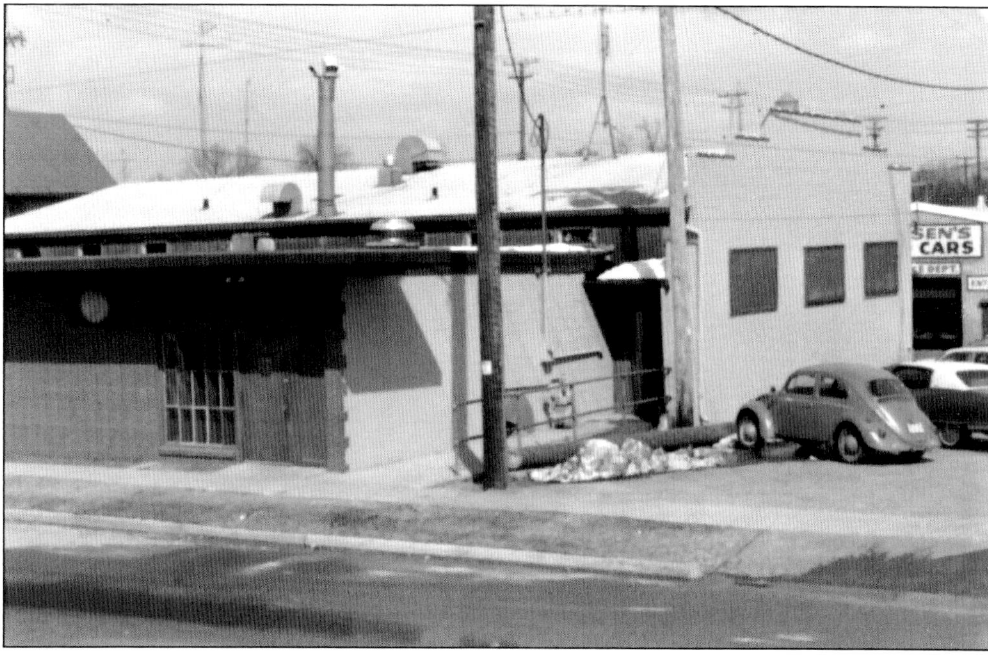

This is the exterior of the Pop House as it looked in 1973 from the railroad tracks across Fifth Street. The 1958 building with its flat roof is visible. The ballroom is behind it with the pitched roof. The main entrance is next to the front window. The stage entrance is at the end of the sloped walkway adjacent to the railing between the utility poles. (Courtesy of Dr. William Fitzgerald.)

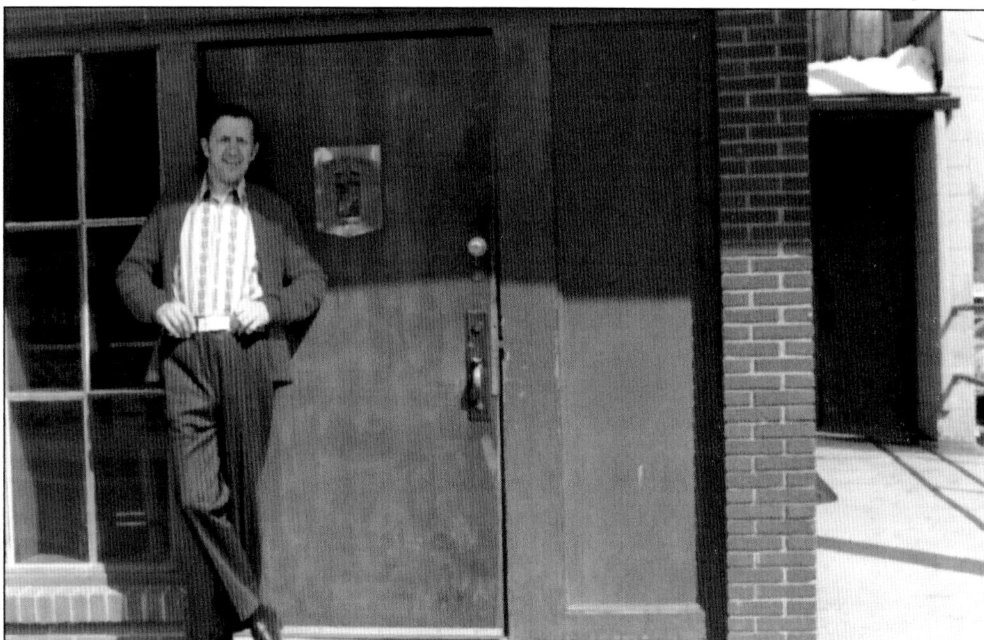

Fastened to the door is a replica of the Pop House logo that had hung on the outside of the original building in 1954. Over the years, the window adjacent to the door underwent various changes. At times, the opening was filled in with stone or glass blocks. The stage door can be seen to the right. (Courtesy of Dr. William Fitzgerald.)

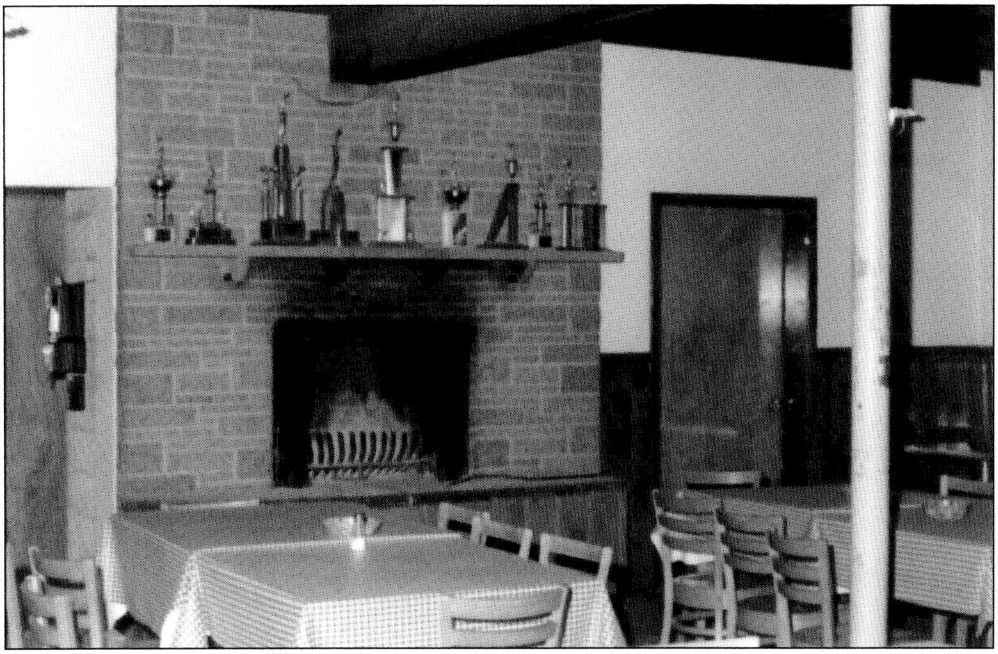

The photograph here looks north into the main dining room at the brick fireplace that was built as part of the 1958 addition to the original building. The mantel is filled with trophies won by Pop House sports teams from the early days. The door on the right led to the patio in 1959 and then to the ballroom after 1964. (Courtesy of Tom Roehl.)

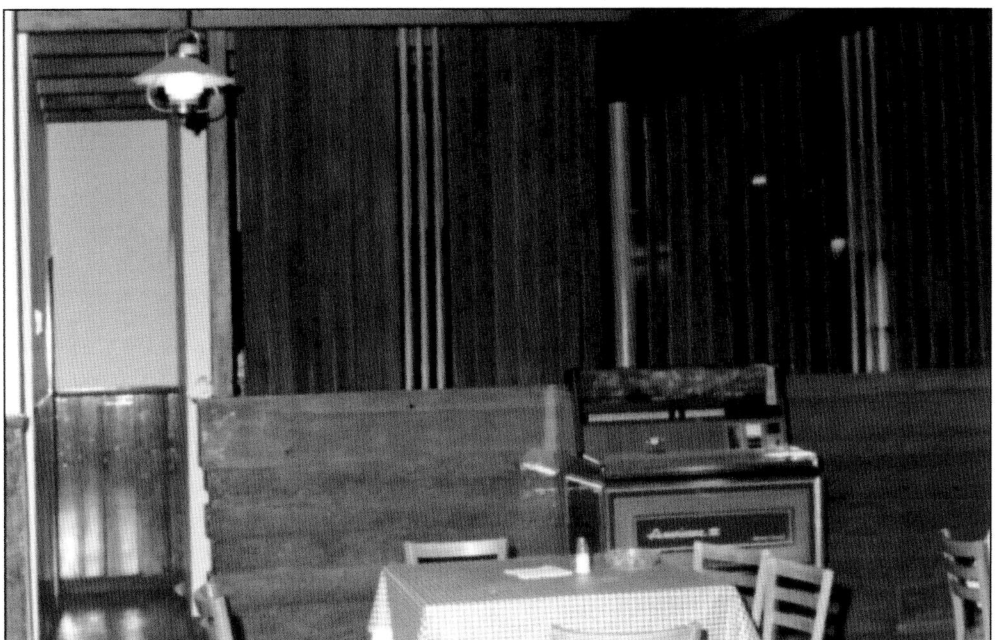

The Wurlitzer jukebox was positioned at the south end of the main dining room in front of the wall separating it from the lunch counter and kitchen area. On the left is the walkway to the restrooms and the kitchen around the corner. The jukebox always had the best music in town, especially at five plays for a quarter. (Courtesy of Tom Roehl.)

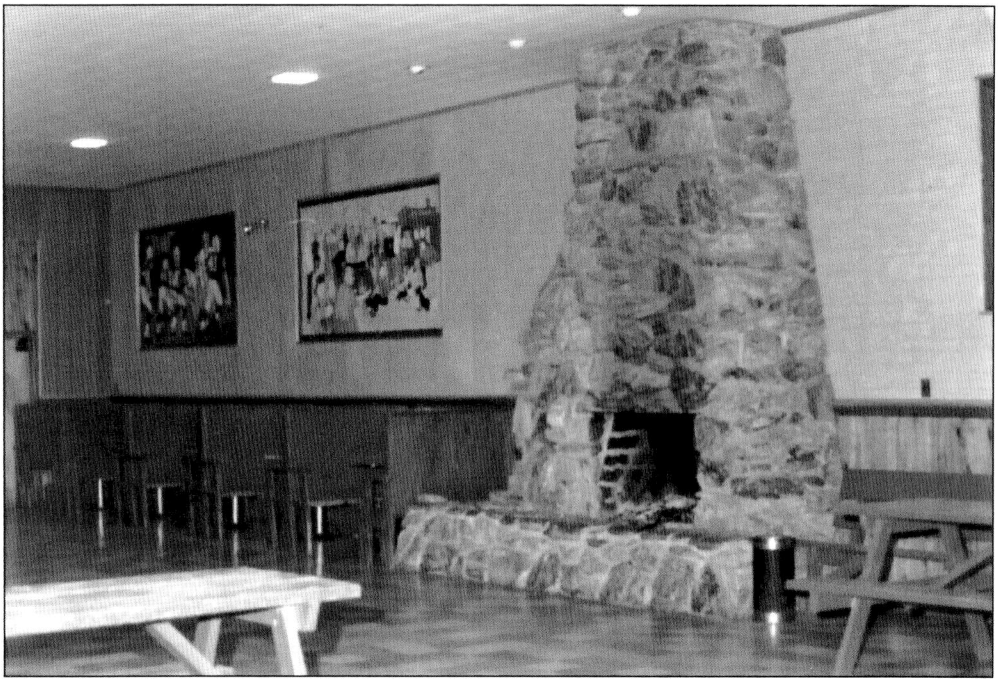

The Pop House ballroom had undergone a number of changes from the time of its construction in 1964. The original walls were concrete block, and the stone fireplace always dominated the east wall. Eventually wainscoting was added all around and a stone facade was installed over the interior walls. New murals filled the spaces that were once windows as a better ventilation system was put in. Several booths and bench seats were added along the walls. The photograph below provides a closer view of the Pete Leonard/Herb Ludtke mural that was replicated for the ballroom many years after the first one was lost during demolition of the original building. (Courtesy of Tom Roehl.)

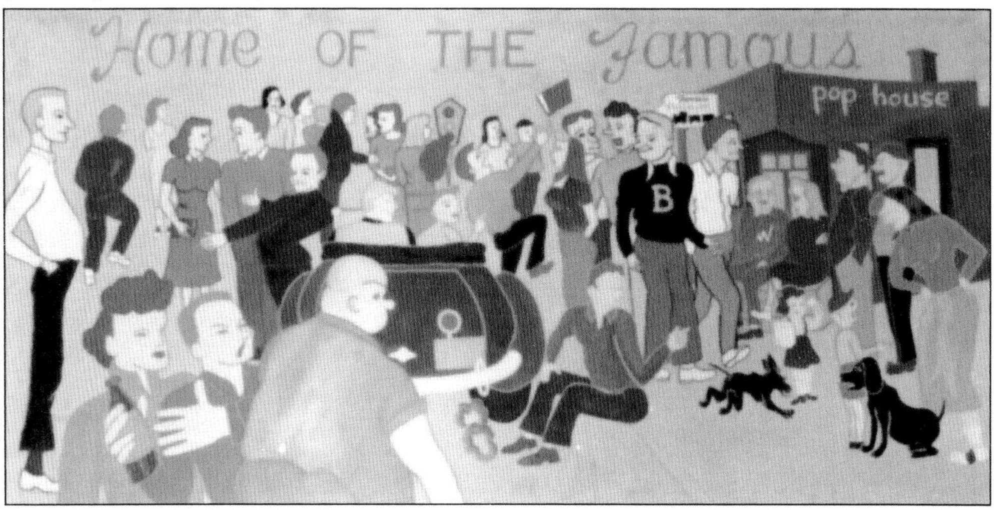

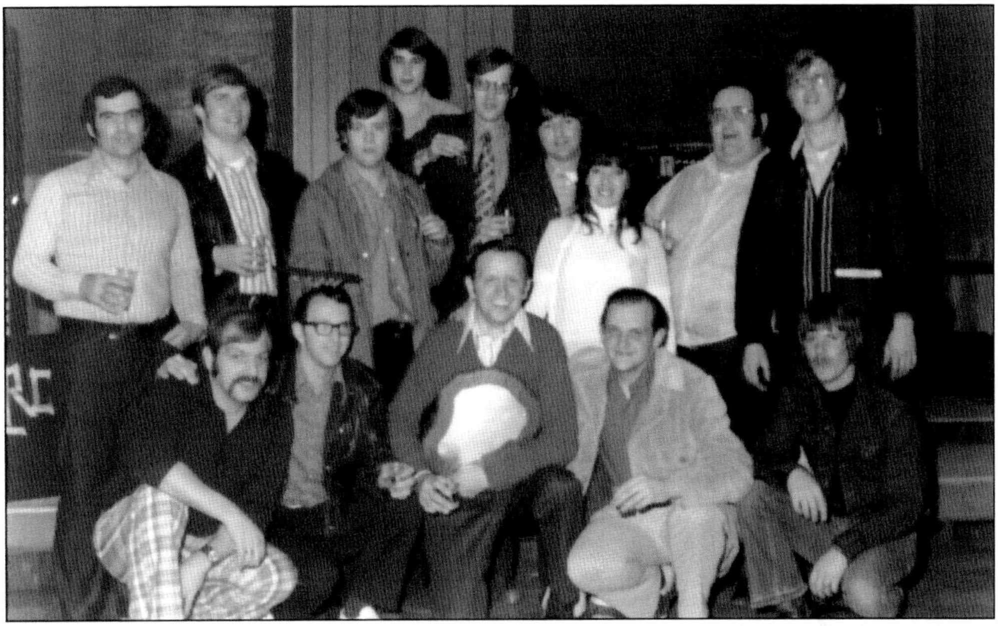

George Stankewitz announced his retirement in April 1973. By then he had served two generations of Beloit youth and through the years had received many plaques and awards for his work with teenagers. To honor him again, a group of past and present grillmen gathered at the last Pop House dance to present him with a plaque expressing their gratitude for his friendship and guidance. (Courtesy of Dr. William Fitzgerald.)

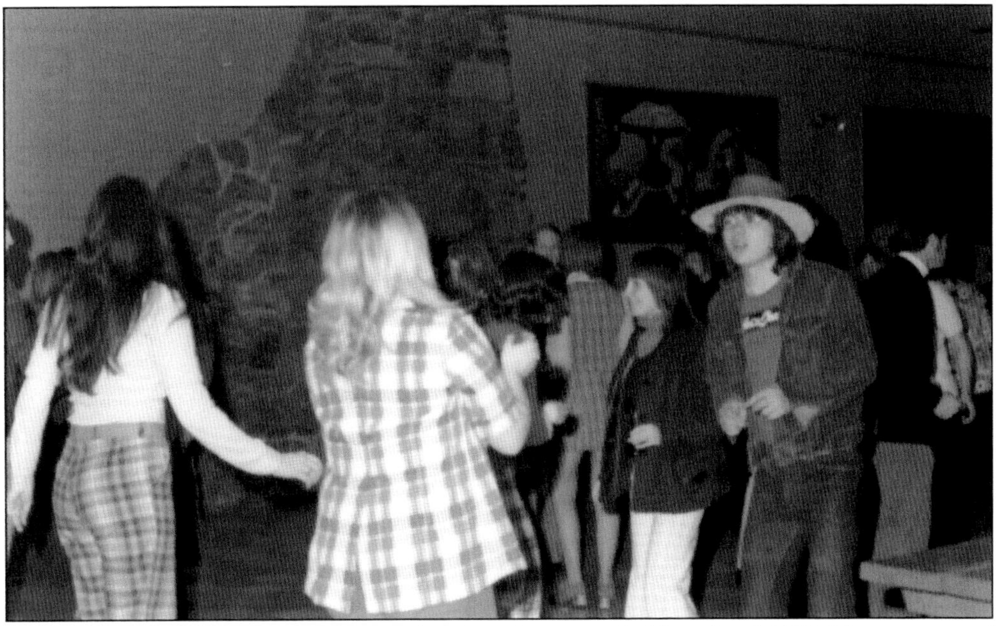

The last dance before the Pop House closed its doors was held in April 1973. Here a group of young adults dances to the music of a band named Crosswind. Business declined after the new drinking age law was passed and Stankewitz converted the teen club into a bar. Still, he would put away the liquor and hold several dances for younger teens who were not old enough to enter a tavern. (Courtesy of Dr. William Fitzgerald.)

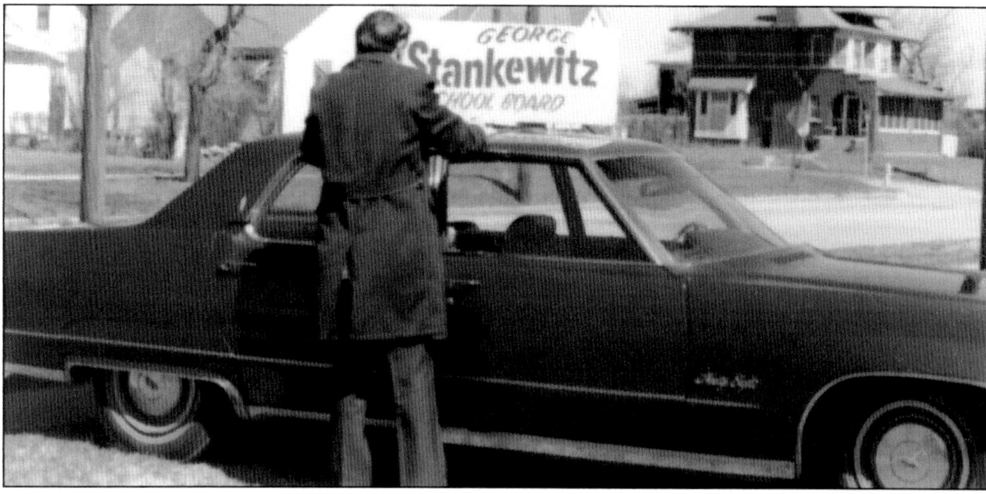

In addition to his career as owner of the Pop House, George Stankewitz also had an interest in local affairs. He was elected to the Beloit School Board in 1974, during a time of growth and building in the district. He had previously served on the Rock County Board of Supervisors where he was involved in planning for construction of the University of Wisconsin Center–Rock County. (Courtesy of Ida and Richard Lenz.)

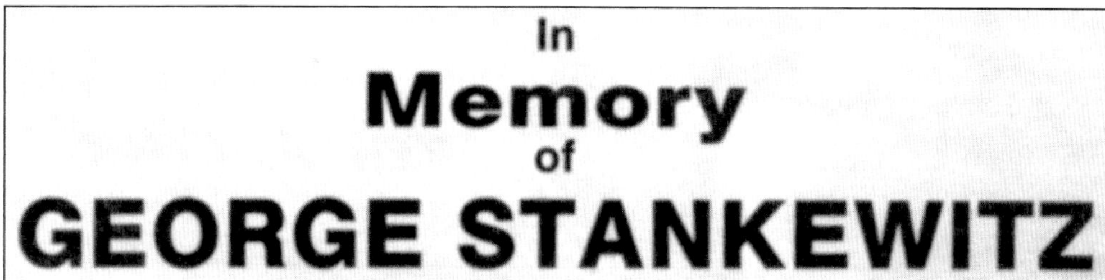

Everett Haskell ran for reelection to the Beloit City Council in the spring of 1992 and dedicated his campaign to the memory of his old friend Stankewitz. An advertisement appearing in the April 5, 1992, *Beloit Shopping News* included a photograph of campaign treasurer Tom Roehl (left), Haskell (center), and Stankewitz pointing to a sign outside the former Pop House, now the Alumni House. (Courtesy of Tom Roehl.)

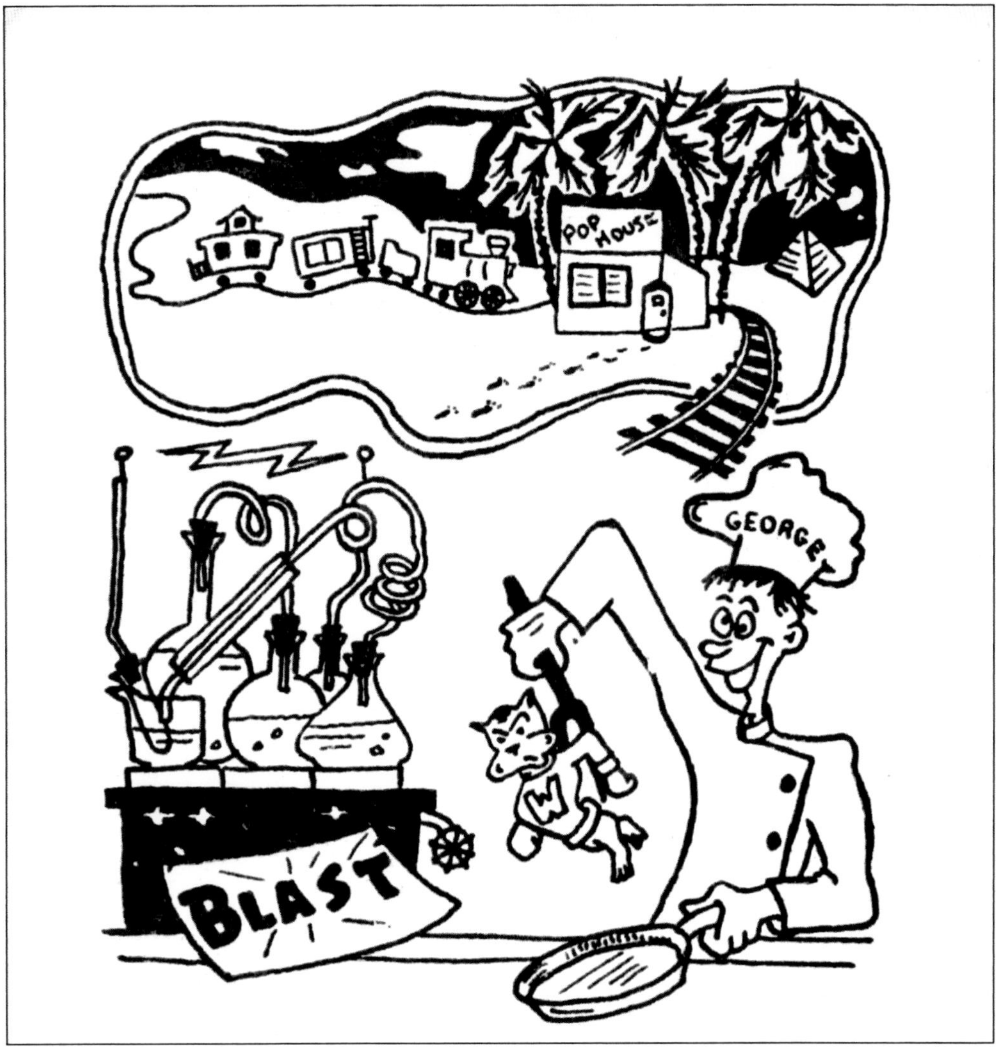

The Pop House provided great fun for two generations of students who were loyal customers. Most would describe it as "someplace special" and a place they enjoyed returning to years after high school graduation. Even returning for a visit several years later, many people could carry on a conversation with George Stankewitz as if no time had elapsed since they last spoke. It was a place where Beloit teenagers could feel at home, have some fun, eat a hamburger, and see top-tier entertainment for a dollar or so. When the Pop House closed its doors, there was a sense of loss that many found hard to describe. There simply was no other place around that compared to the Pop House and what it offered. Before reopening the business as the Alumni House some years later, Stankewitz sponsored a Club Pop House alumni holiday party in December 1981. Pictured here is the illustration that was on the front of the invitation. The event was held at the Wagon Wheel in Rockton for $2.50 per person. (Courtesy of the Pop House collection.)

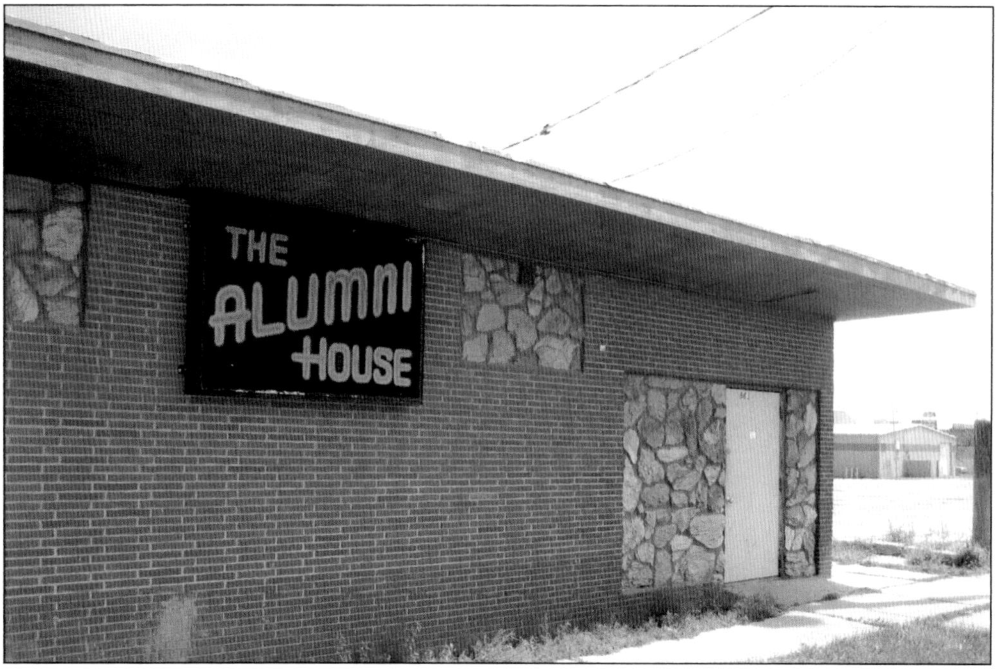

After George Stankewitz got out, the old Pop House tavern business underwent name and ownership changes. With a desire to rekindle the business, he took it back in the mid-1980s and began running the old Pop House once again as a restaurant and bar, fittingly named the Alumni House. Graduates of Beloit schools who lived in the area would come to the Alumni House with their families for a reasonably priced meal and to rekindle old memories. Alumni from Beloit schools who returned for class reunions often would hold events there. Not surprisingly, Stankewitz would remember many faces and have stories to share with a number of the returning guests. On election nights, local candidates would head down to the Alumni House to greet voters and meet friends after hearing the final returns. (Above, author's collection; below, courtesy of John and Fran Tangye.)

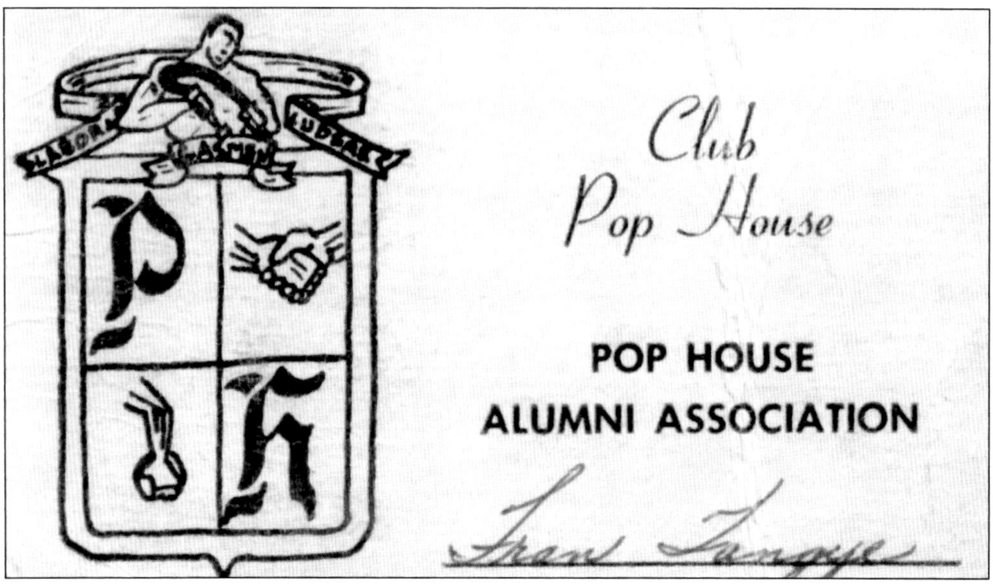

The Alumni House offered inexpensive lunches and dinners, and it boasted a fully stocked bar. It often served as a "meet and eat" place for community organizations. Numerous trophies decorated the fireplace mantel in testament to the long tradition of Pop House sports and games. Hand-painted murals continued to adorn the walls, as did many bronze plaques and other awards presented "in appreciation and fun" from Beloit Memorial High School graduating classes. The menu was trimmed down but still offered the traditional Lugieburger as well as the Hollywood and the Snead. French fries still came in three colors, and the 12:01 and Smiley were available as meatless alternatives. (Courtesy of the Pop House collection.)

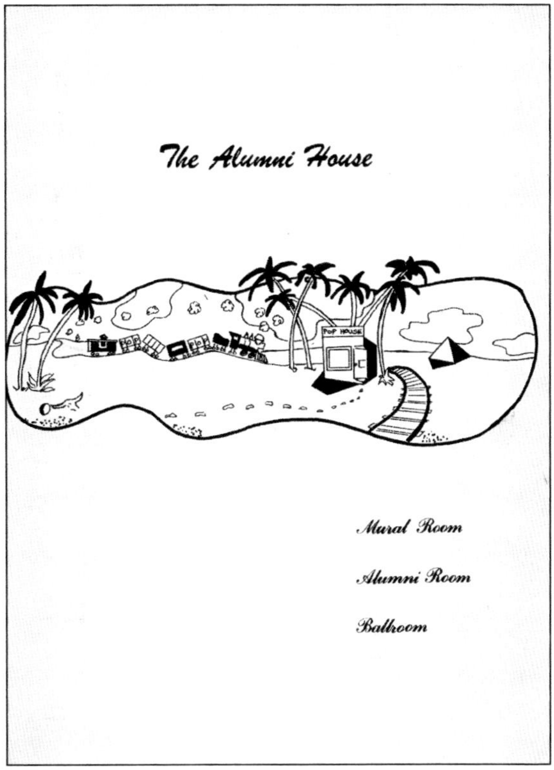

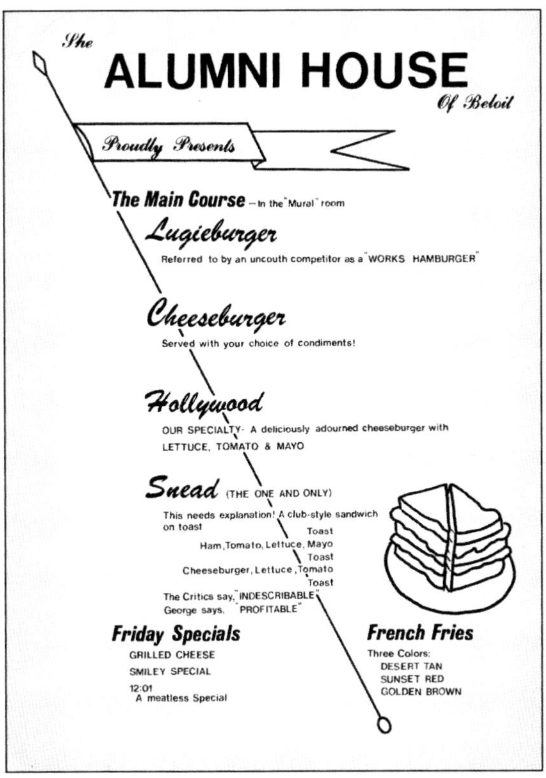

The ALUMNI HOUSE Of Beloit

Proudly Presents

The Main Course – In the "Mural" room

Lugieburger

Referred to by an uncouth competitor as a "WORKS HAMBURGER"

Cheeseburger

Served with your choice of condiments!

Hollywood

OUR SPECIALTY- A deliciously adourned cheeseburger with LETTUCE, TOMATO & MAYO

Snead (THE ONE AND ONLY)

This needs explanation! A club-style sandwich on toast

Toast
Ham, Tomato, Lettuce, Mayo
Toast
Cheeseburger, Lettuce, Tomato
Toast

The Critics say, "INDESCRIBABLE"
George says, "PROFITABLE"

Friday Specials

GRILLED CHEESE
SMILEY SPECIAL
12:01
A meatless Special

French Fries

Three Colors:
DESERT TAN
SUNSET RED
GOLDEN BROWN

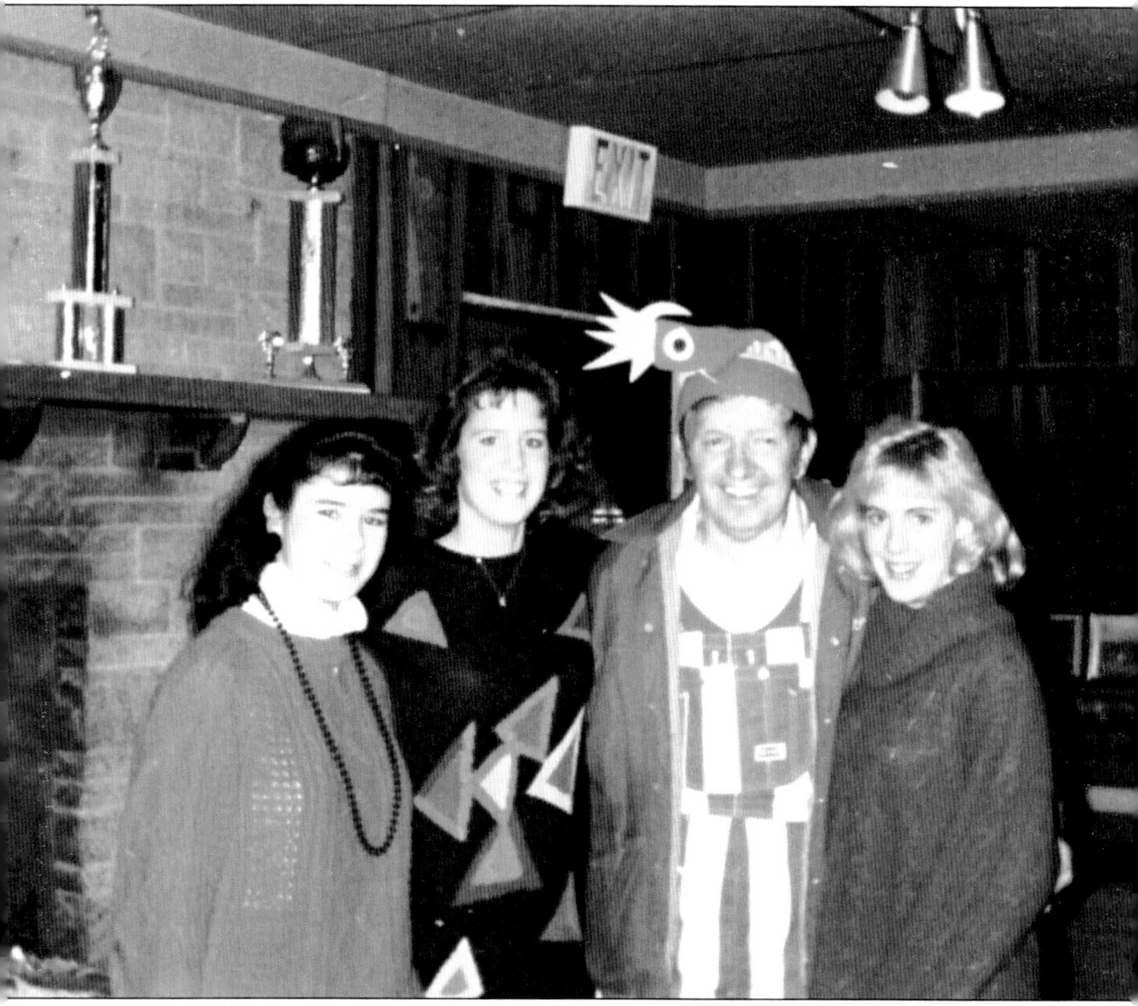

The annual Turkey Bowl, first organized by George Stankewitz in 1941, continued throughout the years. The first game involved Pop House members from the east and west sides of town, but the event was put on hold during World War II. Subsequent games were played against other Beloit taverns. The teams, players, and locations have changed over the years, but the tradition continues to keep the Pop House spirit alive. In typical Pop House fashion, there are pregame activities every year that include coronation of a Turkey Bowl queen, a parade to the playing field, and a postgame awards ceremony. Pictured here with Stankewitz before the 39th annual event in 1986 are, from left to right, Julie Terranova, queen Sue Nyre, and Christi Harrer. Commissioner Stankewitz is wearing red and white striped overalls and sports the traditional turkey hat. On the mantel is the Turkey Bowl traveling trophy that continues to be awarded to the winning team. (Courtesy of the Pop House collection.)

Paul "Rufus" Terry and Vince Stankewitz, manager of the Alumni House team, are pictured here on the sidelines during the 39th annual Turkey Bowl game in 1986. Stankewitz, always an outstanding athlete and sportsman, was inducted into the Beloit Historical Society's E. L. "Ted" Perring Sports Hall of Fame on June 21, 2007. (Courtesy of the Pop House collection.)

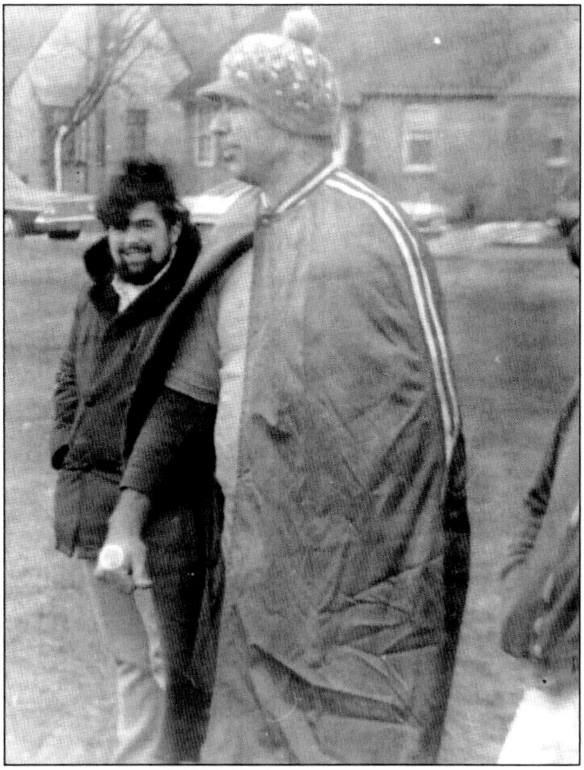

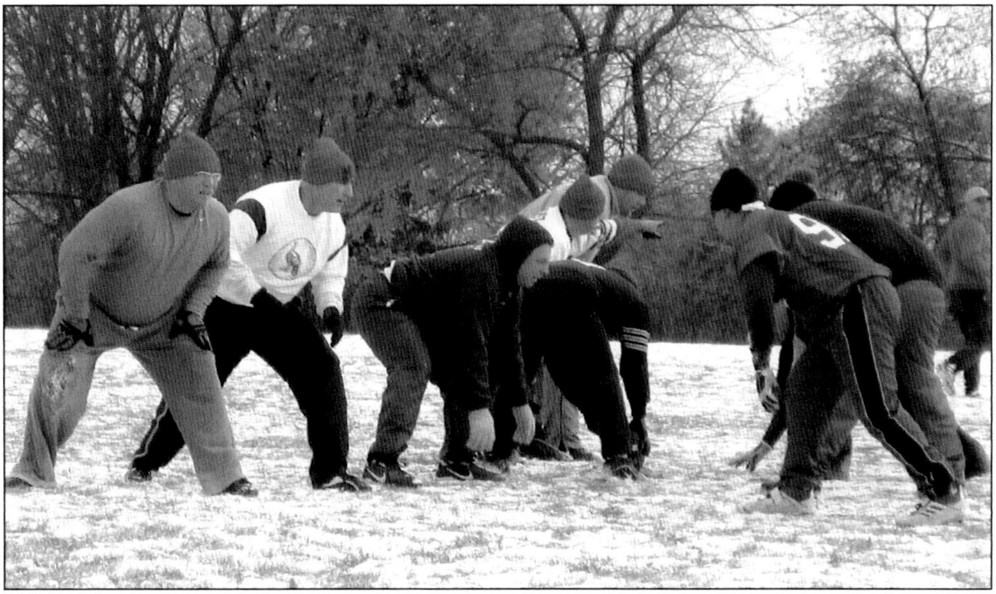

Continuing to keep the spirit alive, the 60th annual Turkey Bowl in 2007 pitted the Hog Cabin and the Mouse taverns against each other in the time-honored Thanksgiving touch football game. Among the customers of both establishments are Pop House alumni and their families who are committed to preserving the tradition. This photograph shows the Hog Cabin and the Mouse teams lined up in the snow moments before the opening snap of the game. Hog Cabin won the contest 22-2. (Author's collection.)

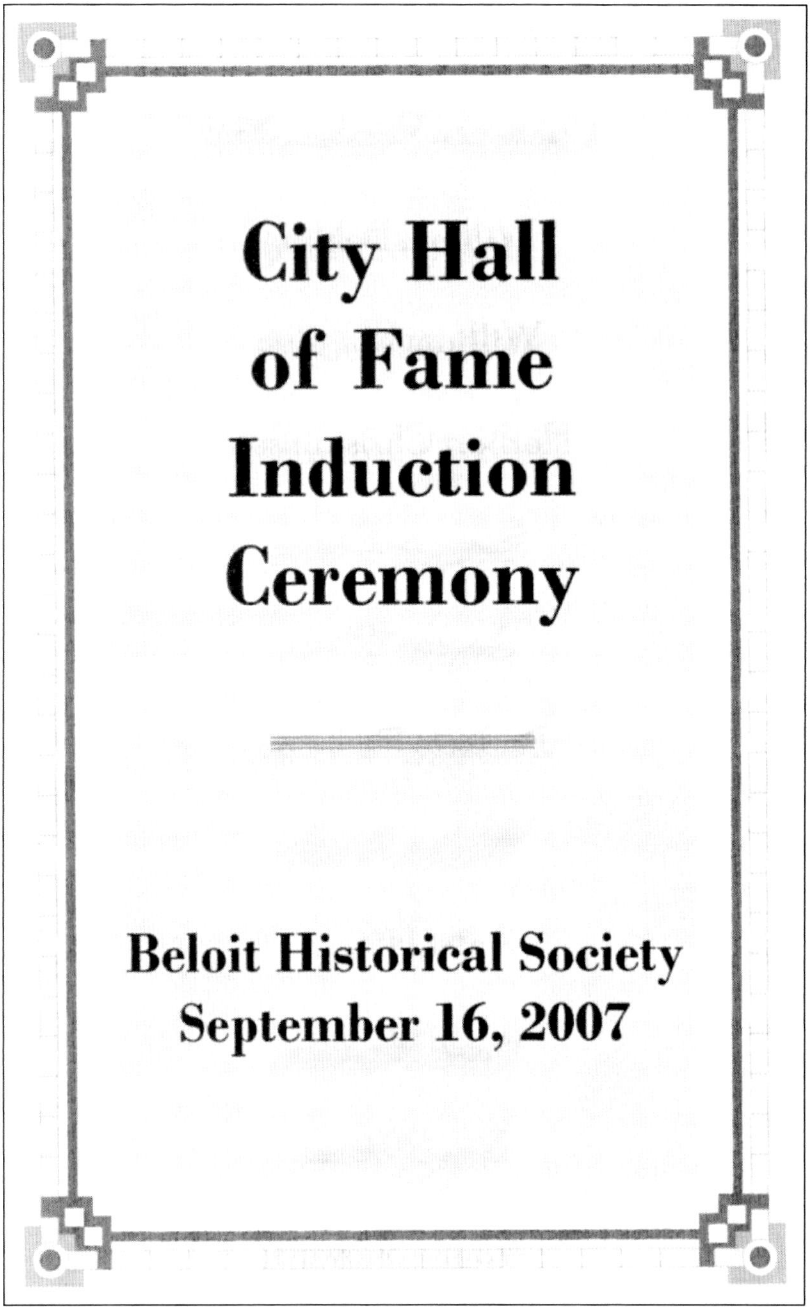
City Hall
of Fame
Induction
Ceremony

Beloit Historical Society
September 16, 2007

On September 16, 2007, the name of George Stankewitz was added to the roster of honorees in the Beloit Hall of Fame. George Stankewitz was inducted 16 years after his death in a ceremony at the Beloit Historical Society. The distinguished award for "unselfish and dedicated service to the city of Beloit" was presented by former Beloit police chief Wayne Showers, who called Stankewitz one of the most highly respected people in Beloit. Showers said he remembered only one police call to the Pop House, and by the time they arrived everything had been taken care of. Vince and Delores Stankewitz were present to accept the honor. (Courtesy of the Beloit Historical Society)

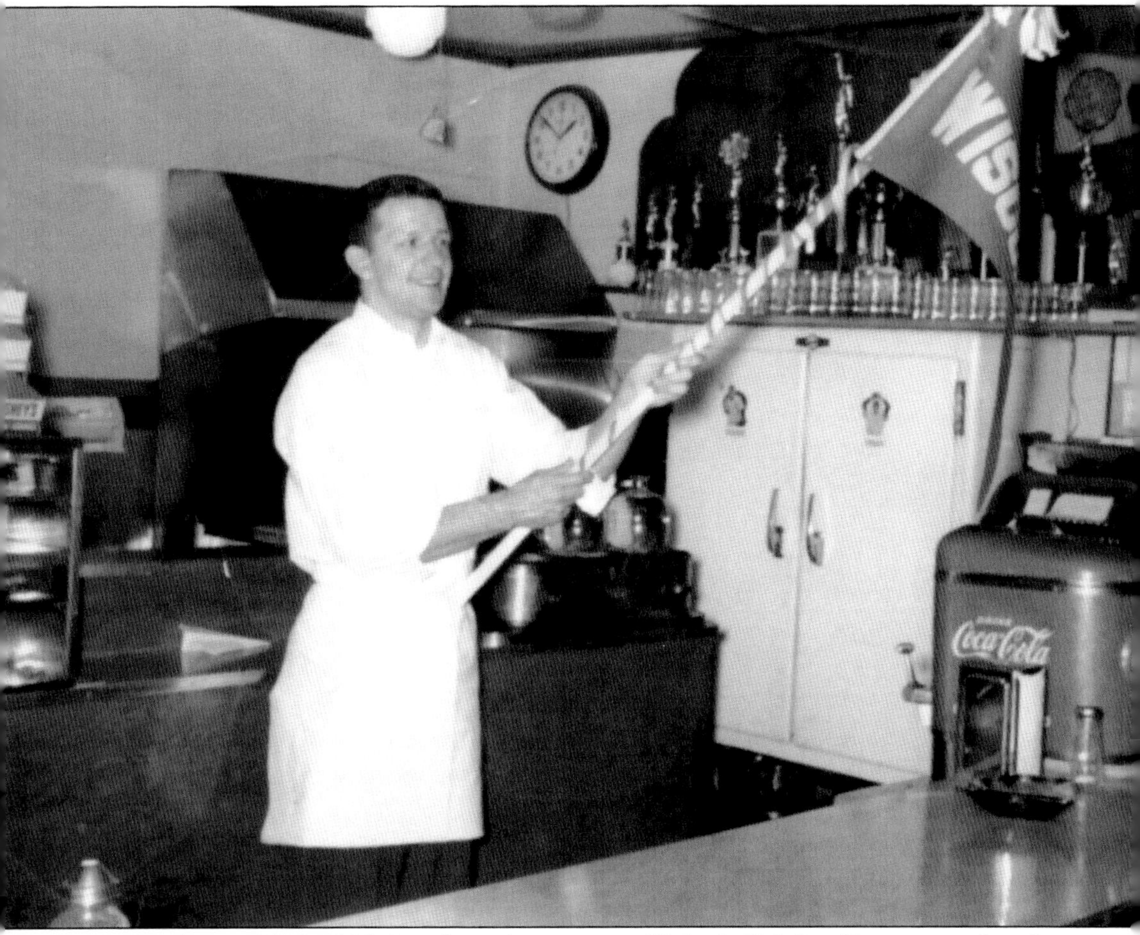

George Stankewitz (1923–1991), founder and proprietor of Beloit's Club Pop House, was a friend and father figure to hundreds of Beloit youth. (Courtesy of Ida and Richard Lenz.)